IMAGES
of America

PIKEVILLE

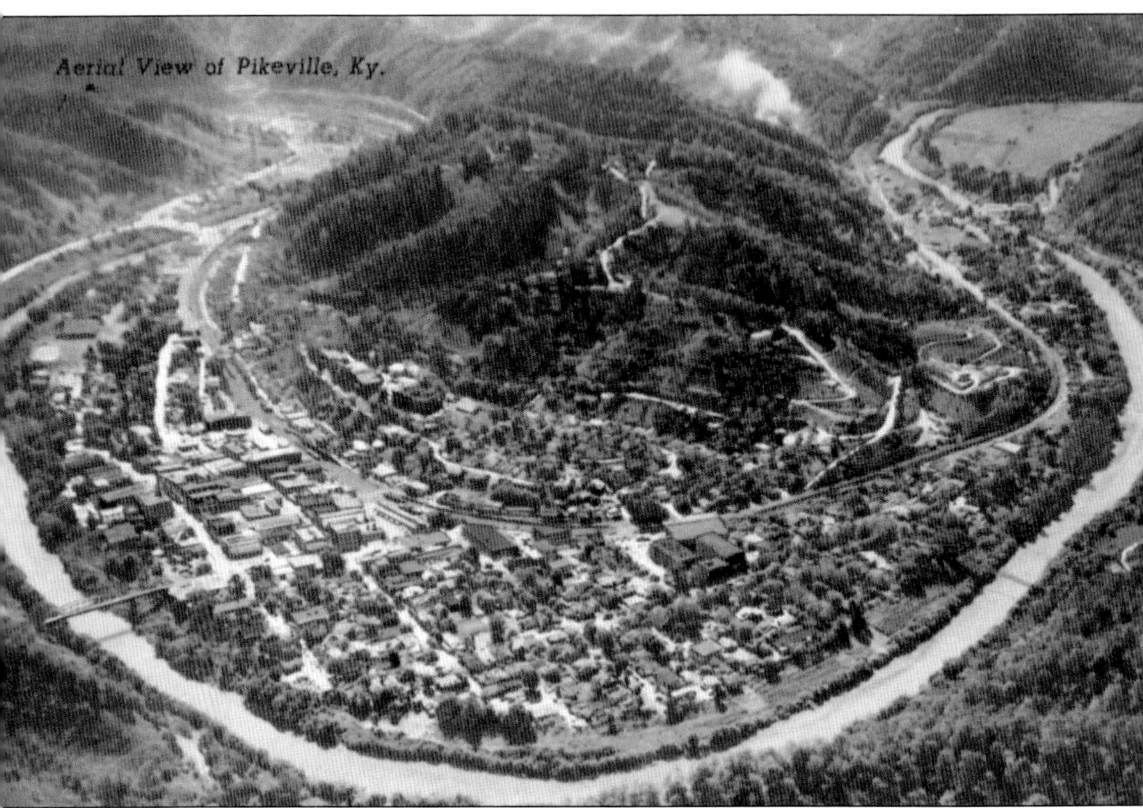

This postcard shows downtown Pikeville in about 1950. The three traffic bridges that crossed the river can be seen beginning at the upper left and following downstream along the long bend in the river that cradled the city. At top center is Peach Orchard Mountain before construction of the Pikeville Cut-Through. (Courtesy of Sam Hatcher.)

On the Cover: Main Street was the heart of the city in 1934 just as it is now, though it does not look quite the same. Traffic is moving in the "wrong" direction, and only half of the buildings shown remain. The differences make sense as this was a decade past the halfway point between Pikeville's beginning and today. (Courtesy of Brenda Hays, John Doug Hays collection.)

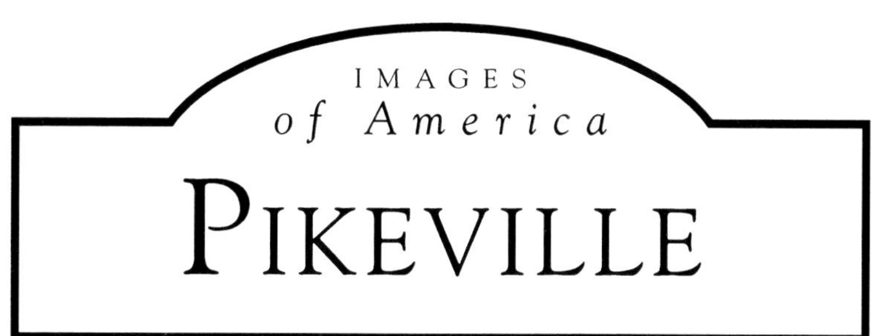

Bradley Slone on behalf of
the City of Pikeville
Foreword by Mayor James A. Carter

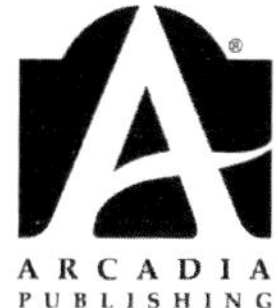

ISBN 978-1-4671-0935-2

Published by Arcadia Publishing
Charleston, South Carolina

Printed in the United States of America

Library of Congress Control Number: 2022946524

For all general information, please contact Arcadia Publishing:
Telephone 843-853-2070
Fax 843-853-0044
E-mail sales@arcadiapublishing.com
For customer service and orders:
Toll-Free 1-888-313-2665

Visit us on the Internet at www.arcadiapublishing.com

The City of Pikeville dedicates this book to all the people who have worked for nearly 200 years to make Pikeville a special place.

Contents

FOREWORD

From humble beginnings to a city full of lively attractions, Pikeville's heritage is built on the natural beauty and resources of the region. This book, compiled in honor of the City of Pikeville's bicentennial, serves as a reminder of the deep and important history of Pikeville.

Our city has come a long way, but there is much to learn from our fascinating past. Famed explorers like Daniel Boone charted new waters in the region in 1767. The land's ample natural resources marked it as an 1800s hub for hunting and logging. And the Civil War saw sweeping changes to the region, with Pikeville acting as both a battleground and swing city between opposing forces.

Then came the city's 20th-century evolution—from a coal mining hot spot to a regional leader in education, arts, and healthcare —earned through hard work, innovative leadership, and a commitment to lifting the entire Appalachian region and her people.

Pikeville's origins can be traced back over 200 years, so detailing the historical timeline and corresponding photographs was no small task. Bradley Slone, chairman of the Big Sandy Heritage Center Museum, rose to the occasion and created this wonderful celebration of Pikeville. Inside, you will find unique stories about the city and its scores of inhabitants over the years. Each period has its own characters who laid the foundation for what we now experience and enjoy.

It is an honor to serve as the mayor of Pikeville, a place I have loved all of my life. While the city continues to grow, its spirit has always been strong. Visitors continue to come back to experience our slice of heaven here in Eastern Kentucky.

Now, as a leader in art, history, and tourism for the entire Appalachian region, the city of Pikeville shines as a beacon of inspiration. I am proud to call myself a lifetime resident of such a uniquely wonderful place. It's exciting to think of the history we'll make over the next two centuries. I hope you enjoy these stories as much as I do!

—Mayor James A. Carter
City of Pikeville, Kentucky

Acknowledgments

This book is, in part, being done in anticipation of 2024 marking 200 years since Pikeville's founding. I appreciate city manager Philip Elswick, Mayor James A Carter, and the city's commissioners—Steve Hartsock, Pat McNamee, Allison Powers, and Bob Shurtleff—entrusting me to write this book on the city's behalf.

I have been most fortunate to have a group of local historians and lovers of history who were willing to review the text to help me avoid factual errors. For that, I thank David Deskins, Sara George, Kevin Hall, Sam Hatcher, Rusty Justice, Randall Osborne, and Reed Potter. Special thanks to Sara for her gracious editing advice. Please give them credit for many of the things I got right but no blame for anything I got wrong.

Gathering the photographs proved to be demanding, but thanks are due to all who are credited in the captions, and special thanks to Charlene Hopkins and the Pike County Public Library, Elisha Taylor and the University of Pikeville's Allara Library, the Big Sandy Heritage Center Museum, Lukas Burchett and Pikeville Independent Schools, and Brenda Hays for providing the bulk of the images.

Thanks to my parents, Kenneth and Janice Slone. They are the examples I have always looked to, and have been invaluable resources on this project. I am thankful for the stories my grandparents—especially Sylvia Thacker and Maggie and Noah Nichols—told about days gone by. Thanks to my wife, Catrena. She is my love, my rock, and, unfortunately for her, always my first editor. Our children Caleb and Joshua are my greatest sources of pride.

My experience says that most of us from Pikeville and Pike County love our place. I hope this book helps the reader realize that this is not an accident but is because the people who have lived and worked here made it this way. I hope the reader sees that I am grateful for that fact and that they remember to be grateful, too. Most of all, I hope that all of us remember that Pikeville in another 200 years will be determined, in part, by what we do today.

Introduction

Downtown Pikeville sits inside a bend in the Levisa Fork of the Big Sandy River. Thousands of years before the first colonial long hunters entered the valley of that river, Paleoindians moved through it hunting buffalo, deer, and other game. Perhaps a thousand years ago, this area represented the southern limits of the Fort Ancient culture. Nearby archeological sites tell us that there were seasonal and, perhaps, semi-permanent settlements throughout that long period, but by the time Europeans first entered the area in the late 18th century, the settlements were gone. Still, the Shawnee and the Cherokee made periodic hunting trips along the river.

The first person of European descent known to have passed through what is now Pikeville was Daniel Boone. Boone was one of the long hunters who ventured into the wilderness for months on end exploring and hunting for furs. One such trip in 1767 brought him through the Breaks of the Big Sandy and into Kentucky for the first time. He passed by the future site of Pikeville and spent a winter farther down the Levisa Fork before returning to North Carolina. It is said that around 1790—just two years before Kentucky became a state—Boone led Revolutionary War veteran William Robert Leslie to the place on Johns Creek where Leslie established the first permanent settlement in Pike County.

Initially, Kentucky had only around 74,000 people, and at statehood, it had only three counties. The population tripled in less than a decade and as it continued to grow, more and more counties were created. Floyd County came along in 1800 and a piece of it was made into Pike County in 1821. It was named in honor of the western explorer and US Army officer Zebulon Montgomery Pike. On December 30, 1824, Pikeville was established by the state legislature as the county seat on land owned by Elijah Adkins.

In the first half of the 1800s, the primary occupation was hunting, as bear and deer were abundant due in part to the large number of chestnuts the area produced. This game meat, along with vegetables from the garden, could sustain a family and the furs were valuable to trade. Steamboats began using the river in the 1830s and Pikeville was the farthest town upstream that they could reach. This along with being the county seat quickly turned it into a center of commerce and industry.

Logging had begun to emerge as an industry in the 1850s, but the Civil War put that on hold. After the war, huge stands of trees, especially yellow poplar, were floated downstream while shipments of tools, goods, and equipment were brought back to Pikeville by steamboat. The industry peaked after the appearance of automobiles—which were made largely of wood—but then the Ford Model T switched to an all-metal design in the mid-1920s, and logging nearly vanished.

During most of the Civil War, nearly all civilian government in Pike County ceased as small armies periodically moved through the mountains, and Pikeville changed hands between Confederate and Union forces multiple times. The most prominent Union sympathizer in Pikeville was taken from his home and temporarily jailed hundreds of miles away while the Confederate-sympathizing county judge was shot dead on Main Street by a Union scout. There being no formal law, "home guards" were formed to handle "justice" as best as they could. In other places, after the war, each side went home to live among those who had fought on the same side. Here, however, men who fought on opposite sides were once again neighbors.

It is perhaps unsurprising that the men who led each side of the infamous Hatfield-McCoy Feud had lived through that chaotic, lawless time. Although the violence of the feud took place on the other side of Pike County along a different fork of the Big Sandy, Pikeville played a large role. After the McCoy family home was burned by Hatfields in 1888, the McCoys made their new home in Pikeville. The subsequent murder trials were among the first held in the newly constructed courthouse that still stands on Main Street. Both sides had Pikeville attorneys, and the conclusion of the trial saw a member of the Hatfield clan hang in front of thousands near the Pikeville City Cemetery.

The feud was just a brief episode in Pikeville's story, though, while education was a core value established when the town was little more than a village. The first subscription school opened around 1840. Primary education grew rapidly, with more than 60 such schools being in Pike County by 1860. When the Presbyterian Church began looking for a place to build a secondary school in the Big Sandy Valley in the 1880s, it found that Pikeville was ripe ground for its planting. It is this early and consistent commitment to education that has likely meant more to Pikeville's character than any other single factor. The work of men like John Dils Jr., Dr. James Record, and T.W. Oliver built foundations that continue to support that value decades after their deaths.

Around the turn of the 20th century, coal mining was expanding throughout the region, and the railroad followed shortly thereafter. A railroad depot opened here in 1905. Pikeville maintained its status as the economic center of the region through the booms and busts of the industry throughout the next century.

Eventually though, the railroad proved a hindrance. It physically divided the town and—along with the coal truck traffic resulting from its presence—contributed to dust in the air and severe traffic congestion. The river that had been the source of commerce decades before had always left its banks too frequently. The semi-regular floods repeatedly set back the economic fortunes of the town's citizens and, in some cases, cost them their lives. Mayor William C. Hambley spent decades of his life working to complete an audacious solution. This project, the Pikeville Cut-Through, came to be known as "Hambley's Dream."

Work began in 1973 and was not completed until 1987. In the end, a man-made canyon nearly three-quarters of a mile long was constructed through Peach Orchard Mountain, and now the Chesapeake & Ohio Railway (C&O), the Levisa Fork, and a modern, four-lane highway pass through that channel.

Today, Pikeville is home to a rapidly expanding regional hospital, a university featuring colleges of osteopathic medicine and optometry, several local financial institutions including the second largest bank holding company domiciled in Kentucky, and an independent school district that consistently ranks among the best in the state. Our businesses and venues provide diverse offerings for shopping, dining, and entertainment while our people enjoy a high quality of life with good schools, a healthy economic base, and a parks system that provides a variety of active and passive recreational opportunities.

As Pikeville approaches its bicentennial, it is remarkable to consider that the original incorporated area of about three square blocks has expanded to its present size of over 20 square miles. The pages that follow speak to the talent, hard work, service, and leadership that the people of Pikeville have shown over these last two centuries and will undoubtedly demonstrate in the centuries to come.

One

Early Days

Pikeville was founded by a vote of the Kentucky state legislature to be the seat of Pike County on December 30, 1824. Elijah Adkins owned the land previously called Peach Orchard Bottom, likely the largest piece of bottom land along the Levisa Fork. When the legislature acted, Adkins donated an acre of land for the courthouse and its public square. A year later, he was awarded a license for the first ferry crossing the river to the new town.

Pikeville was more hamlet than city for decades after its founding, with more acreage taken up by farmland than buildings. At its first census in 1830, only 49 people lived in Pikeville. Even in 1860, it is reported that there were only a dozen homes, with Main Street (then called Front Street) the only road. This single street snaked down on each end to access the ferries at Ferguson's Branch or Chloe Creek. The post–Civil War timber industry stimulated commerce, though, and the population grew by over five percent per year from 150 in 1870 to nearly 3,400 in 1930.

These boom years brought significant lifestyle changes. The last few decades of the 1800s saw the city's first two hotels—the Williamson House and the Connolly House—open their doors as more people came to conduct business in Pikeville. Telephone service soon followed. Public water service started in 1904, supplied by a reservoir built in a small hollow near Lover's Leap, but the service only consisted of a single faucet in each yard. The Pikeville Light and Power Company opened that same year, as did an ice plant.

Other signs of growth include the first steam-driven lumber mill in the Big Sandy Valley and the arrival of a passenger train depot in 1905. The streets were paved in 1913 and a factory for building spokes for automobile tires started production shortly thereafter.

As a result of these rapid changes, Pikeville left its adolescence behind.

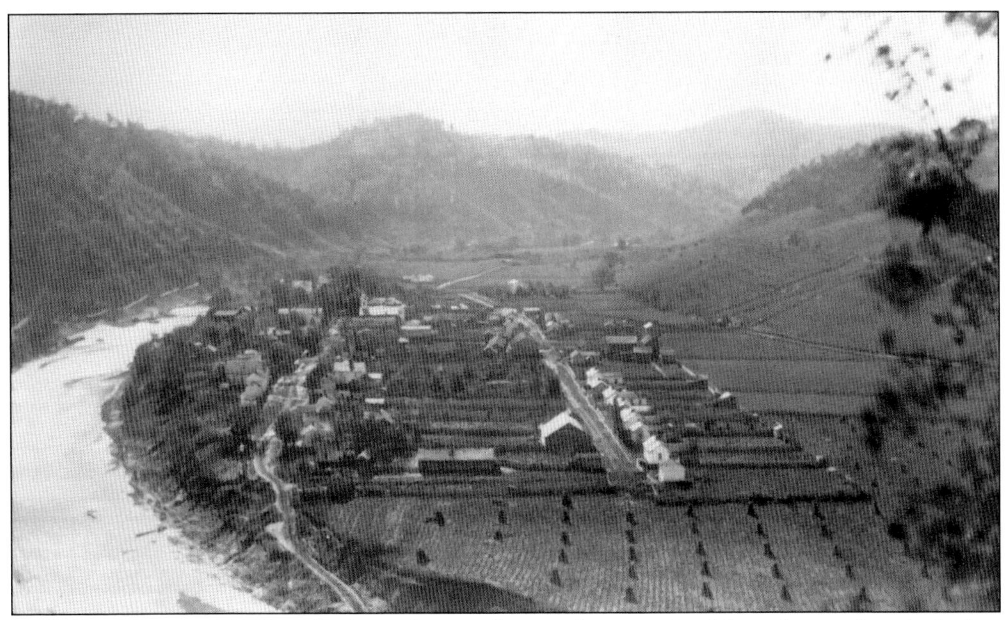

This c. 1883 view of Pikeville from the north was photographed less than a decade before construction began on the current courthouse in 1889. The original was built with logs in 1824. The white church with a steeple on Main Street (left of center) was the original location of the Methodist Episcopal Church South. (Courtesy of the Big Sandy Heritage Center Museum.)

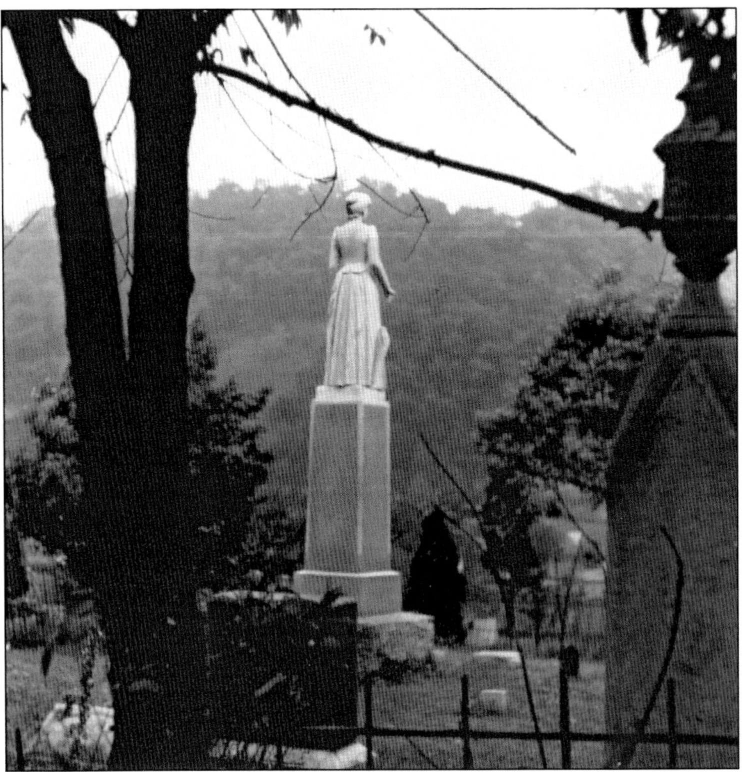

This statue marking the grave of Octavia Hatcher overlooks downtown Pikeville. She was the wife of prominent businessman James Hatcher and passed in 1891 after losing a child. Legend says that a sleeping sickness caused her to be buried alive. When James realized what may have happened, she was exhumed, revealing scratches inside the top of her coffin. (Courtesy of the Pike County Public Library.)

Daisy Thornbury married John Bowling in September 1897 at the Christian church in possibly the most extravagant wedding held in Pikeville up to that point. It was attended by most prominent citizens including future mayor Ralph Hellier (fourth man from the right) and John Paul Riddle's parents (immediately to the left of the groom). (Courtesy of the Pike County Public Library.)

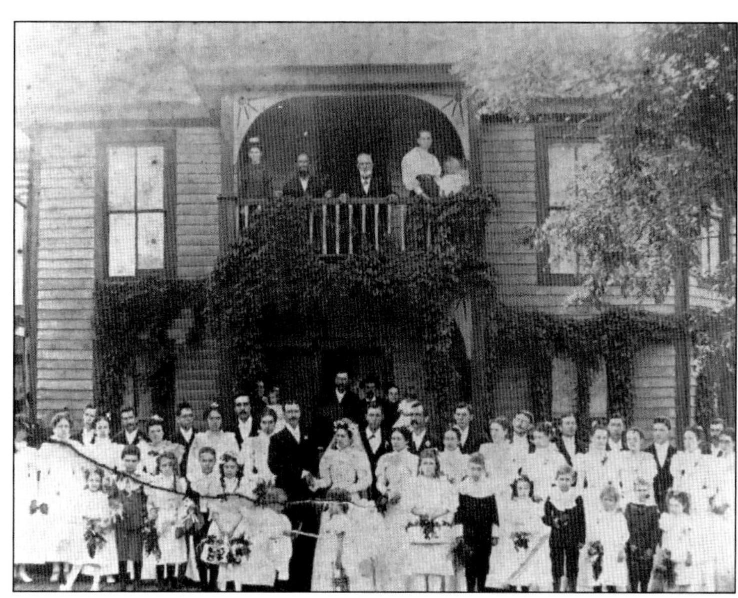

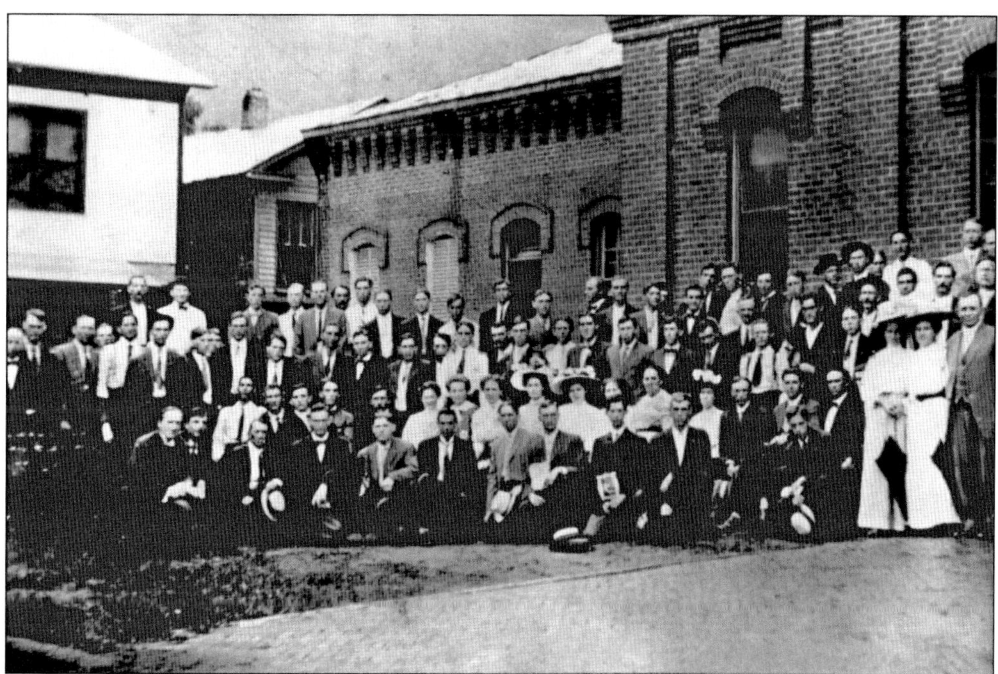

This c. 1898 photograph was taken in courthouse square. The brick building is the courthouse near the Division Street entrance, then the primary entrance. Most large meetings, graduation ceremonies, and similar gatherings were held in the courthouse in those days as it offered the most spacious meeting room in town. (Courtesy of the Pike County Public Library.)

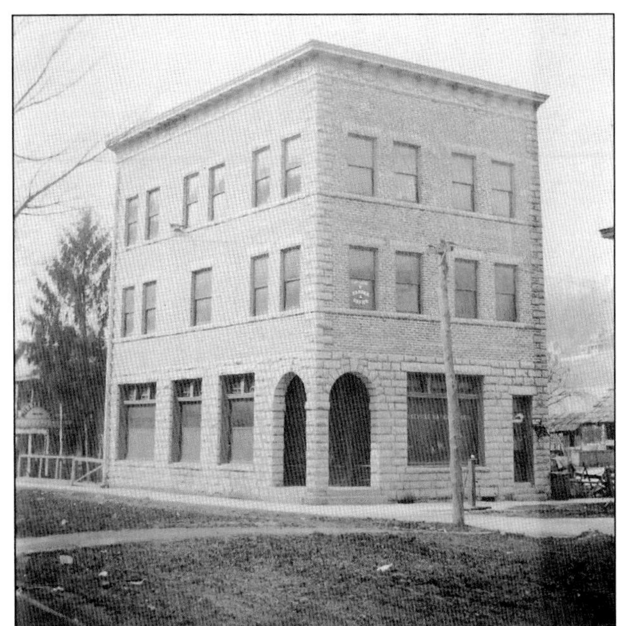

Community Trust Bank—formerly Pikeville National Bank—is perhaps the oldest business still operating in Pikeville. It was approved to operate as a national bank in 1903. John Yost was its first president, and Fon Rogers was its first cashier. Construction on this first building on the corner of Main Street and Grace Avenue finished in 1904. (Courtesy of Community Trust Bank.)

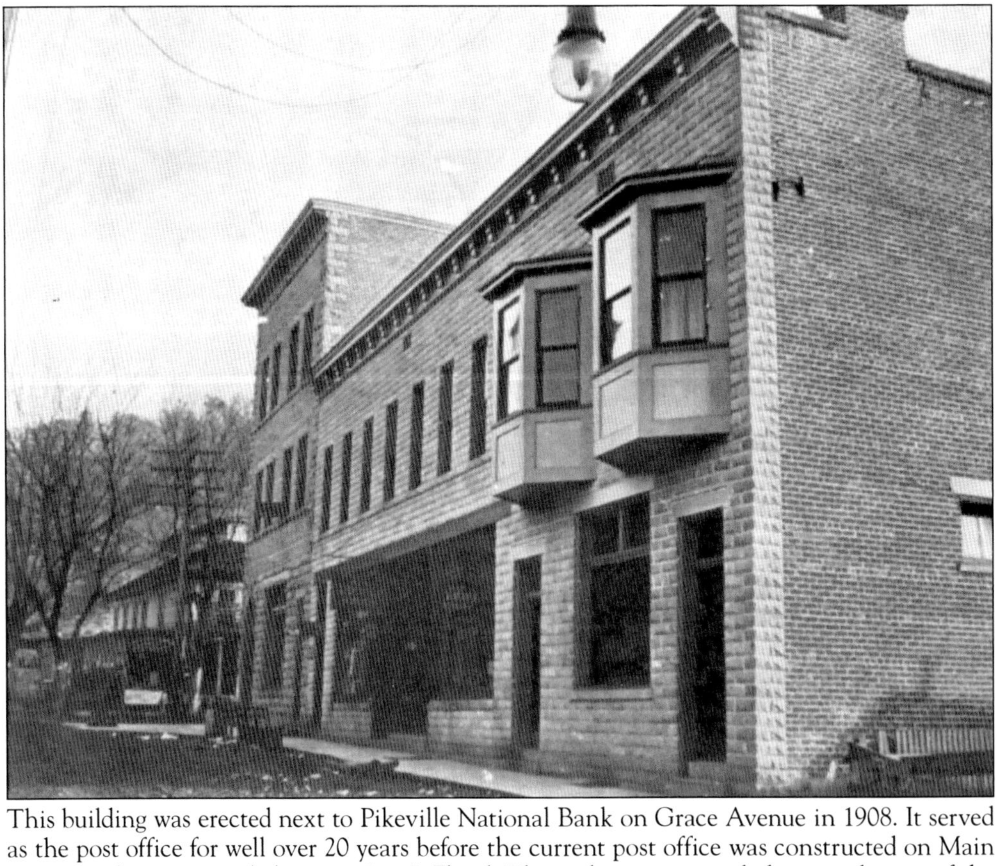

This building was erected next to Pikeville National Bank on Grace Avenue in 1908. It served as the post office for well over 20 years before the current post office was constructed on Main Street, and it is currently home to Levi's Floral. The carbon arc street light near the top of the photograph was among Pikeville's first. (Courtesy of Brenda Hays, John Doug Hays collection.)

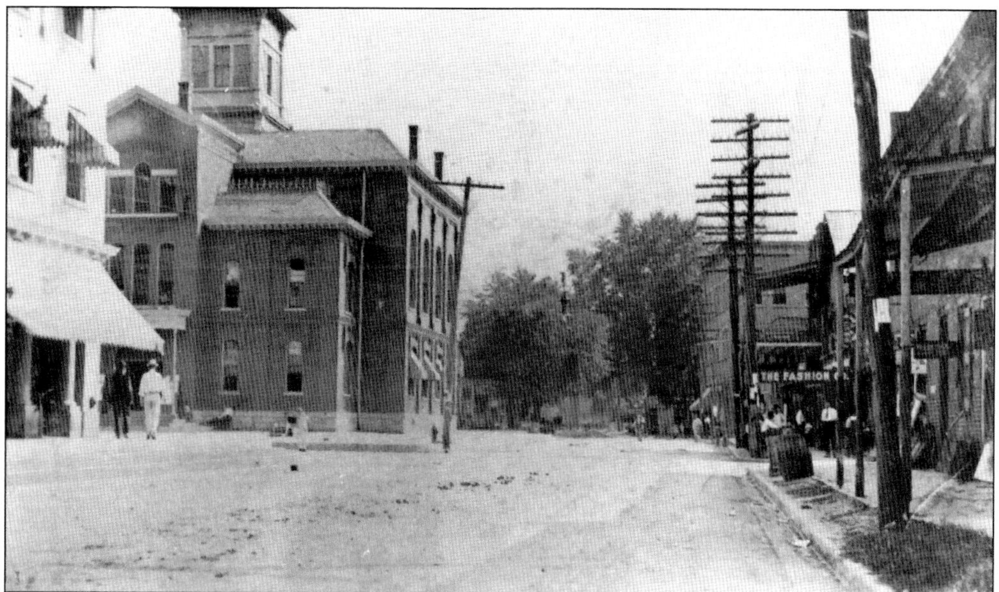

This is Main Street around 1910. There was not yet an entrance to the courthouse facing Main Street. The absence of cars and bricks or pavement dates the photograph and makes the town seem empty. Pikeville's population had just topped 500, but the emergence of the coal industry would soon contribute to rapid expansion. (Courtesy of the Pike County Public Library.)

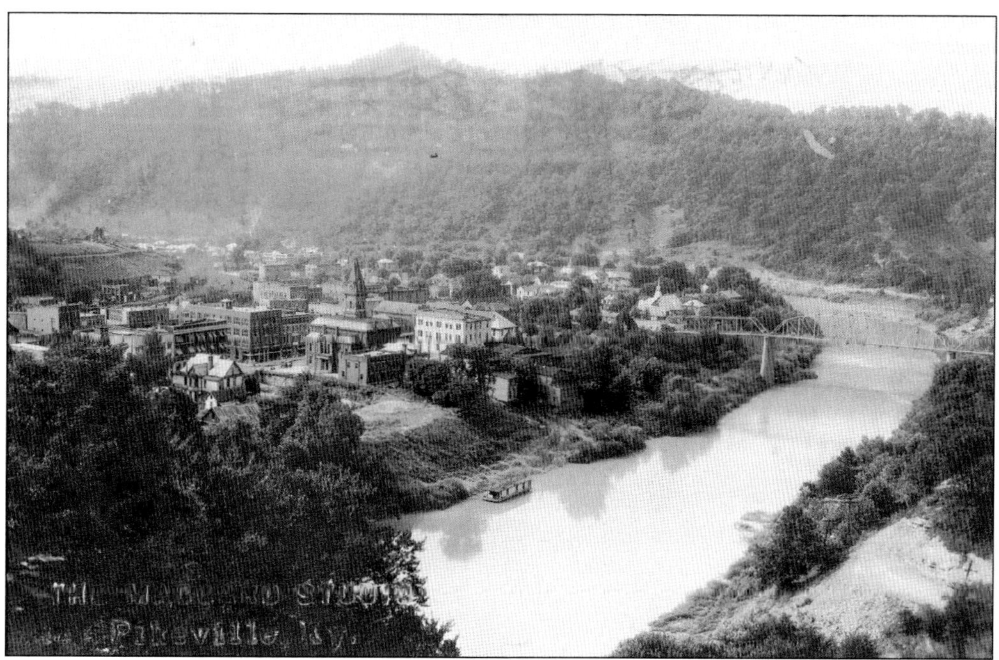

This postcard is of downtown Pikeville around 1915. The courthouse is just left of center and the Hotel Anthony can be seen across Main Street with an early automobile sitting on the street between them. The Middle Bridge spans the river on the right. Bypass Road leading from there to Chloe Creek had not yet been built. (Courtesy of the Frank M. Allara Library, University of Pikeville.)

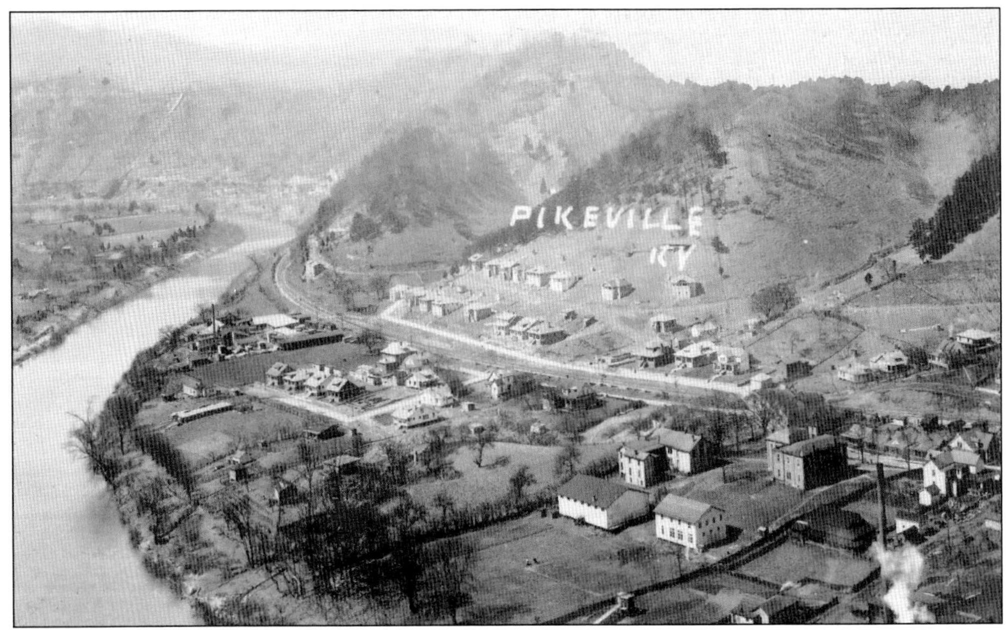

This is Pikeville's upper end in about 1915. The Pikeville Collegiate Institute's Academy Building can be seen near the lower right, while the spoke factory is on the left near the river, the current location of Damron Furniture. Many of the homes seen in this photograph still stand today. (Courtesy of Brenda Hays, John Doug Hays collection.)

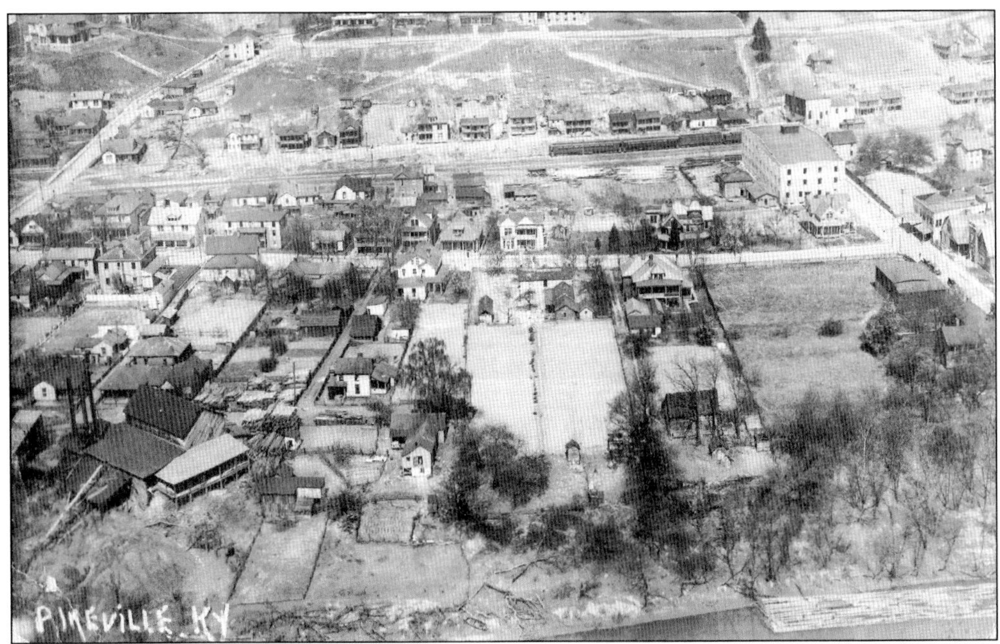

A steam-powered lumber mill is on the lower left of this photograph of the College Street area taken around 1920 while the York/Creekmore Mansion is at top left. The present-day location of the City Park is on the right, and what is known today as the Garfield House can be seen just to its left. (Courtesy of the Frank M. Allara Library, University of Pikeville.)

Two

Education

Pikeville's citizenry has long valued education. John Dils Jr. arrived around 1837 and opened Pikeville's first subscription school in 1840 when just one-sixth of Kentucky's school-age children attended.

The Pike County common school system grew rapidly, but there were no secondary schools until 1889. Dr. William Condit and Dr. James Hendrick convinced the Presbyterian Church of the need for a school for the "mountain boys and girls" of the region. Dils was among those who convinced the church's site committee that Pikeville was the right fit. Pikeville Collegiate Institute opened in September 1889 with David Blyth as principal.

Dr. James Record arrived in August 1899 and found a school with promise but also on the brink of collapse. He poured himself into the role and—minus a four-year absence—remained until 1932. When he left, the academy had become the thriving Pikeville College and had the foundation needed for a bright future.

In 1915, Pikeville High School opened at the joint expense of the city and county boards. Tybee William Oliver, a University of Chicago graduate, became superintendent in 1923. He held that position until his death in 1949. Oliver was a remarkable intellect and administrator and is credited with establishing the long tradition of educational excellence at the school.

A segregated common school opened around 1890 after changes to state law pushed through by Perry Cline made it possible. These efforts were remembered in 1938 when the school was renamed in Cline's honor. The school's students transferred to Pikeville without incident after desegregation in 1957. It closed entirely in 1966 when the new elementary school opened on Chloe Road.

Pikeville's current secondary school opened in 1976, and the school system consistently ranks among the best in the state.

Pikeville College ended high school classes in 1957 and became a fully accredited four-year college in 1961. Beginning in the late 1990s, the school started six graduate programs including medical and optometry schools. A final name change to the University of Pikeville in 2011 reflects this growth.

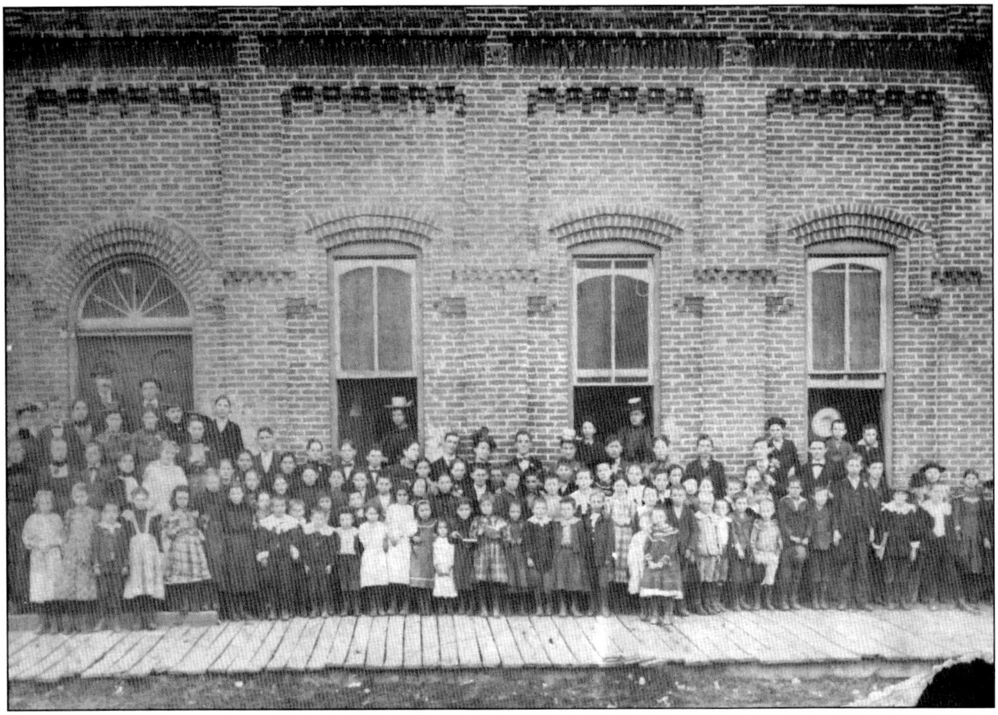

Prior to the 1915 construction of Pikeville High School near today's intersection of Hambley Boulevard and Fourth Street, this brick building housed a subscription school that instructed children in grades one through eight. The tall man in the hat on the left is thought to be Tandy Riddle, the last principal of the school. (Courtesy of the Frank M. Allara Library, University of Pikeville.)

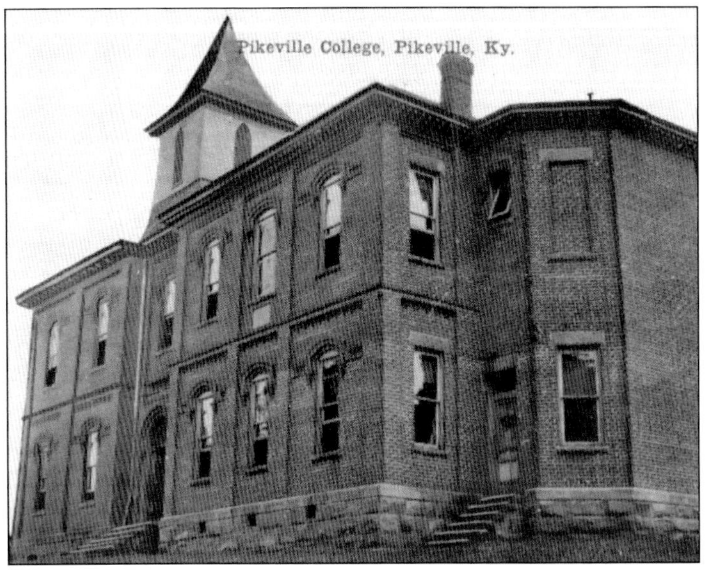

The Pikeville Collegiate Institute's Academy Building was erected in 1890 using locally cut stones for the foundation and hand-made bricks. Dr. Blyth is said to have worked tirelessly for nearly three years before resigning after becoming ill during a typhoid epidemic. The building is currently home to the University of Pikeville's Coleman College of Business. (Courtesy of Brenda Hays, John Doug Hays collection.)

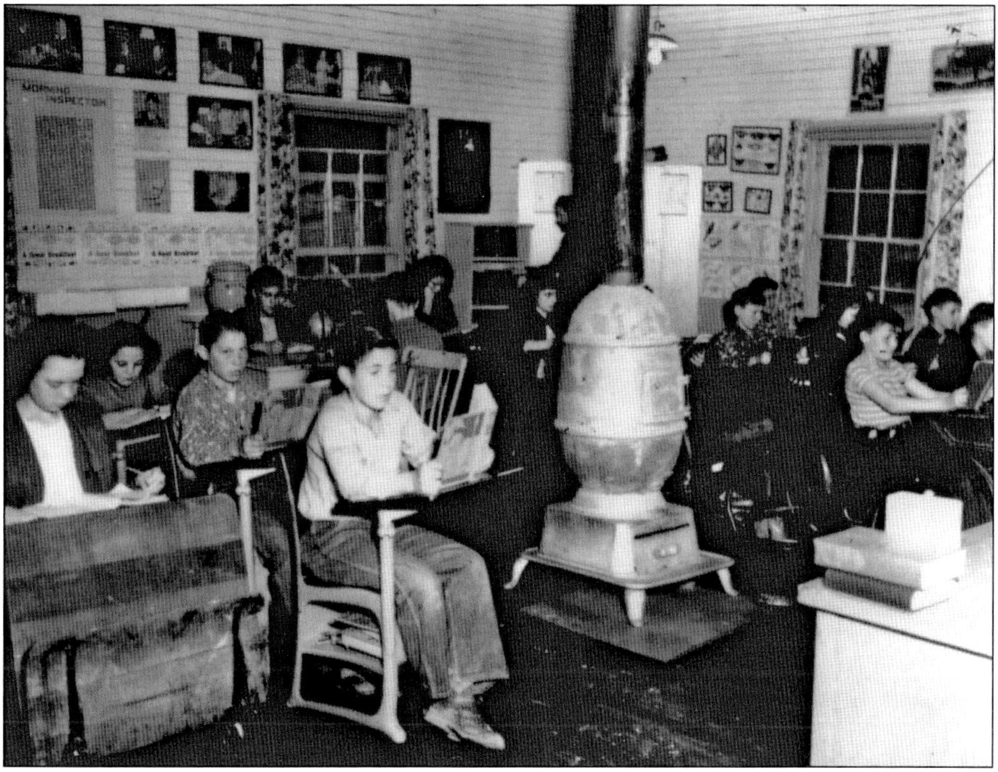

This is a typical school room of the mid-1900s, and it probably was not too different from earlier classrooms. The most prominent feature was the chimneyed, wood-burning stove set in the middle of the room for heat. In earlier days, metal desks were preceded by desks of wood. (Courtesy of the Pike County Public Library.)

The first class from Pikeville Collegiate Institute graduated in 1894. They were, from left to right, Nona Connolly, Sidney Grey, and Elizabeth Syck. The graduation ceremony was held in the courthouse and celebrated by the community. The principal at the time was Kathleen Vreeland, and Dr. Blyth obliged when asked to return to hand out diplomas. (Courtesy of the Frank M. Allara Library, University of Pikeville.)

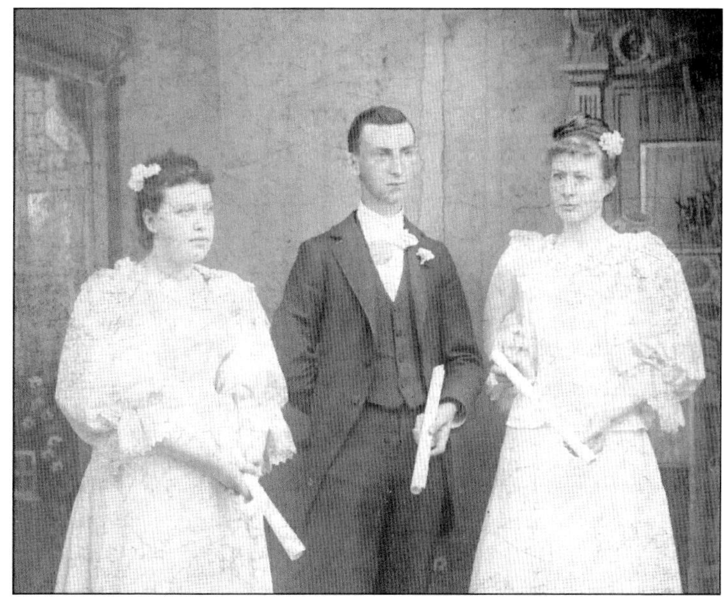

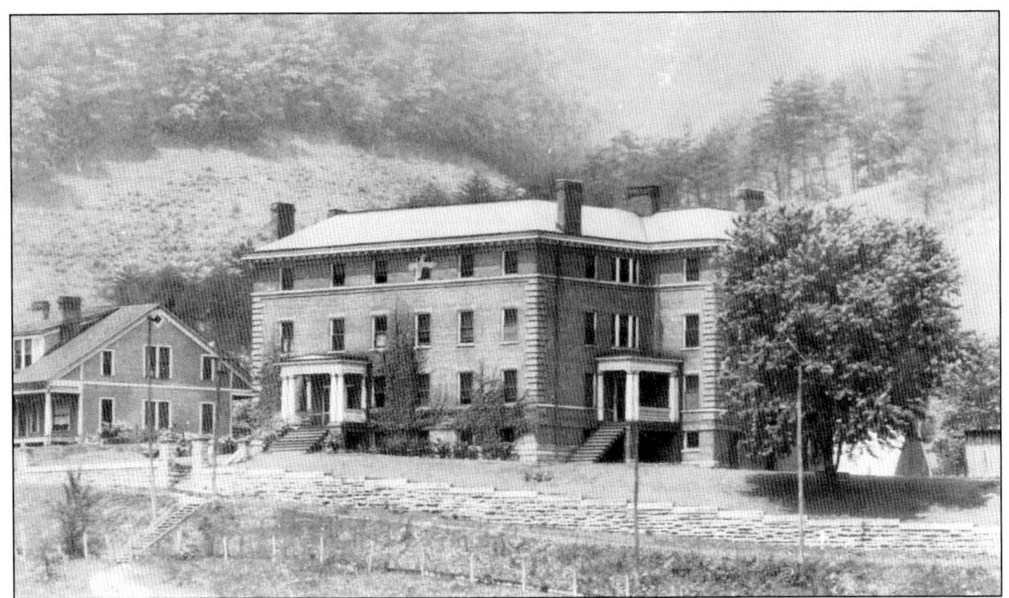

Derriana Hall is a dormitory constructed for women in 1908, one year before the institute became Pikeville College. John Simpson funded its construction, and it was named in honor of his sister Derry. Pikeville was also ahead of its time in emphasizing the need for women's education. (Courtesy of the Frank M. Allara Library, University of Pikeville.)

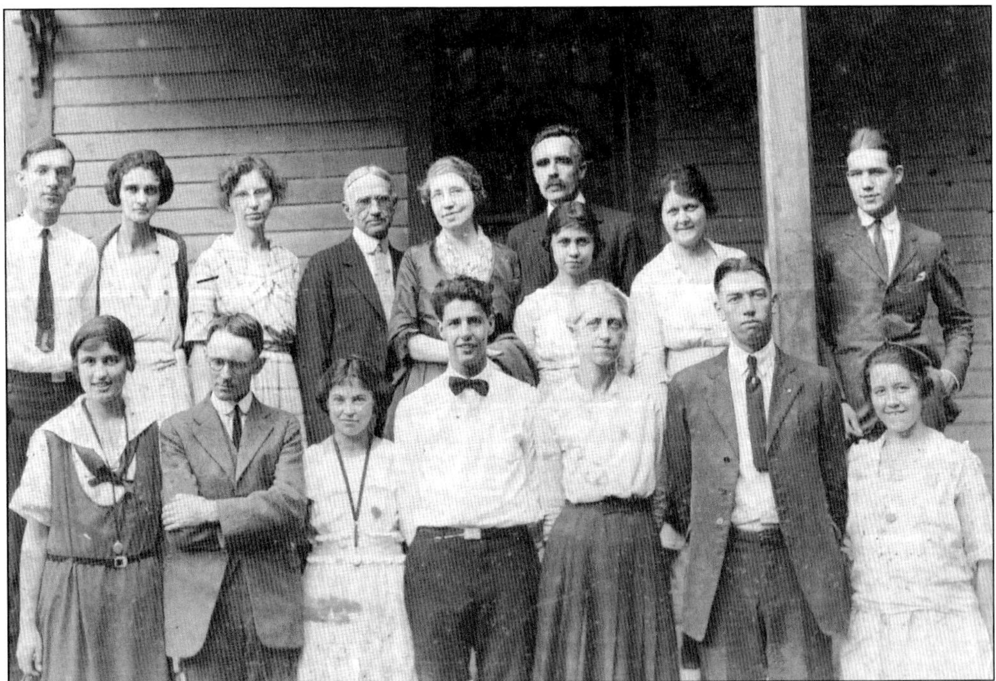

Dr. James F. Record (second row, fourth from left) began offering teacher's training classes in 1901. This group includes some of his teachers as well as others in training around 1922. Dr. Record is regarded as one of the most important citizens in Pikeville's history as he helped establish the university as an important force for education. (Courtesy of the Frank M. Allara Library, University of Pikeville.)

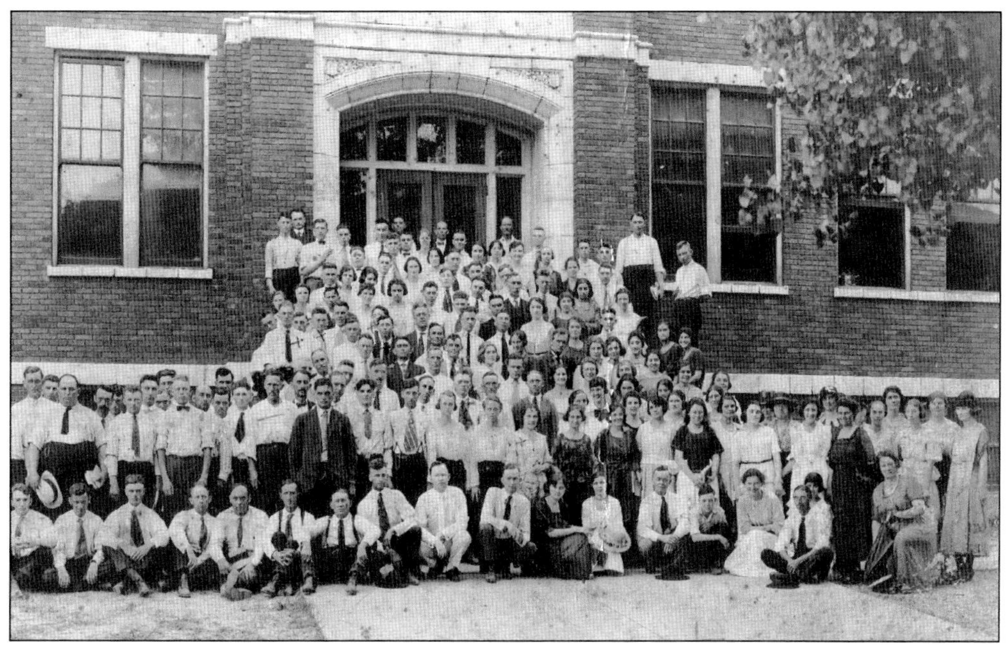

When Pikeville High School opened in 1915, the brick building was described as "the finest in the state" by a state inspector. There were around 150 students in grades one through twelve taught by nine teachers. The Summer Institute for Teachers was taught at the school for two years by Mary Spilman (fourth from right, kneeling). (Courtesy of the Frank M. Allara Library, University of Pikeville.)

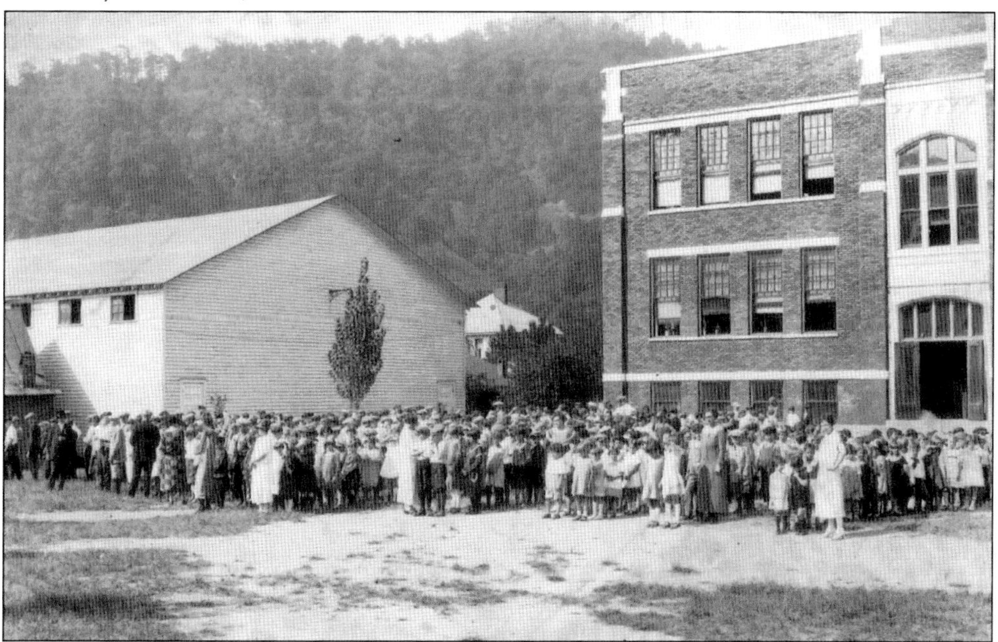

Though a new elementary school was constructed on the grounds in 1929, this photograph taken in 1947 shows elementary-age children lined up in front of the high school, apparently by grade. The building on the left was the school's first gymnasium made of wood and known as the "cracker-box" gym. (Courtesy of Pikeville Independent Schools.)

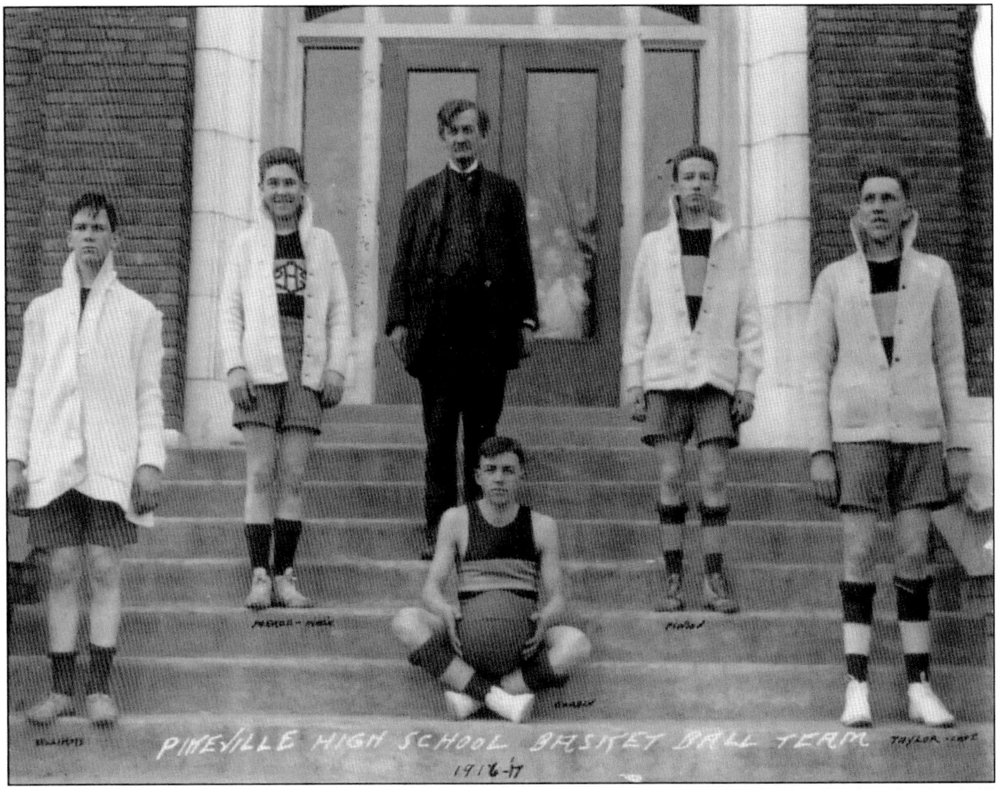

Athletic competition was almost immediately taken up by the new school. This is the first basketball team along with its coach and the first superintendent, Tobias Kendrick. They competed the first year the school opened, but the closest high school they could play was in Ashland. They filled their schedule with games against teams from churches and coal companies. (Courtesy of Pikeville Independent Schools.)

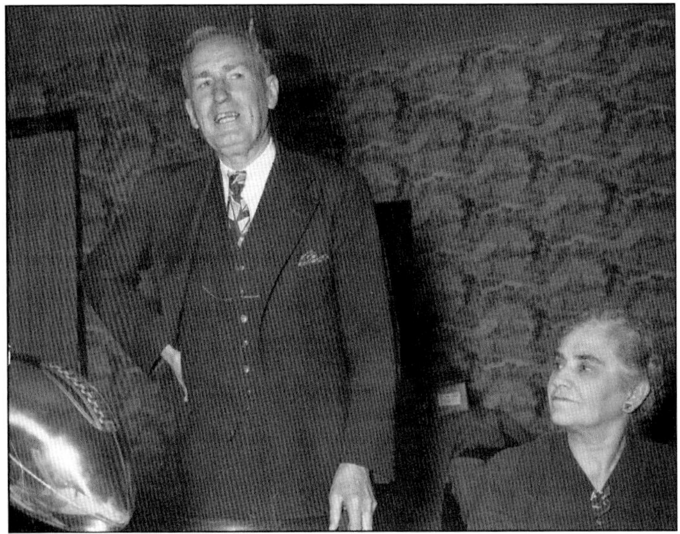

Tybee W. Oliver (standing) was born in Sturgis, Kentucky. He earned both bachelor's and master's degrees at the University of Chicago and a certificate of superintendency at Columbia University. He was an education professor at Morehead State and superintendent in Middlesboro before coming to Pikeville. The 1950 school yearbook said, "For him no task was too great, no child was too small." (Courtesy of Pikeville Independent Schools.)

Pikeville High School soon had a women's basketball team. The first to compete may have been earlier, but the earliest recorded was in 1923. However, this photograph of the 1926–1927 team is the first team photograph known to exist. The women's team stopped playing after 1930 and only resumed in 1974. (Courtesy of Pikeville Independent Schools.)

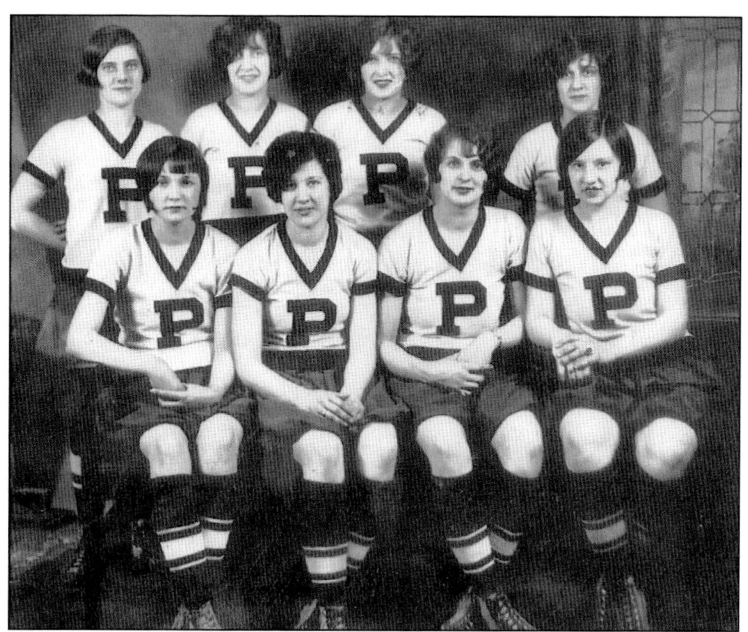

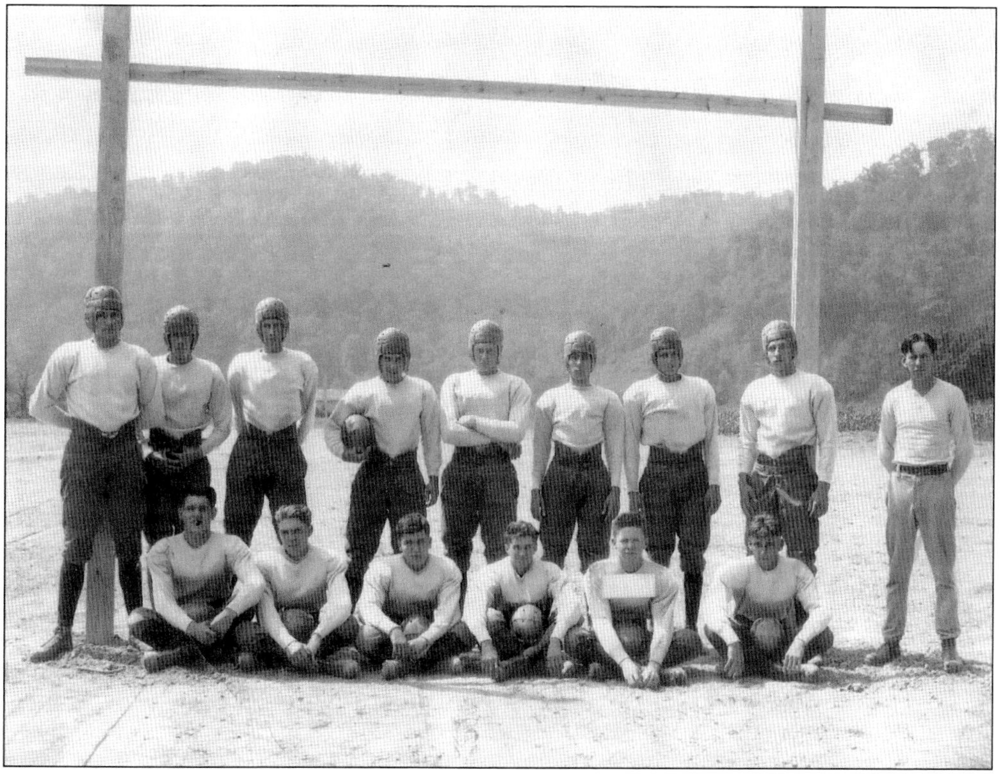

The first Pikeville High School football team is seen here on its first day of practice in 1925. Cassius "Cack" Hatcher is seated second from right. He played at Kentucky Wesleyan before returning to Pikeville to coach basketball and football. His basketball teams won 131 games and lost 135, but his football teams had 57 wins, 21 losses, and 8 ties. (Courtesy of Pikeville Independent Schools.)

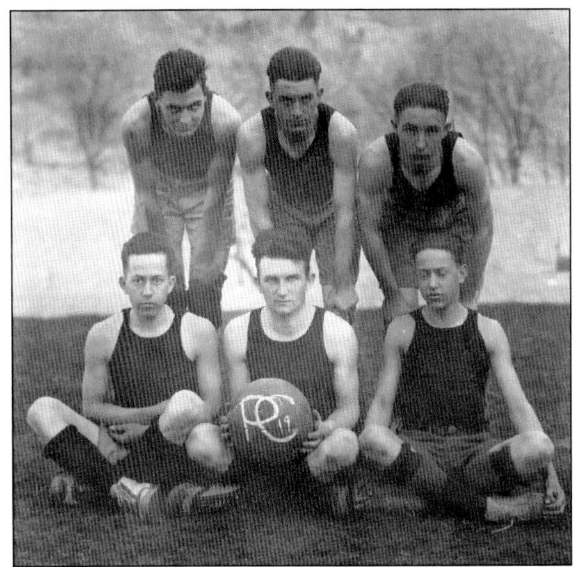

Pikeville Collegiate Institute also had a basketball team take the court in 1919. It is not known if this was the first team. The players are, from left to right, (first row) ? Scott, Dorris Music, and Cecil Greer; (second row) Walter Walters, John Paul Riddle, and unidentified. (Courtesy of the Frank M. Allara Library, University of Pikeville.)

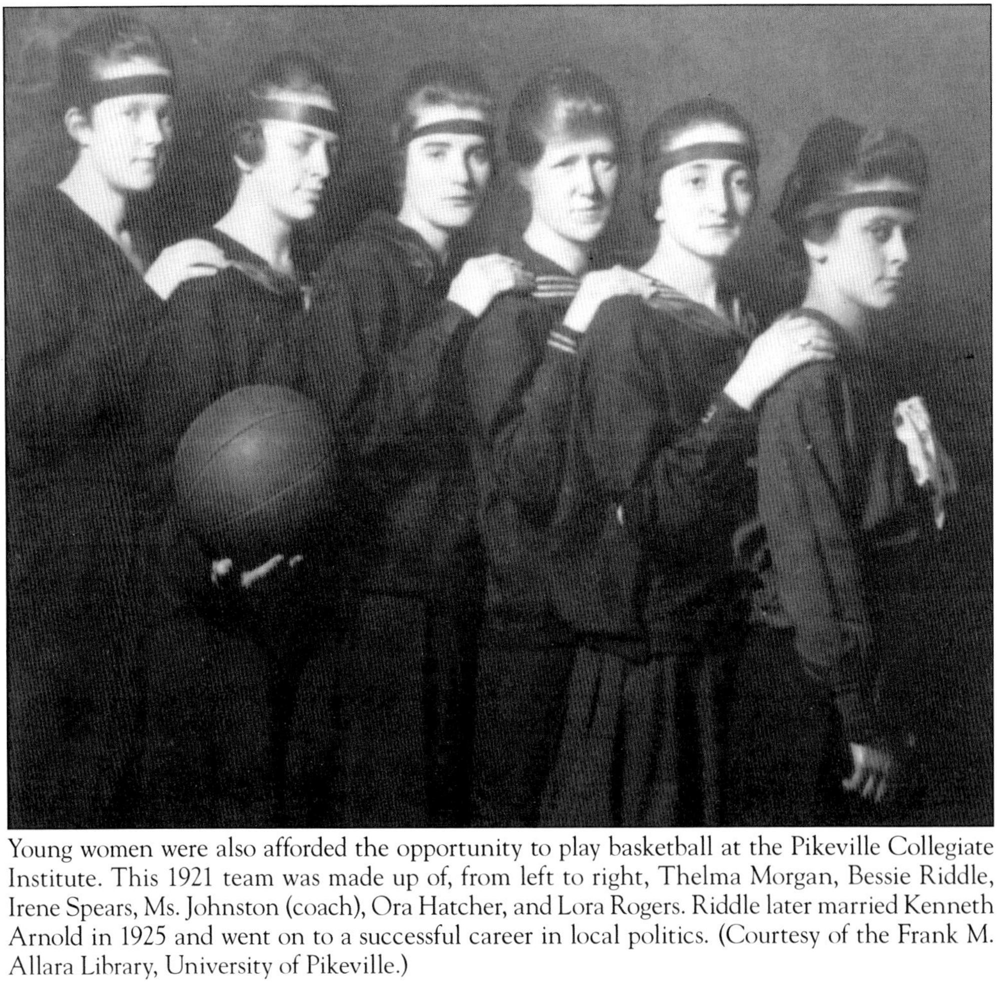

Young women were also afforded the opportunity to play basketball at the Pikeville Collegiate Institute. This 1921 team was made up of, from left to right, Thelma Morgan, Bessie Riddle, Irene Spears, Ms. Johnston (coach), Ora Hatcher, and Lora Rogers. Riddle later married Kenneth Arnold in 1925 and went on to a successful career in local politics. (Courtesy of the Frank M. Allara Library, University of Pikeville.)

In 1925, the community attended the placement of the cornerstone for Pikeville College's new Administration Building. The man second from left is E.L. Howerton, pastor of First Baptist Church; Dr. Record stands at the far right. He retired in 1932, but his contributions were honored 30 years later with the naming of Record Memorial. (Courtesy of the Frank M. Allara Library, University of Pikeville.)

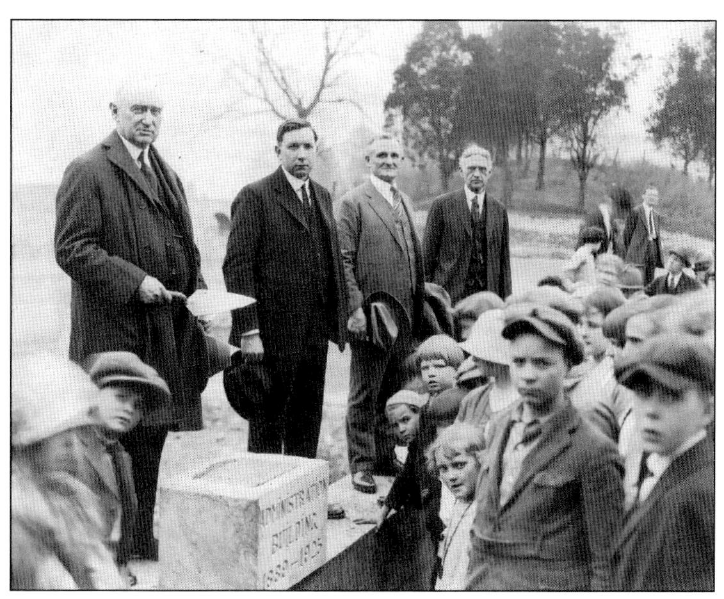

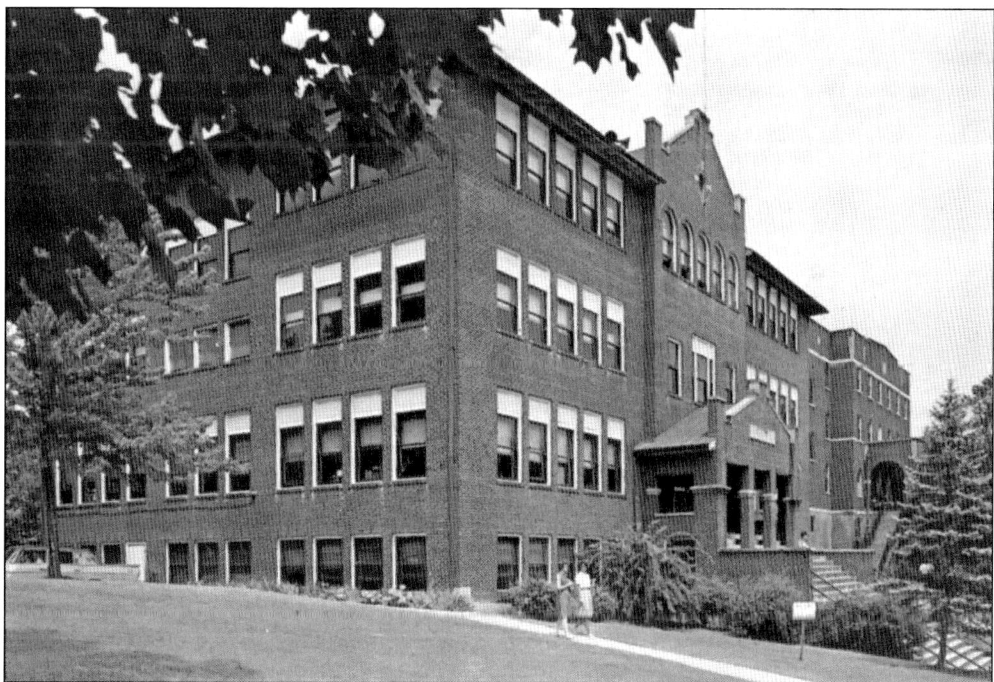

The state approved the school's application to teach college classes in 1909, but it was over a decade before a full curriculum was offered. By the time the Administration Building opened in 1925, it filled a sore need for the growing college by providing classrooms, offices, and a library. (Courtesy of Brenda Hays, John Doug Hays collection.)

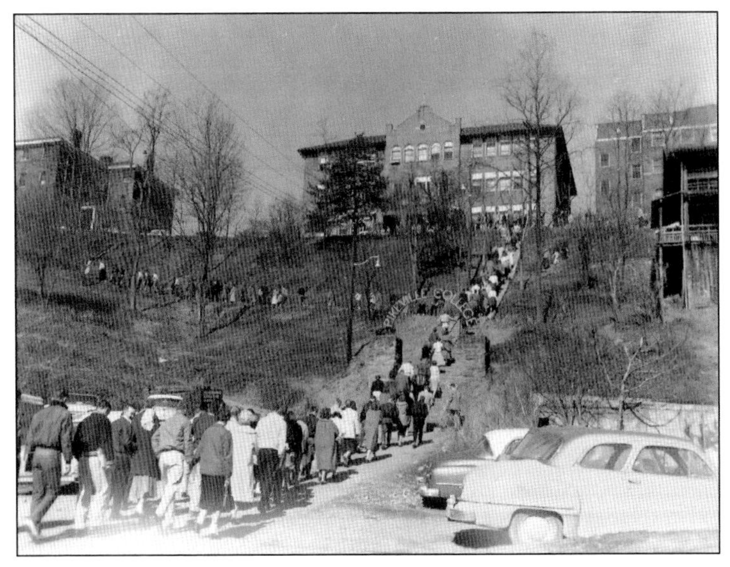

The iconic 99 steps that lead from Hambley Boulevard up to the Administration Building were originally 88, and they were built in the 1930s. The other 11 steps were added after Record Memorial was built. The steps are seen here around 1955 before Record Memorial and the Coal Building were erected on either side. (Courtesy of the Frank M. Allara Library, University of Pikeville.)

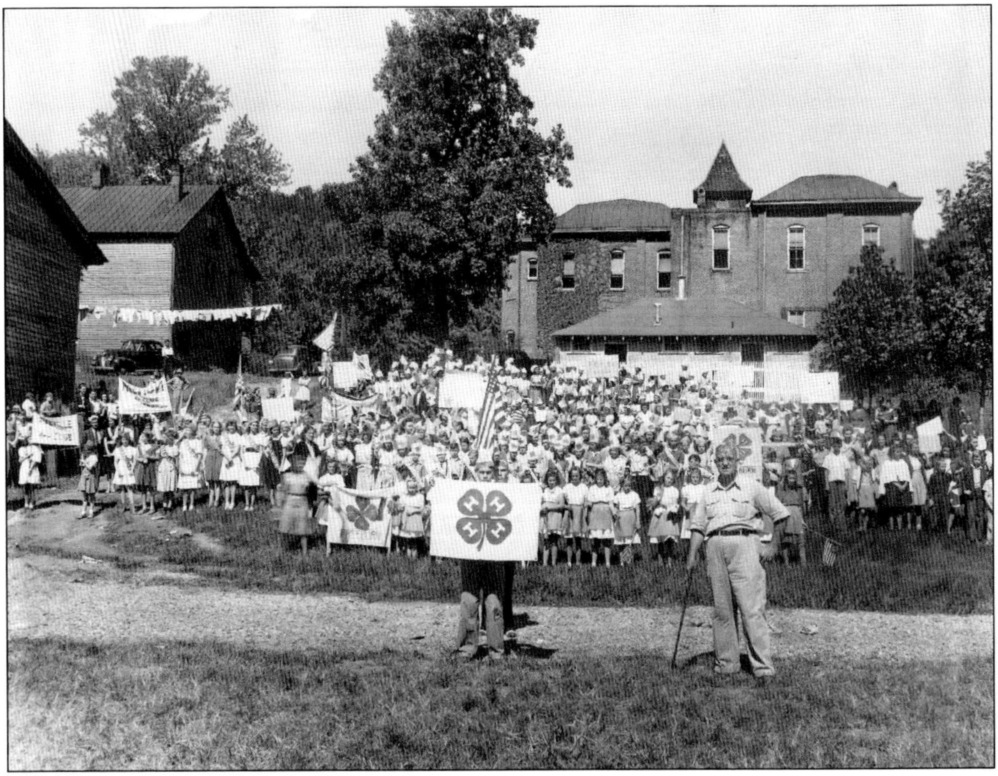

Dozens of schoolchildren from all over Pike County took part in a 4-H rally behind the Academy Building around 1940. The children are holding up signs with the names of their schools. Signs from Pikeville, Blackberry, Freeburn, Hellier, Millard, Heenon, Ball Fork, Sidney, Piso, and Belfry can be seen. (Courtesy of the Frank M. Allara Library, University of Pikeville.)

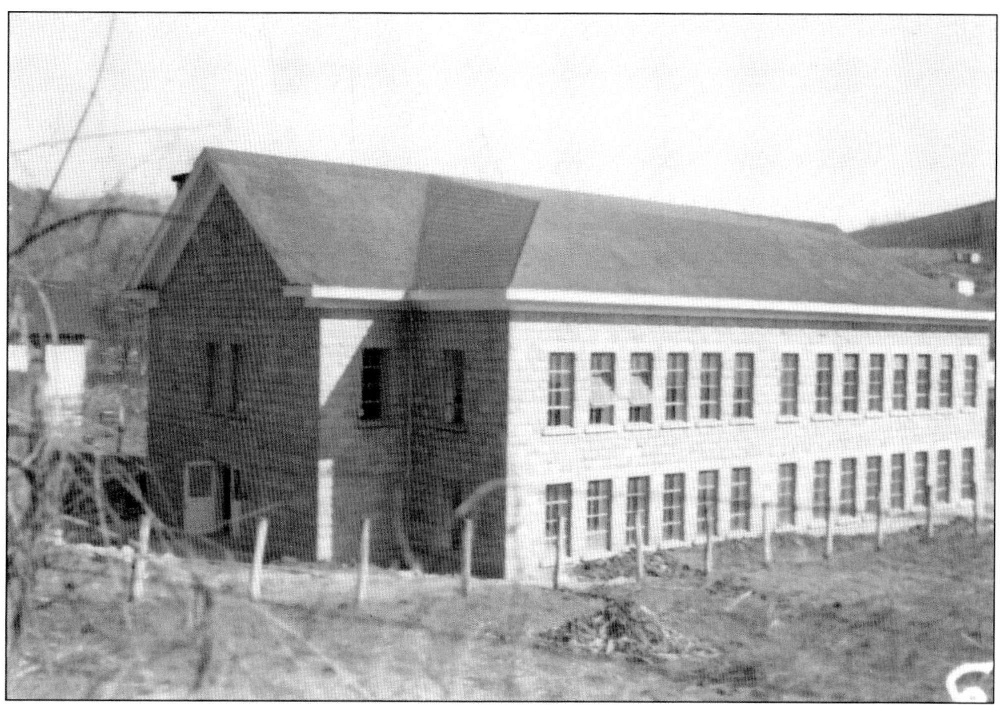

Perry A. Cline High School was built in 1938 as a Works Progress Administration project for $75,000. This allowed the school district's Black children to receive an accredited high school diploma for the first time. Principal William Cummings offered night classes to adults who had not previously had the opportunity to earn their diplomas. (Courtesy of the University of Kentucky Libraries Special Collections Research Center.)

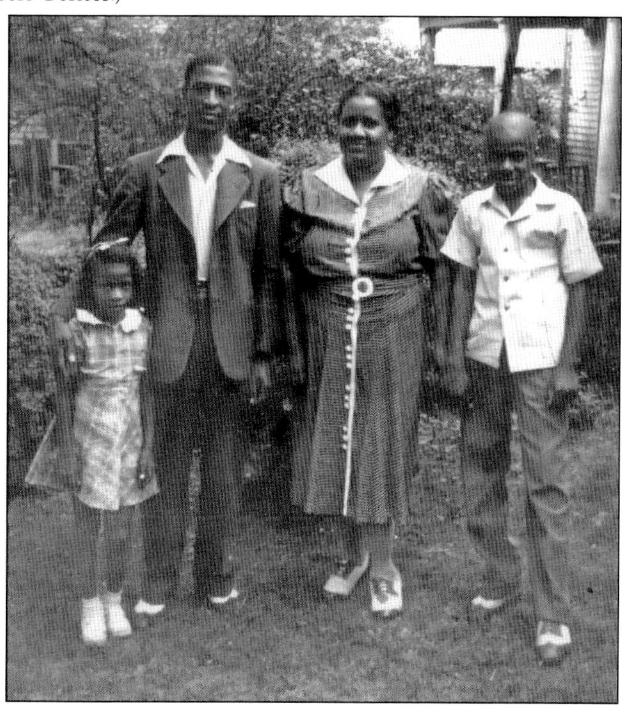

This is the Cummings family in about 1940 with, from left to right, daughter Ann, William Sr., Alberta, and William Jr. William Sr. was principal at Perry Cline from its opening until 1945, while Alberta taught lower grades. The school had a stellar reputation statewide, as William Sr. earned an award for distinguished service and the school was named the state's most progressive school in 1944. (Courtesy of the Cummings family.)

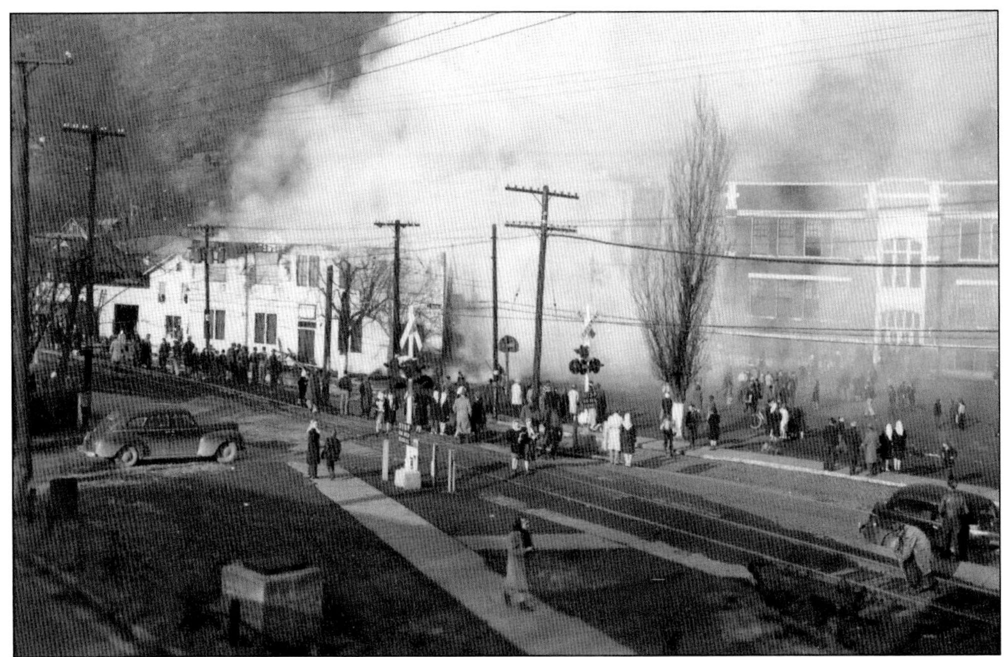

In 1947, the wooden gymnasium and elementary building burned almost completely. Here, the public is watching the fire, helpless to prevent the destruction. Supt. T.W. Oliver and John Bill Trivette, head basketball coach, began planning for a new gymnasium on the site soon thereafter. Unfortunately, Oliver died months before the new gymnasium was opened in 1949. (Courtesy of Brenda Hays, John Doug Hays collection.)

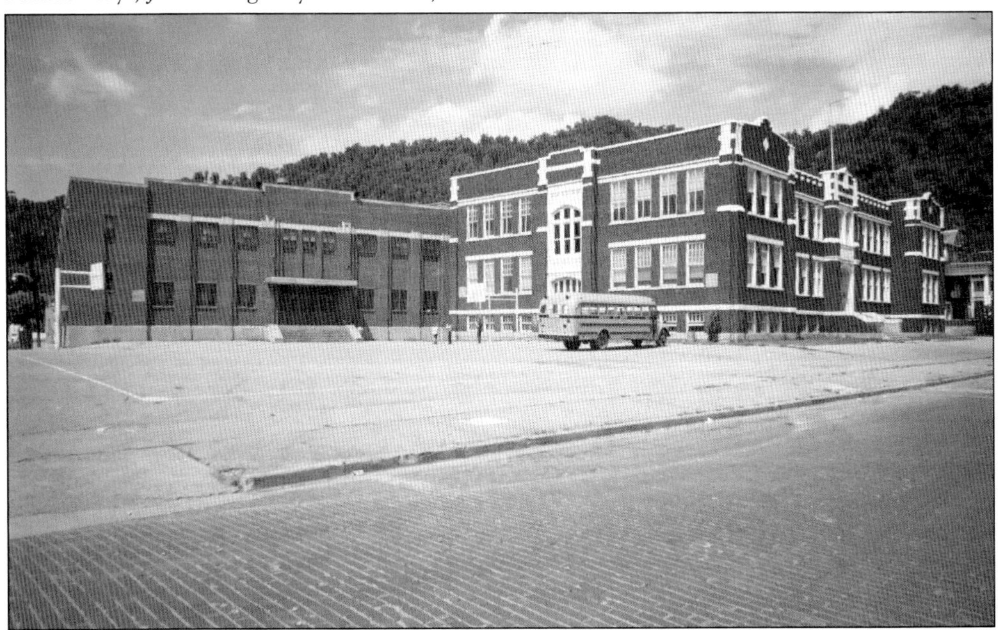

This is Pikeville High School around 1965, with the 3,200-seat T.W. Oliver Memorial Gymnasium on the left. This gymnasium also burned in 1969 and a metal building called "the Blue Goose" was erected in its place. Modern-day Pikeville High School has an attached gymnasium, which also bears Oliver's name. (Courtesy of David Hefner.)

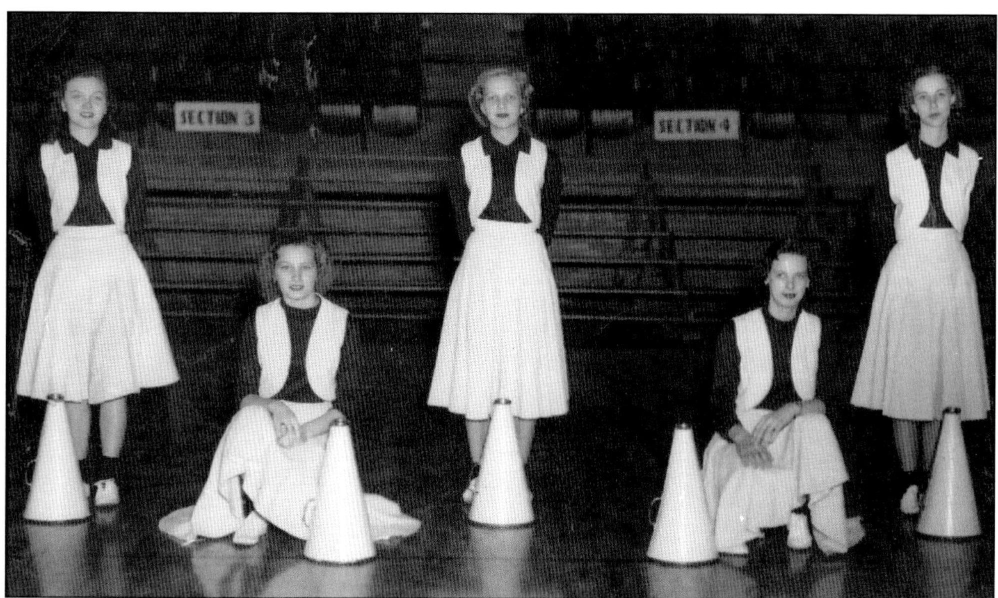

Pikeville High School has had a varsity cheerleading team since at least 1938. The 1950 squad is shown here. To say this program has excelled in competition is a gross understatement. They have won 32 regional, 11 state, and 7 national championships since 1972. The national championships came in 2001, 2002, 2016, 2017, 2018, 2021, and 2022. (Courtesy of Pikeville Independent Schools.)

The first Pikeville High School band was organized in 1925 by John Lewis, and the school has continued to have a strong band program throughout its history. This is an early 1970s band marching on Main Street during the annual Christmas parade. The band is led by field commander Betsy Elder; the band director at the time was C.J. Birch. (Courtesy of Pikeville Independent Schools.)

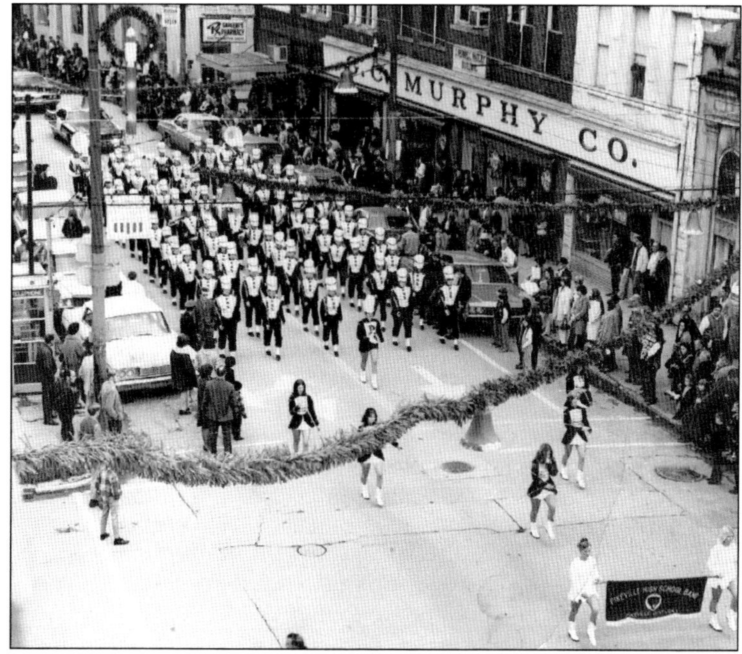

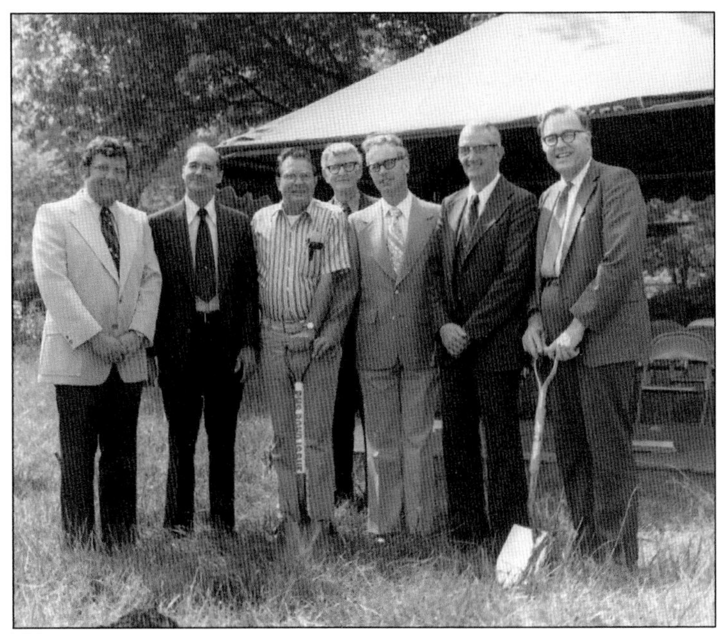

A new high school was built on the Mary Coleman property. Mayor William C. Hambley (far right) attended the groundbreaking. He believed that education was critical for the community's economic well-being. To help the school focus on that mission, the City of Pikeville built and maintains Hambley Athletic Center, with the school compensating the city for its use. (Courtesy of the Pike County Public Library.)

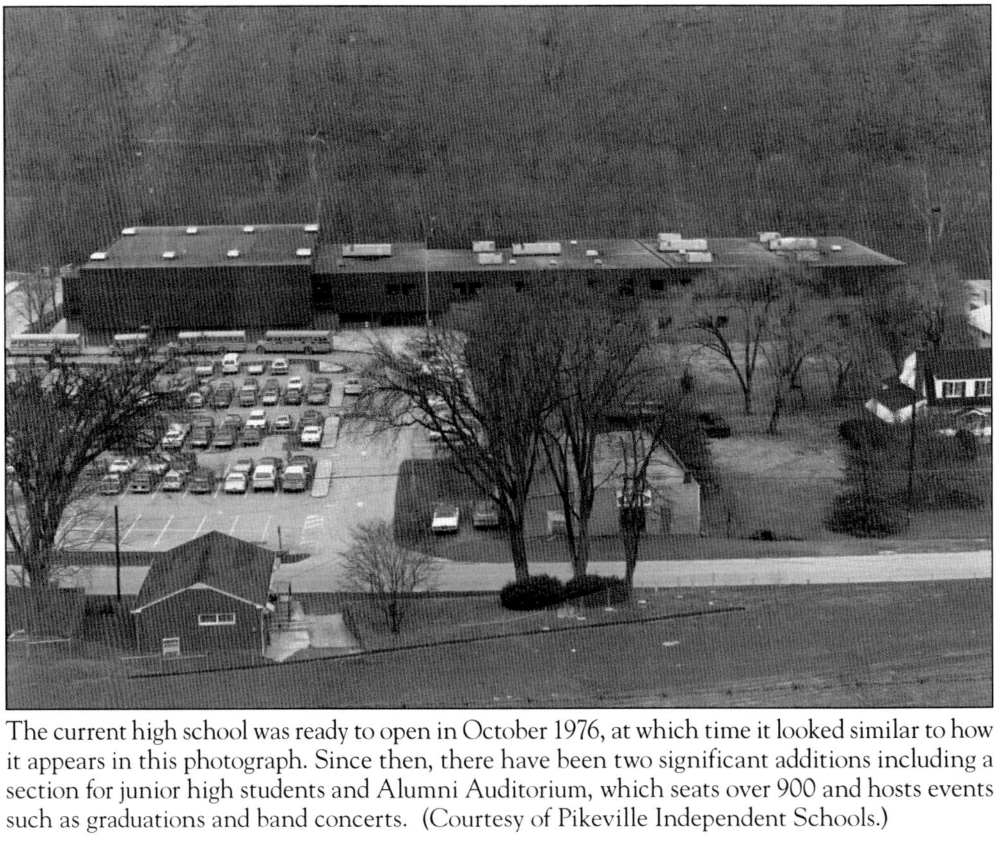

The current high school was ready to open in October 1976, at which time it looked similar to how it appears in this photograph. Since then, there have been two significant additions including a section for junior high students and Alumni Auditorium, which seats over 900 and hosts events such as graduations and band concerts. (Courtesy of Pikeville Independent Schools.)

John Bill Trivette was the Pikeville High School basketball coach between 1942 and 1960. Trivette played in college for Adolph Rupp. He was among the first coaches to employ a full court press defense. From 1949 until his retirement, the Panthers won the district 11 times and the region seven times. Their best finish in the Sweet 16 was third place in 1957. (Courtesy of Pikeville Independent Schools.)

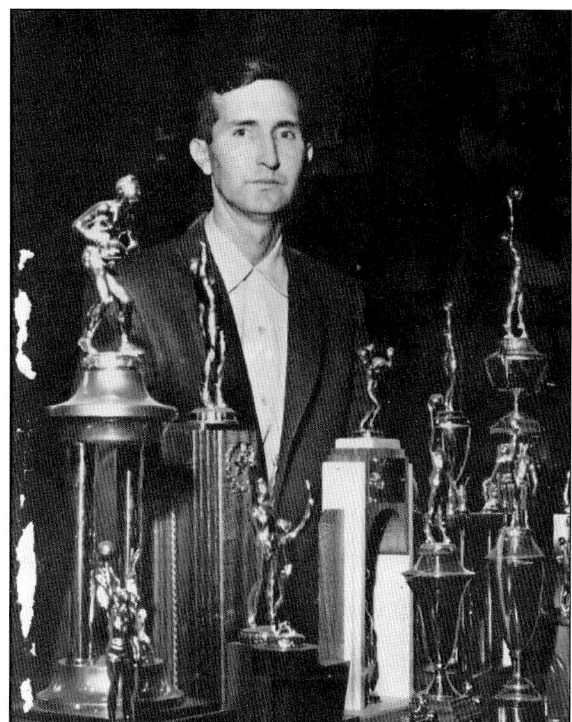

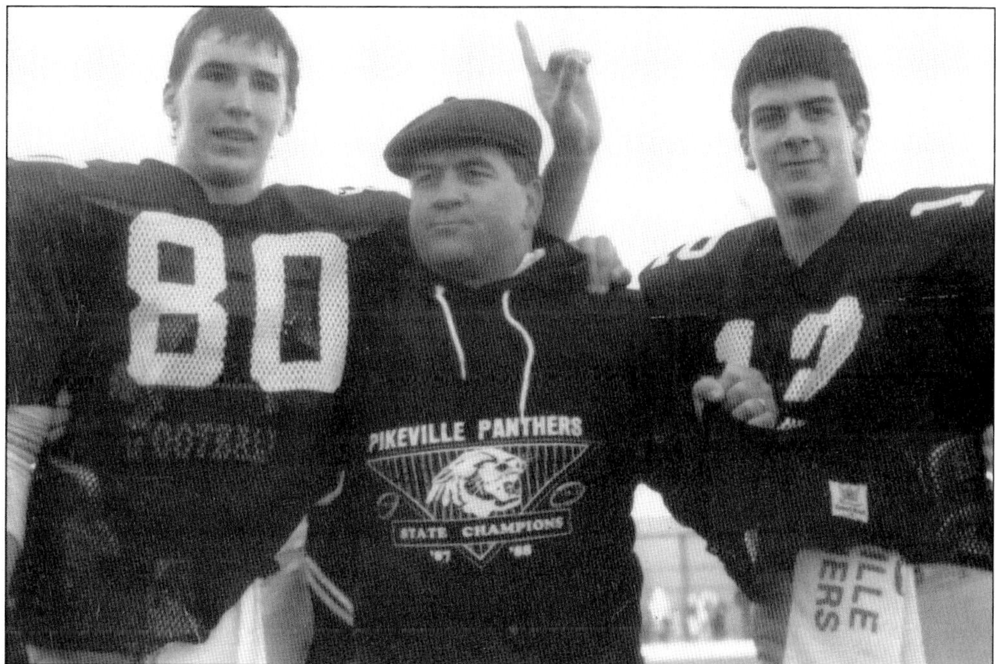

Hillard Howard (center) is seen here with his son, Jason (right), and Jason Justice. Howard built Pikeville's football program into a powerhouse over two decades. He won 208 games, 12 Class A regional championships, and three consecutive Class A state championships from 1987 through 1989. He was inducted into the Kentucky High School Athletic Association Hall of Fame in 2017. (Courtesy of Pikeville Independent Schools.)

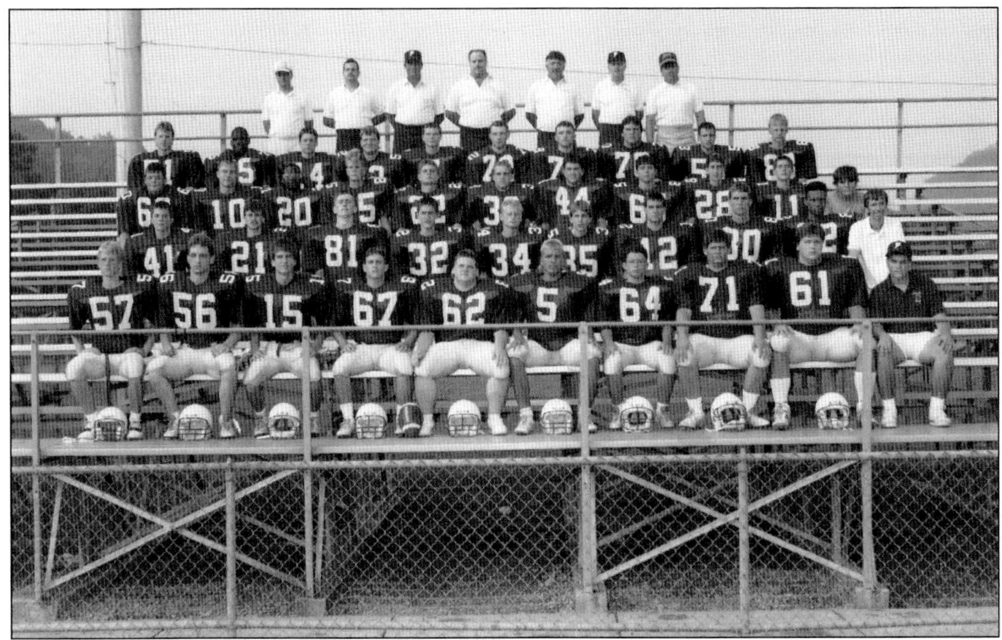

The 1989 Pikeville High School football team was the school's third consecutive Class A state champion team. The Panthers won 33 straight games before falling to Belfry in the fifth game of the 1989 season, but then won 10 straight, including the championship game. Coach Chris McNamee has continued the tradition, with state titles in 2015, 2019, and 2021. (Courtesy of Pikeville Independent Schools.)

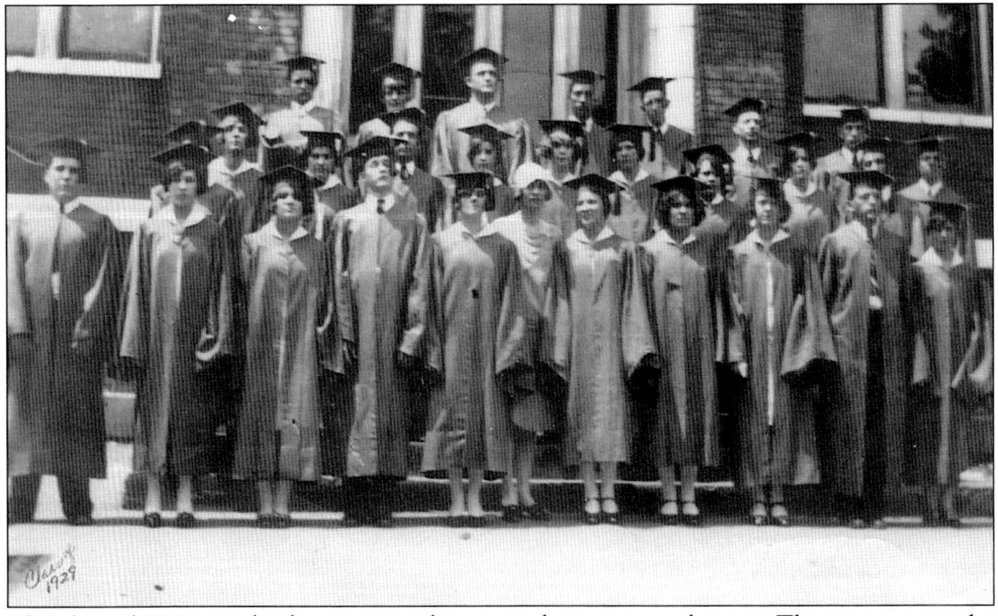

The class of 1929 was the first to wear the cap and gown at graduation. They are a reminder that, though athletic accomplishments deserve to be celebrated, they are secondary. Recent test scores and rankings by various organizations consistently place the school among the top 15 in the state. Academic excellence is the true legacy the school's leaders and faculty leave behind. (Courtesy of Pikeville Independent Schools.)

Three

Commerce and Industry

Other than trade in furs and ginseng, commerce in Pikeville was limited prior to 1860. A logging industry began in earnest in the 1850s, but the Civil War put that on hold.

After the war, logging resumed and huge trees were cut down and tied together into rafts, then floated down to the Ohio River to sell. In 1890, Pike County produced $2 million in timber. Several fortunes were made in the business, but it was dangerous work, and many men were injured or killed.

All of the old-growth forests in the county were gone by the 1920s. Some acreage was timbered a second time, but the smaller trees could not sustain the industry at a high level. Around that time, the Ford Model T switched to an all-metal design and large-scale logging was essentially over.

Coal filled the gap. It supplanted wood for energy use in the United States around 1890, but its use in industry accelerated in the first decade of the 20th century. Pike County's coal deposits were said to be the richest mineral deposits in the world. There had been mines in Pike County in the 1850s, but river transport of coal proved difficult. Extreme demand for the product and the quality of Eastern Kentucky coal brought railroads in to ease transportation concerns. It also brought young attorneys and businessmen to Pikeville—where land deals were recorded and court was held—from all over the country.

The economic impact of coal was many times greater than timber. At 1.5 billion tons, Pike County has produced more coal than any other in the country. There were down cycles, but coal mining was the industrial base of the local economy for over a century. Hundreds of businesses started in that environment. Some lasted more than a century.

As with timber, coal mining was dangerous and could be deadly, but the area has never had a shortage of people willing to work hard and take risks to support their families.

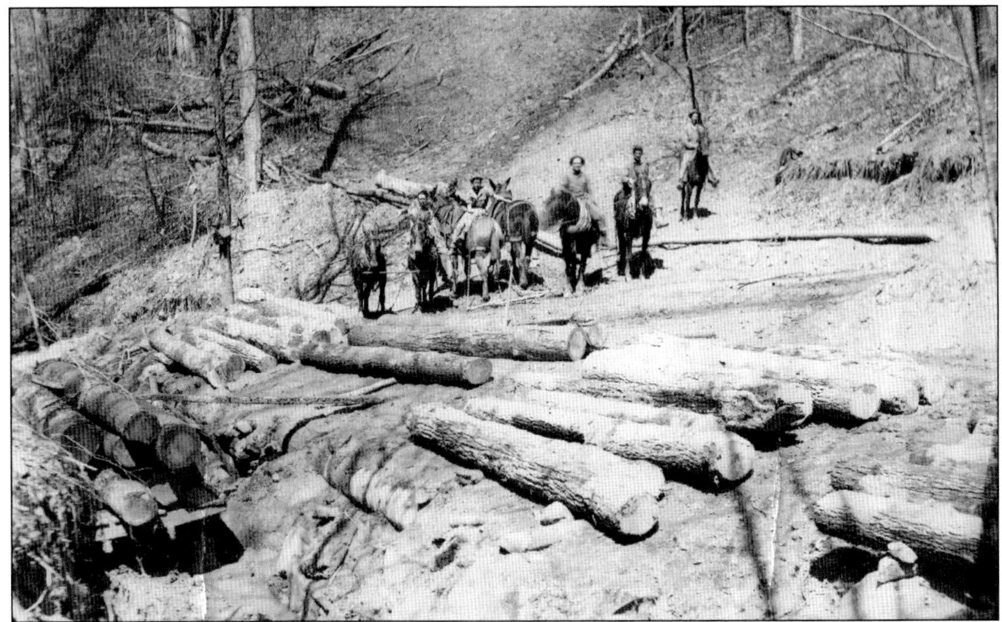

Though this photograph was taken in 1949, with subtle differences, it could be confused with one taken decades before. In 1870, the logs would have been hand cut and the chains would have been hemp ropes, but felled trees were gathered at a landing before mules or horses dragged the logs toward the river just the same. (Courtesy of the Frank M. Allara Library, University of Pikeville.)

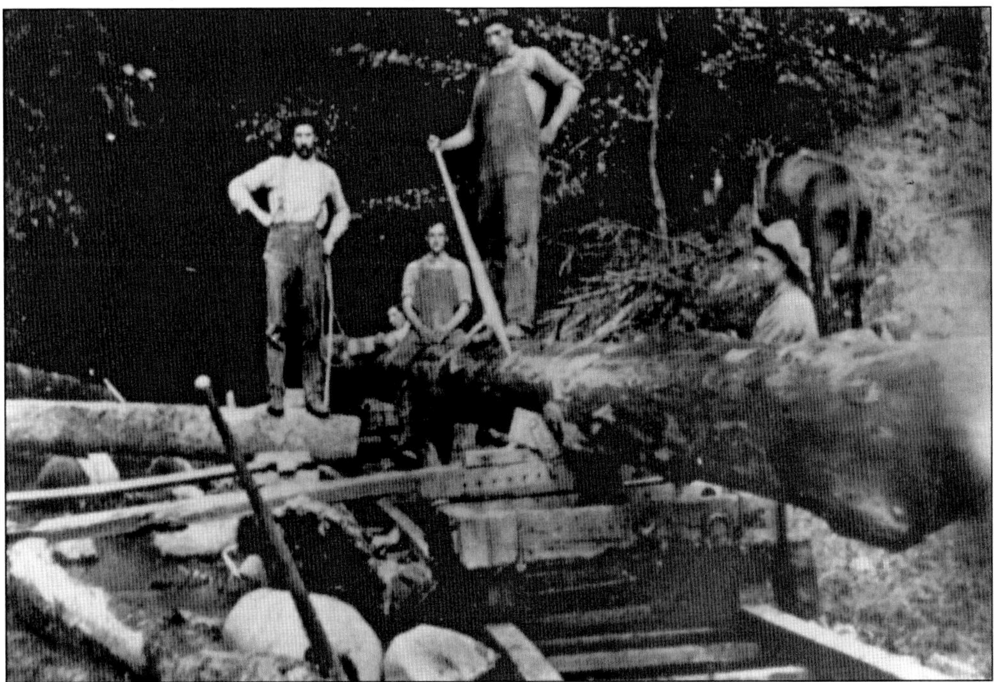

Around 1910, Winfield Ramsey (left) is holding his ox whip while (from right) Dan and Harry Syck help two unknown men secure a log to a hand truck on Peter Fork of Chloe Creek. Ramsey's team of oxen dragged the logs here, then the men transported them downhill using the truck mounted on wooden rails. (Courtesy of the Pike County Public Library.)

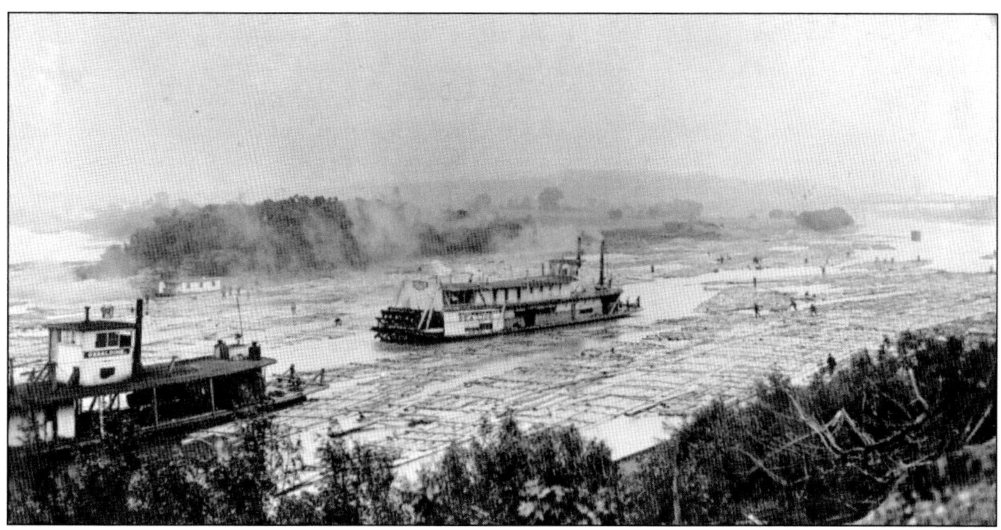

During months when the river was low, the felled logs were gathered in the river and fashioned into rafts. When rains swelled the river, the rafts floated, and men piloted them downriver to market. Thousands of logs each year left the Big Sandy River at its confluence with the Ohio, as seen here in May 1910. (Courtesy of Murphy Library Special Collections/ARC, University of Wisconsin-La Crosse.)

Thomas "Tom" Huffman (foreground) and his twin brother, William, are standing along a narrow-gauge rail near a mine close to Chloe Creek, which the two started in 1909. The rail transported coal to a loadout near today's Reynolds Market. Besides mining, the brothers each had other businesses. Tom—Huffman Avenue's namesake—owned the ice plant, and William owned a grocery store. (Courtesy of the Big Sandy Heritage Center Museum.)

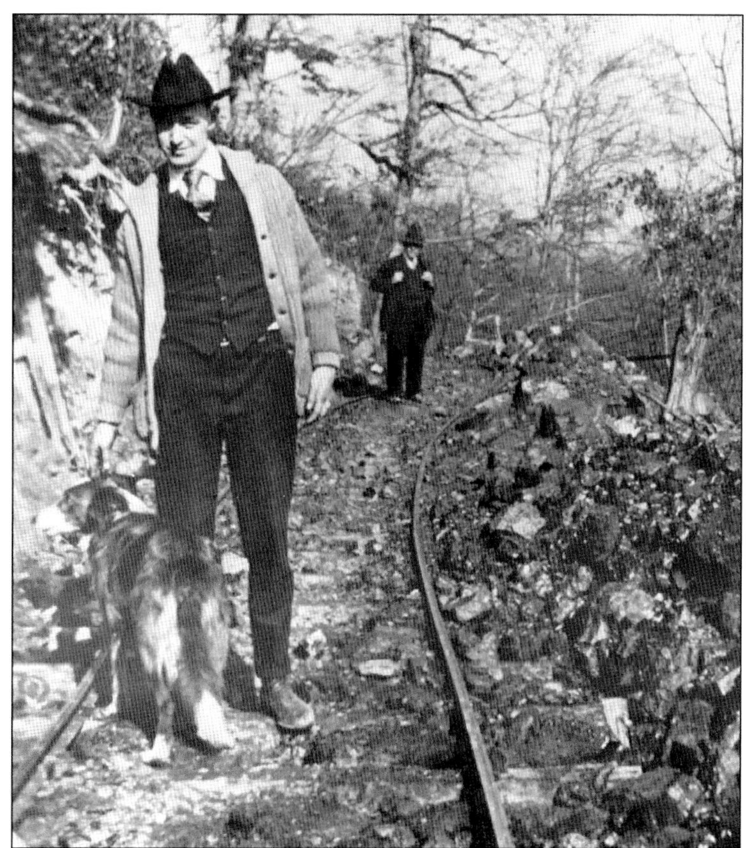

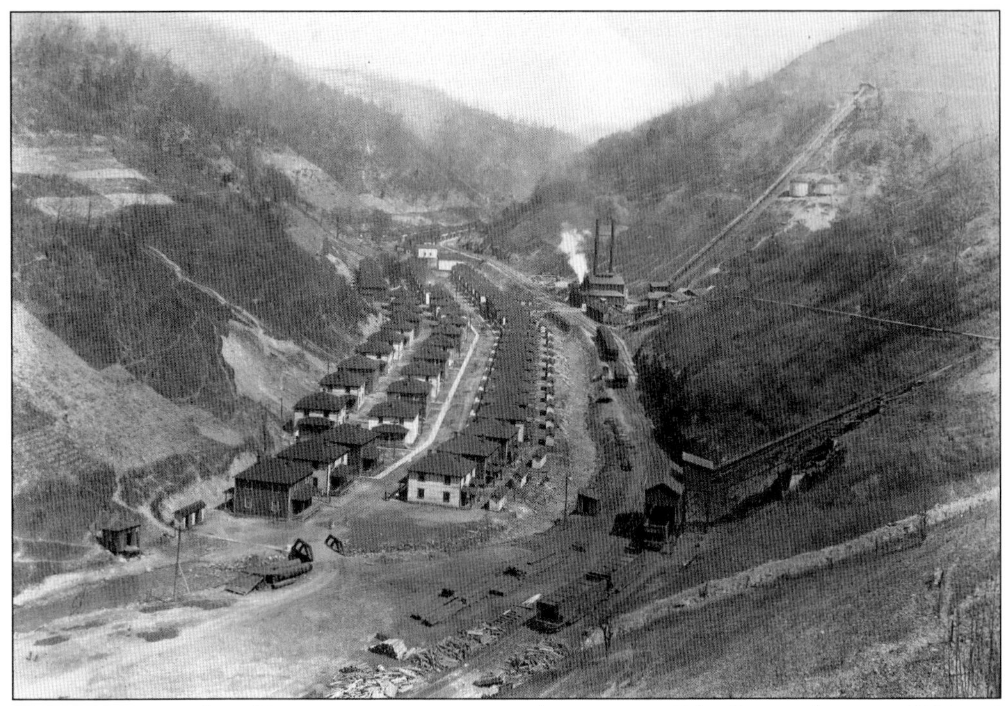

There were more than 50 company towns—or coal camps—in Pike County between 1904 and 1958, and the McKinney Steel Company Mine on Greasy Creek, pictured here, was open between 1923 and 1928. This operation and its twin at Wolfpit employed 1,000 men. The investments in coal camps brought significant capital into Pikeville. (Courtesy of the Frank M. Allara Library, University of Pikeville.)

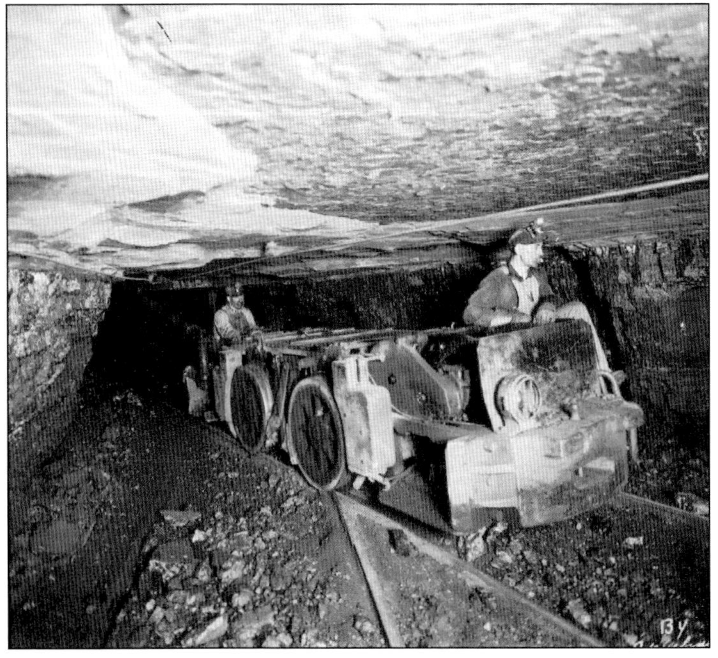

These underground coal miners were in McKinney Steel's Wolfpit mine around 1925. Their personal safety equipment mostly consisted of carbide lights on their caps, but larger companies were replacing mules with electric locomotives like this one. In the first third of the 1900s, many of Pikeville's prominent citizens were managers or agents of mines like these. (Courtesy of the Pike County Public Library.)

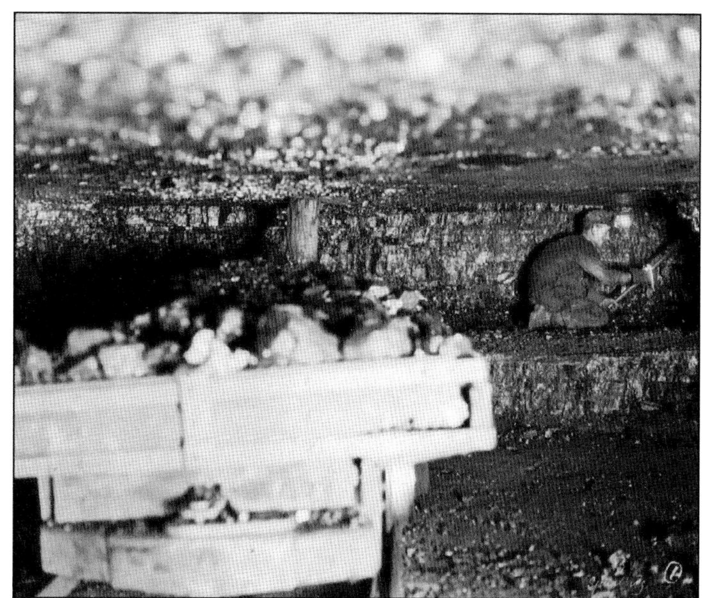

Mining in 1925 meant picking the coal and loading it by hand. Later innovations such as continuous mining machines, roof bolters, and ventilation systems dramatically improved safety, reducing deaths from 2,696 in 1917 to 8 in 2016, while mechanization reduced the need for labor. After World War II, most larger companies closed operations and local mine owners filled the gap. (Courtesy of the Pike County Public Library.)

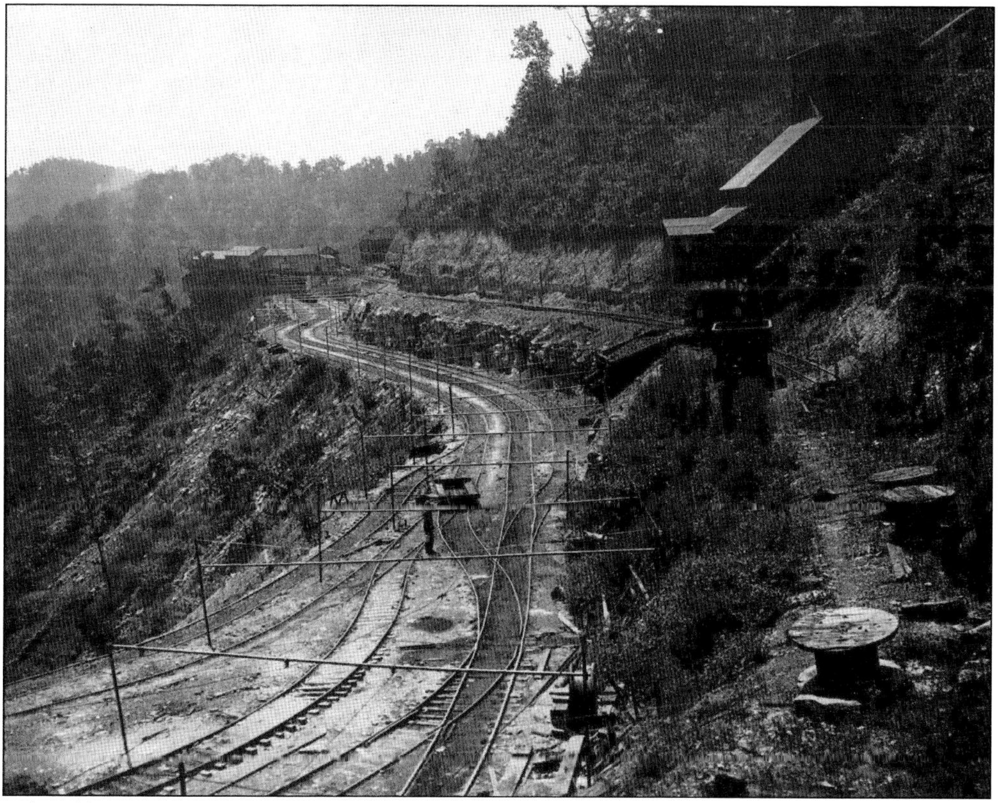

A head house is where miners were told whether their coal was accepted. Wolfpit's head house is seen here at upper left around 1925. Large companies drew on substantial capital to buy large tracts of mineral rights and modern equipment and build rail to the mines. Smaller operators had to be innovative, and dozens of mining-related patents were awarded to Pike County innovators. (Courtesy of the Pike County Public Library.)

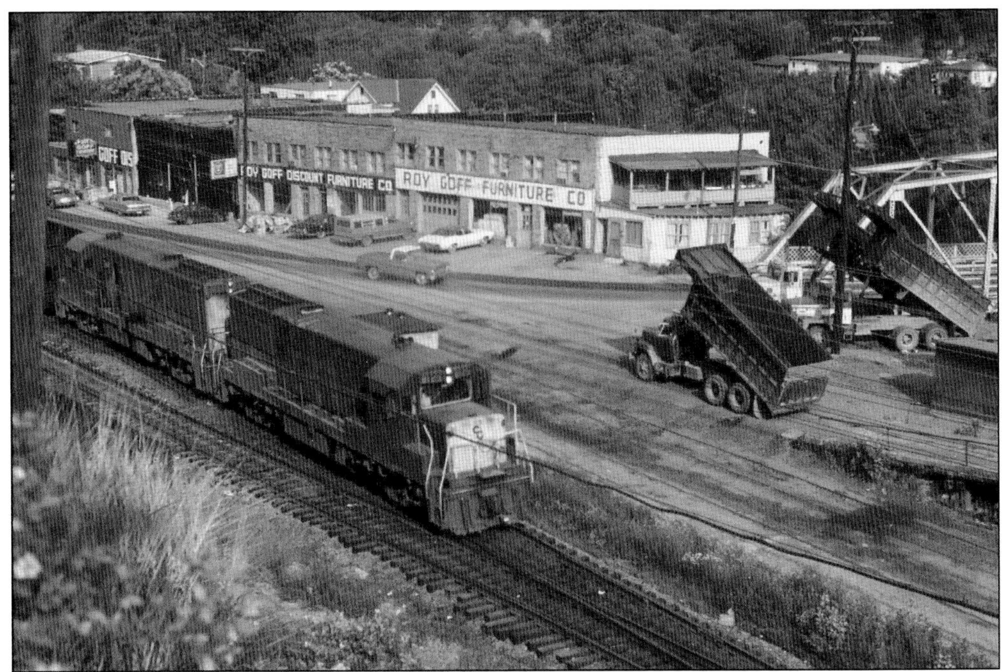

Some small operators started "truck mines"—meaning they hauled the coal by truck to loadouts on the rail rather than depositing the coal directly from the mine into rail cars—as early as the 1930s as a way to reduce capital requirements. Here, unloaded coal trucks have just visited the loadout near the Upper Bridge in 1977. (Courtesy of Everett N. Young.)

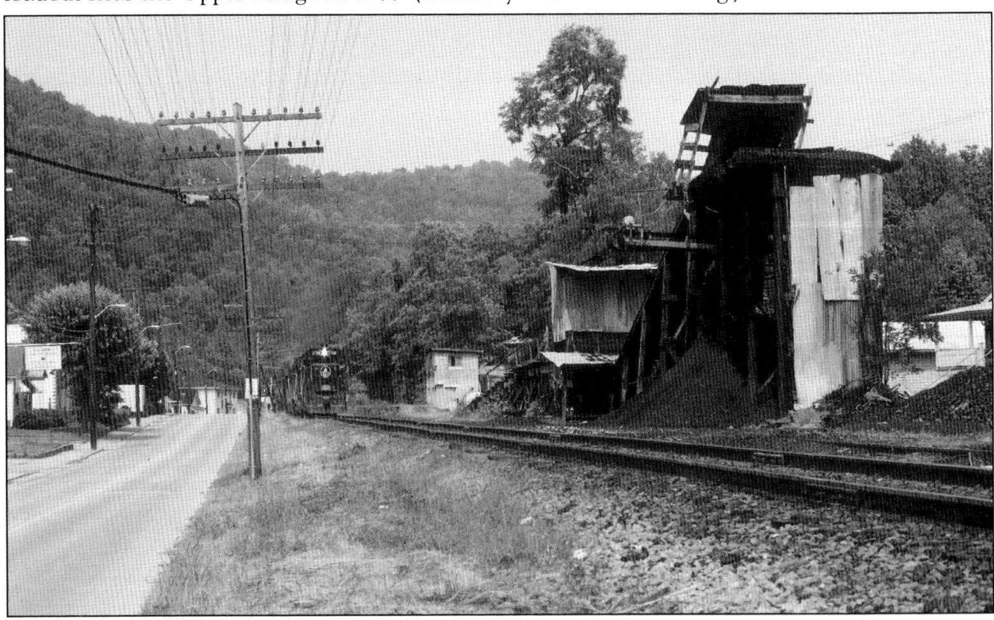

Pikeville had several loadouts supplied by truck mines including East Kentucky Collieries' Dana Sue tipple on Cline Street across from Shurtleff's Laundry, seen here in 1978. A.J. "Jack" Dalton was called "the King of Truck Mines" and once owned over 100. In the early 1950s, it was claimed that he was Pike County's first millionaire. Many others later obtained similar wealth. (Courtesy of Everett N. Young.)

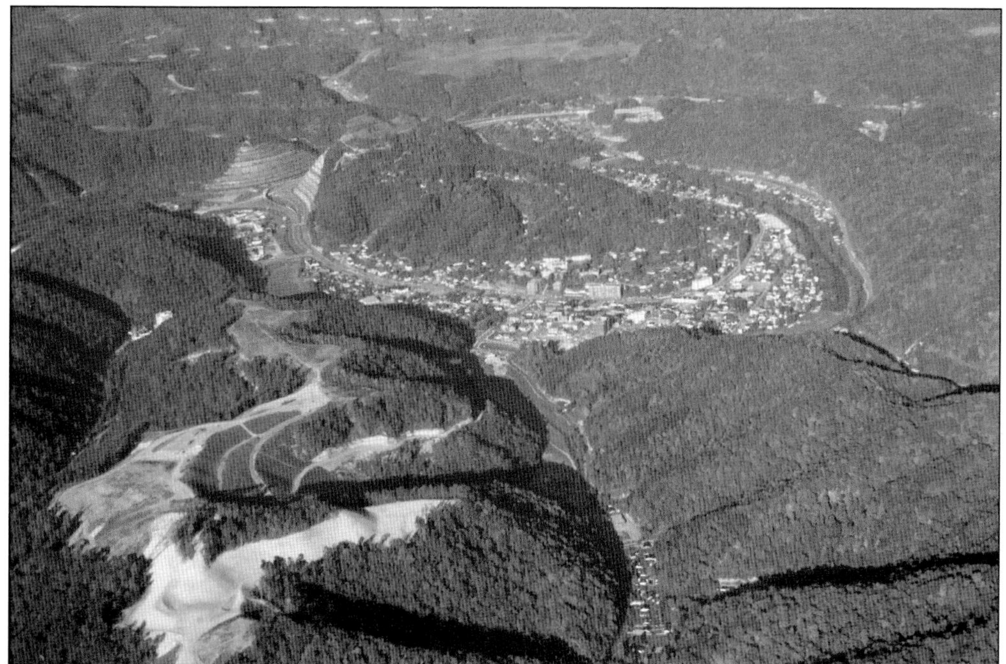

The next technological step in coal mining was mountaintop removal surface mining, where the rock overlying the coal seam is removed using large earth-moving equipment. The coal is hauled away in trucks, and the rock is returned. The large surface mine seen here around 1988 is now a residential neighborhood called Chloe Ridge. (Courtesy of the University of Kentucky Libraries Special Collections Research Center.)

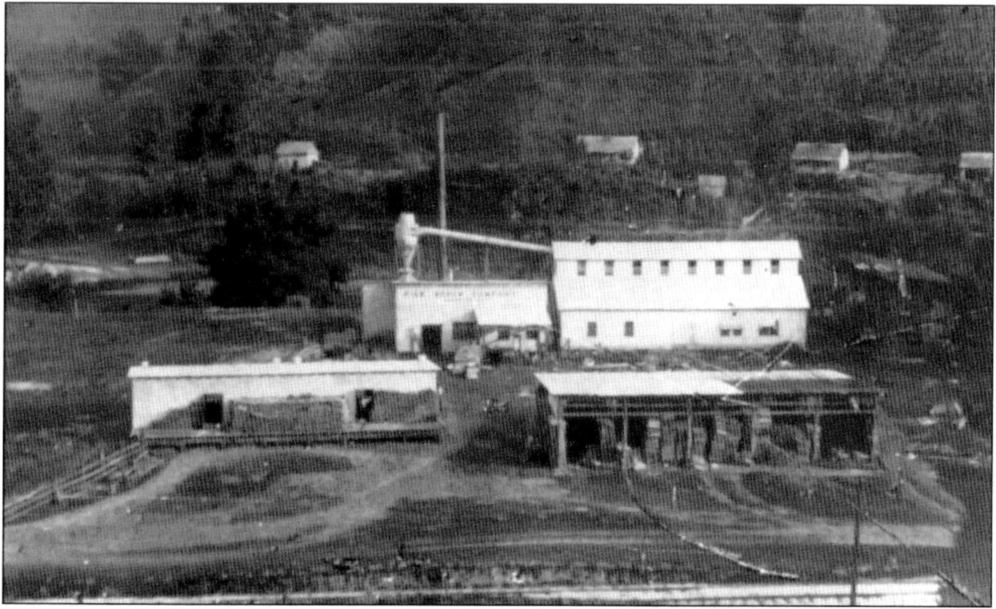

The Pike Spoke Company, near today's Hibbard Street, was founded in 1909 by Jesse Sanders, Henry Sagraves, and Robert Wilson. The spokes were used for wooden automobile wheels. By March 1916, Pikeville Supply & Planing Company owned the factory when one of its boilers exploded. Four men were killed and two injured. (Courtesy of the Pike County Public Library.)

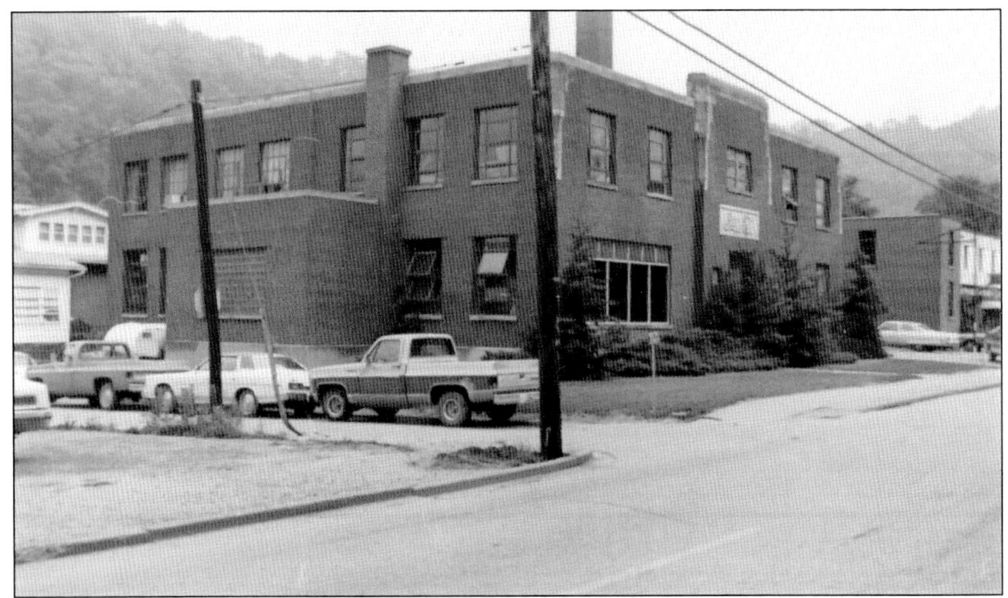

William Huffman and Tom Hatcher founded Pikeville Bottling Company in 1912. This building—seen here in about 1976—was built in 1938 and operated until just before the company dissolved in 1980. Today, it is home to Bit Source, a digital solutions company that earned national attention for transitioning coal miners to the digital workforce. (Courtesy of Mayor James A. Carter.)

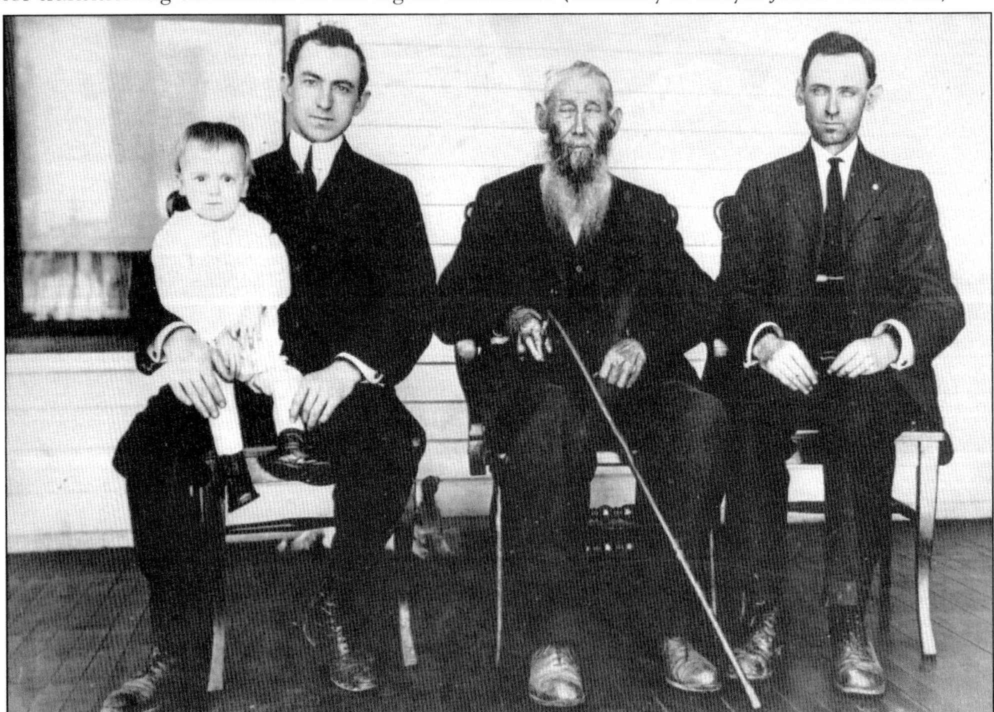

William "Bill" Call moved his family from North Carolina around 1870 and ran a hardware store for many years. His son John Wesley established J.W. Call and Son Funeral Home, one of the oldest businesses in Pikeville. Pictured from left to right are John George, William Perry, Bill, and John Wesley Call. (Courtesy of the Frank M. Allara Library, University of Pikeville.)

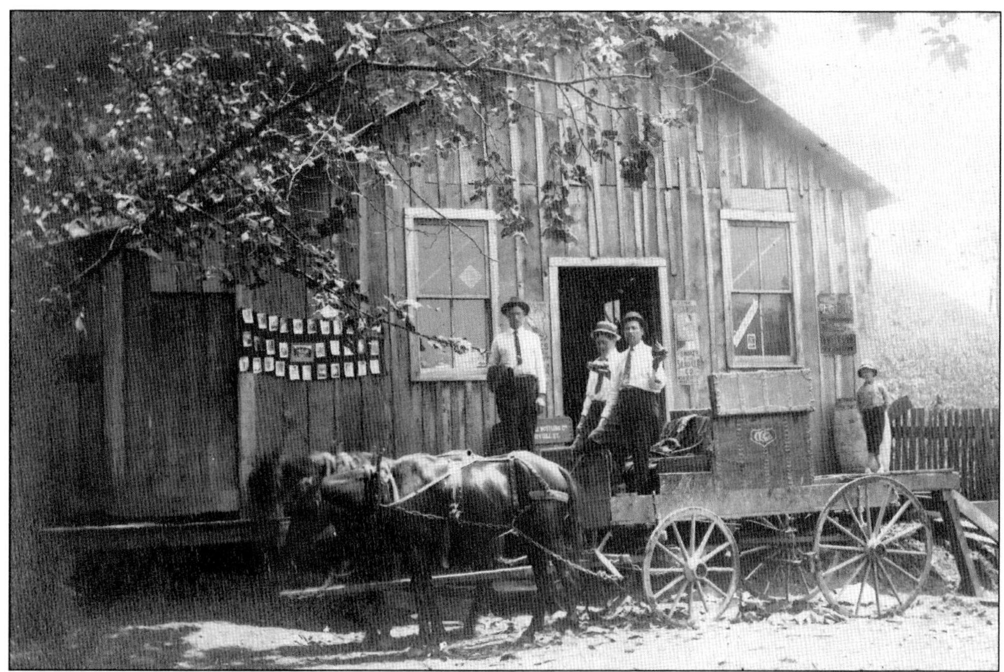

Brothers Sam and Jasper Saad were born in Syria and emigrated to the United States in 1901 and 1904, respectively. The brothers came to Pikeville by 1905 and opened a grocery, but later Sam owned Saad Clothing Co. and Jasper owned a photography studio. Jasper married local girl Clara Sword and took many of the best-known photographs of Pikeville. (Courtesy of the Big Sandy Heritage Center Museum.)

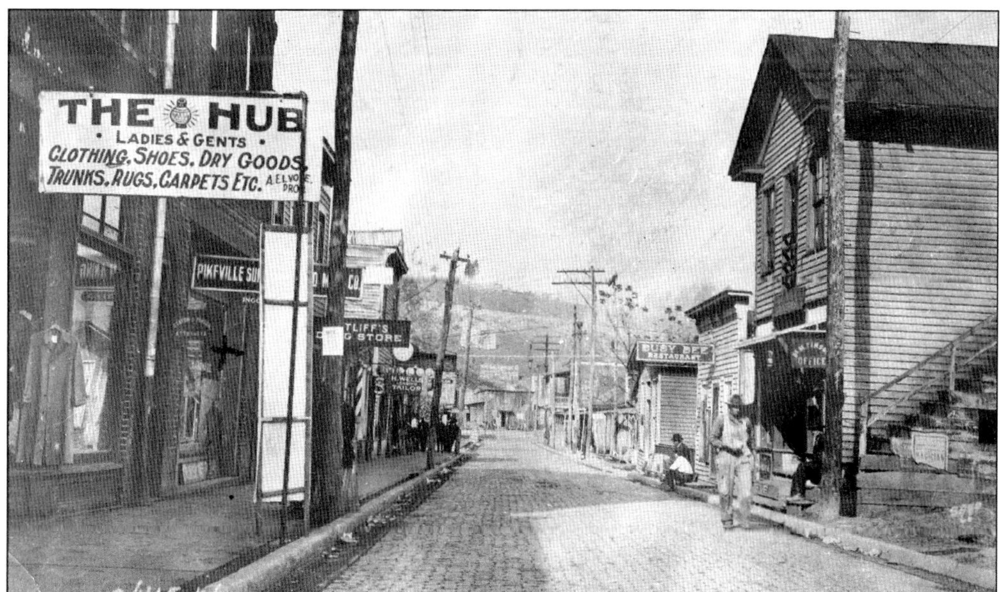

In 1913, Pikeville was the first town on the Big Sandy to brick its streets, as can be seen here on Division Street around 1920. Among the restaurant, grocery, jewelry, and other stores was Ratliff's Drug Store. During the 1918 flu pandemic, this pharmacy was open 24 hours every day. (Courtesy of the Frank M. Allara Library, University of Pikeville.)

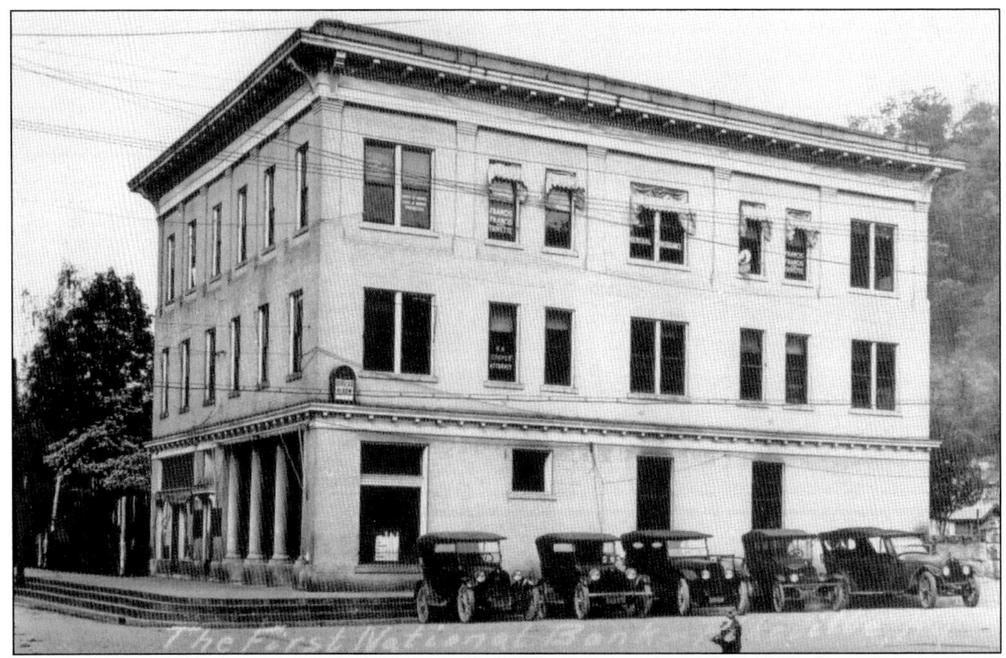

The First National Bank of Pikeville opened in 1889 as a state bank under the name Bank of Pikeville in this building on the corner of Main and Division Streets. The building reportedly required around 76,000 bricks to complete. It was approved to be a national bank in 1903. (Courtesy of the Big Sandy Heritage Center Museum.)

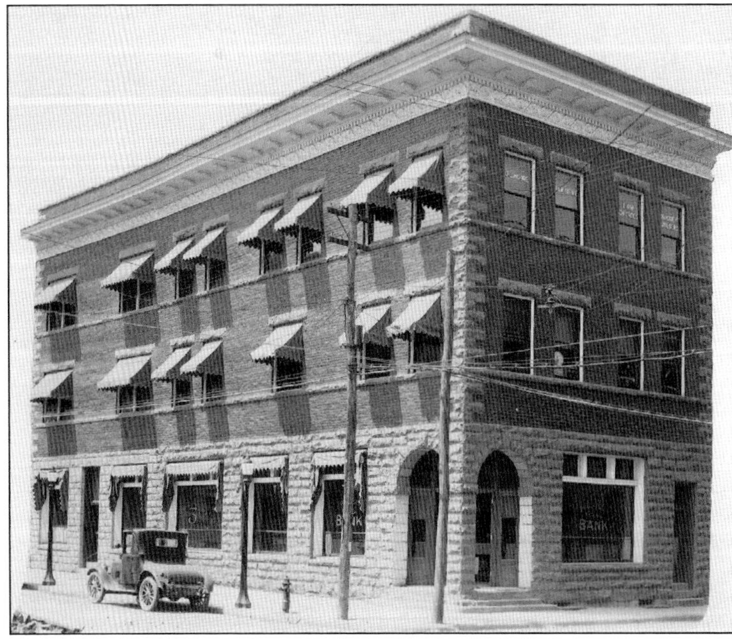

Pikeville National Bank was originally capitalized with just $25,000, but the business grew rapidly, and the first remodel of the building, including the installation of the bank's first vault, was completed in 1921. The surroundings had changed in the 17 years since it first opened. The streets were bricked, a fire hydrant installed, and an electric light hung overhead. (Courtesy of Community Trust Bank.)

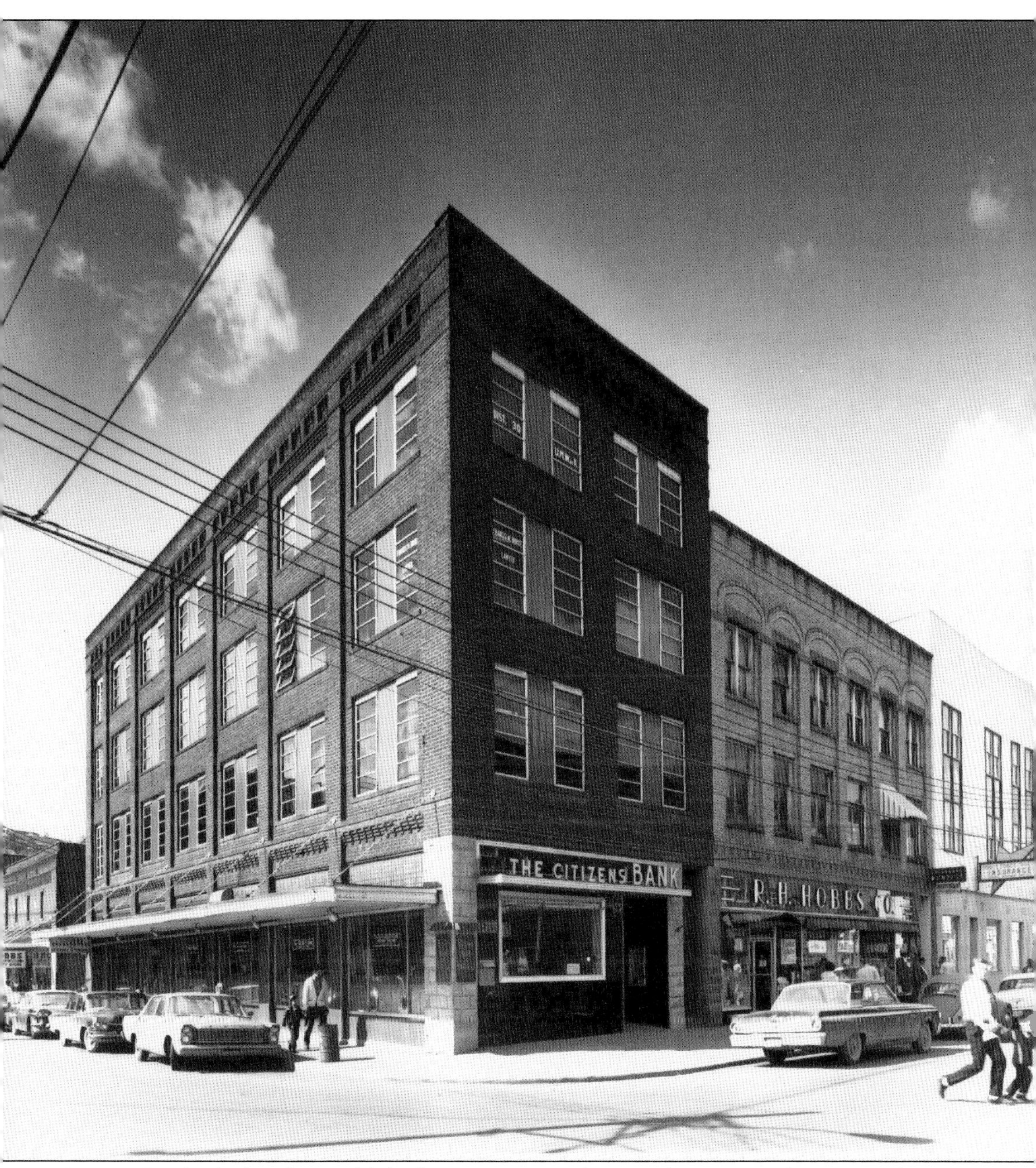

Citizens Bank of Pikeville, established in 1952, is seen here in the 1960s at the corner of Main Street and Caroline Avenue. Close inspection of the upper floors reveals signage for the United Mine Workers of America District 30 and for attorney Francis Burke. Just to the bank's right was the R.H. Hobbs Company department store. Owned by Robert H. Hobbs, originally from Tennessee, this building wrapped around the bank and also had an entrance on Caroline Avenue. It was well known in the area for its snack bar, and Pike County children knew that it was the best place to go for candy and the latest toys. These buildings were renovated in the 1980s to produce a single, larger building for Citizens Bank, which was later acquired by U.S. Bank. (Courtesy of the Big Sandy Heritage Center Museum.)

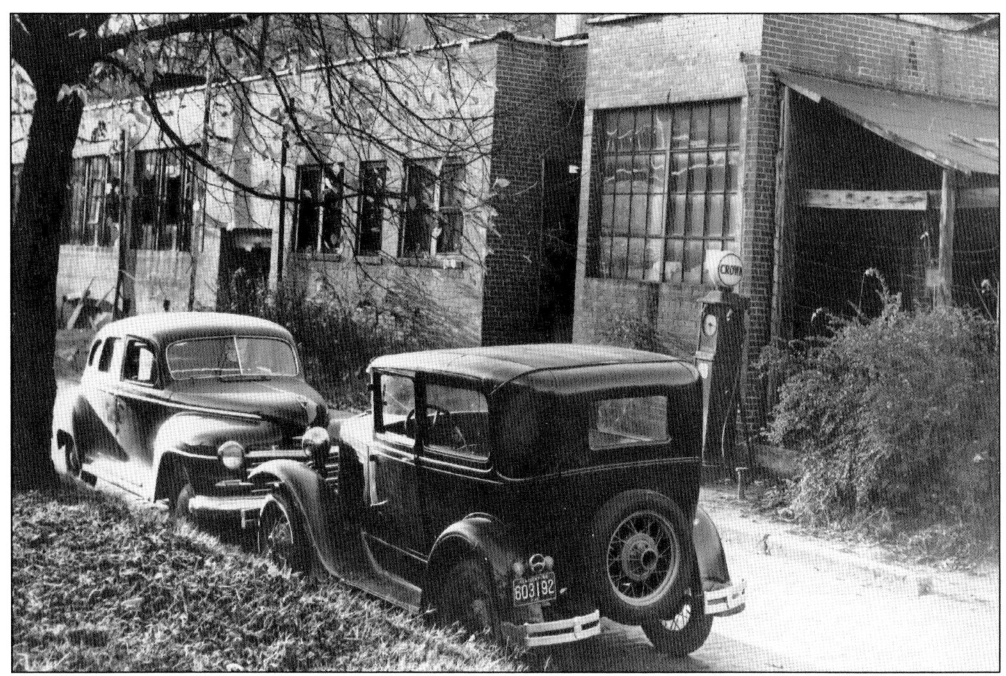

This is Shurtleff's Laundry on Central Avenue around 1946. Ernest Shurtleff, originally from Massachusetts, founded the company in 1921, the same year he married Mae Elliott from Pikeville. A 1914 engineering graduate from the Massachusetts Institute of Technology, he ran the laundry for 30 years before losing his life in an airplane crash. His descendants continue the business to this day. (Courtesy of Shurtleff's Laundry.)

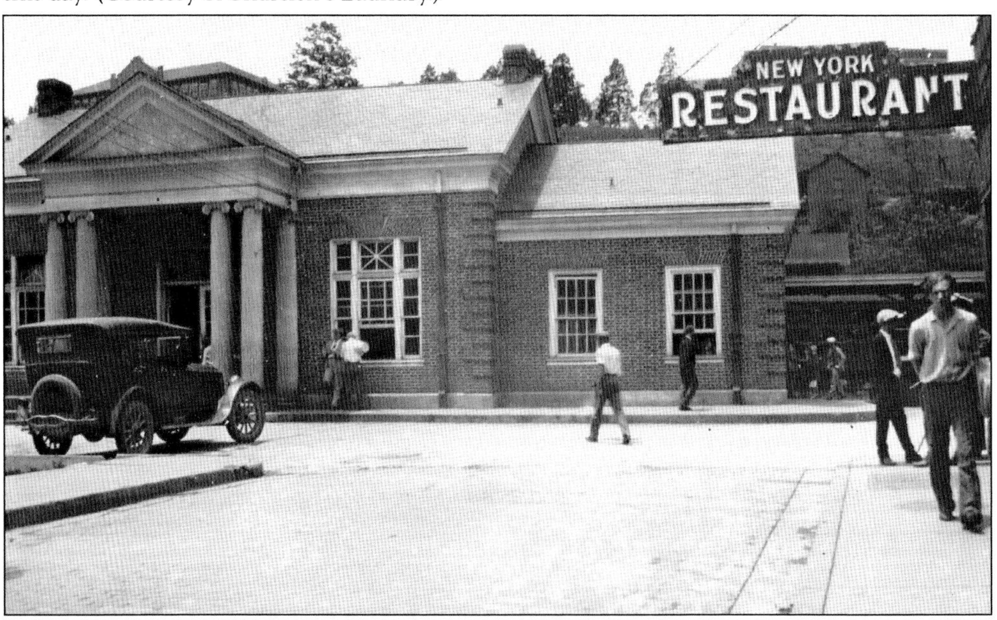

The Railroad Depot was perhaps the busiest spot in town at the time this photograph was taken around 1929, and it was a prime location for an establishment like New York Restaurant. Owned by Christos Petrou, an immigrant from Greece and World War I veteran, the restaurant was in operation through at least the early 1940s. (Courtesy of Everett N. Young.)

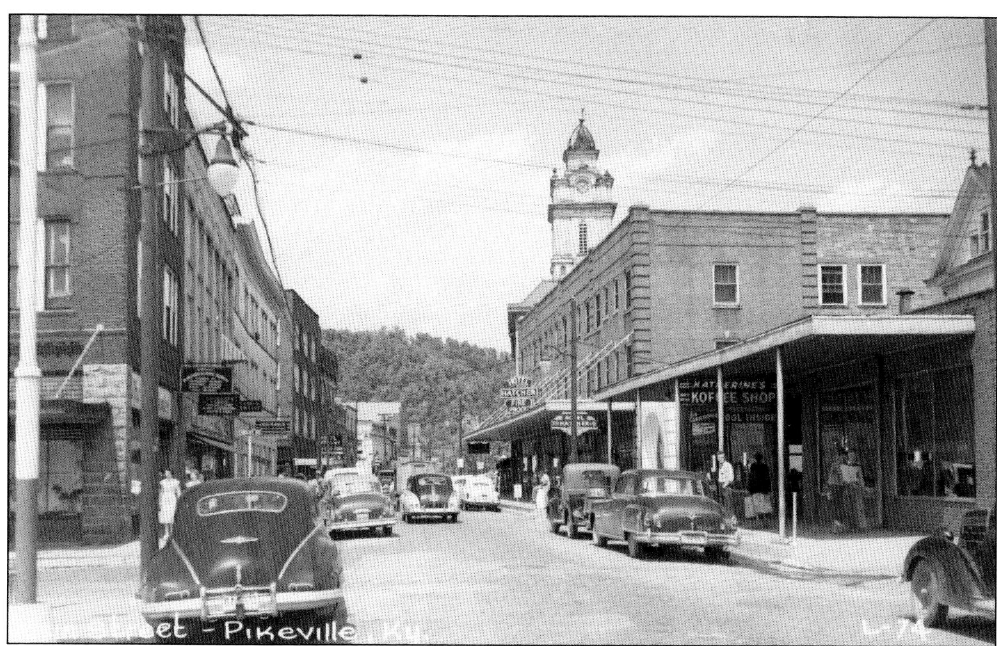

This is Main Street around 1950 as seen from its intersection with Caroline Avenue. There were many businesses on this end of the street, with two hotels, a coffee shop, a dentist, an insurance agency, and department stores all on one block. The Hatcher Hotel on the right had 106 rooms and later became the home of Watson's department store. (Courtesy of Sam Hatcher.)

The Hatcher Hotel was completed by local businessman James Hatcher in 1931 and was reputed to be the finest hotel in Eastern Kentucky. As seen here, Hatcher filled the walls with folklore, statistics, and other bits of wisdom and trivia. On the right is an iron lung display asking for polio treatment donations. (Courtesy of the Pike County Public Library.)

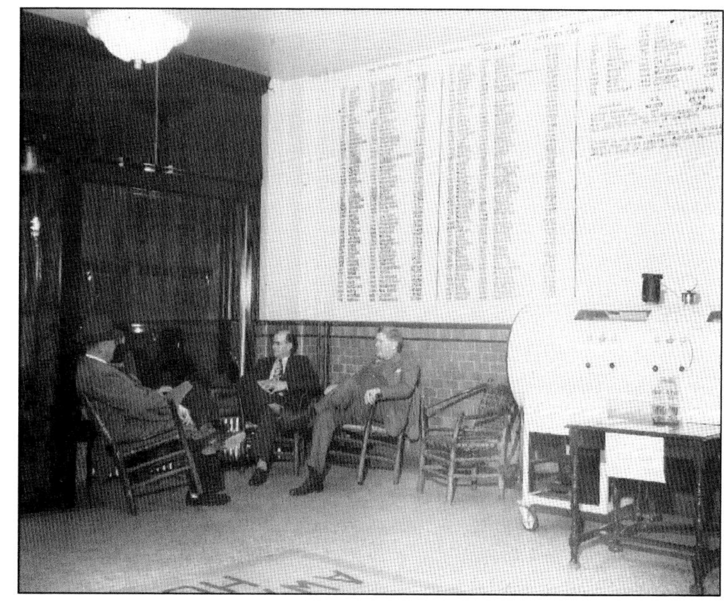

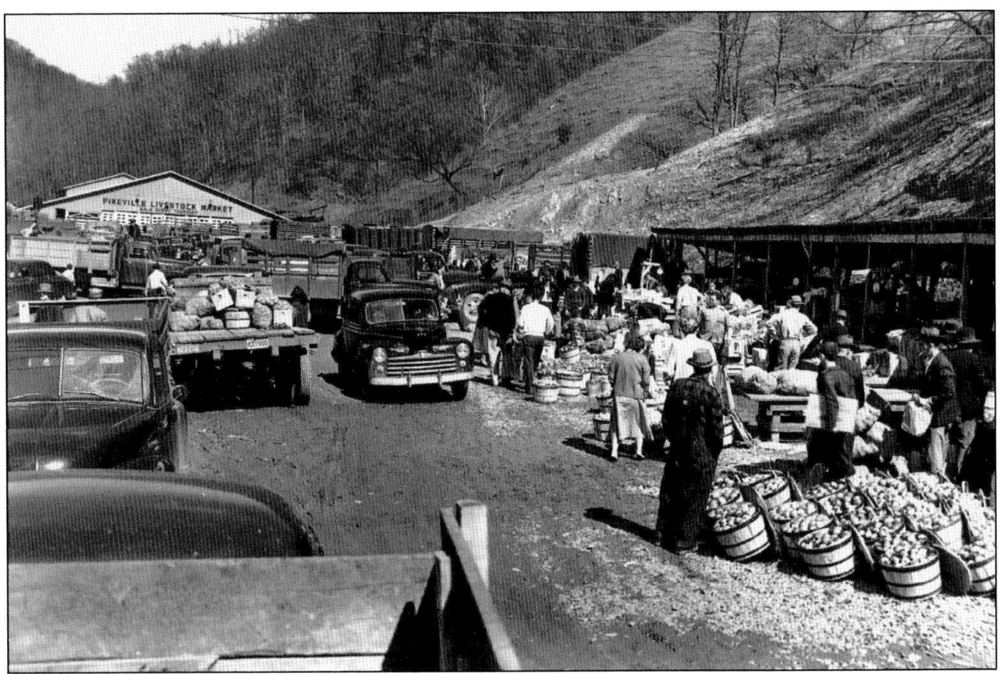

The Pikeville Livestock Market, seen here around 1940, was on Town Mountain Road until the early 1960s, when local businessman Robert Walters developed the land into Town and Country Shopping Center. In addition to livestock, farmers throughout the county and nearby communities sold their fresh vegetables here. (Courtesy of the Pike County Public Library.)

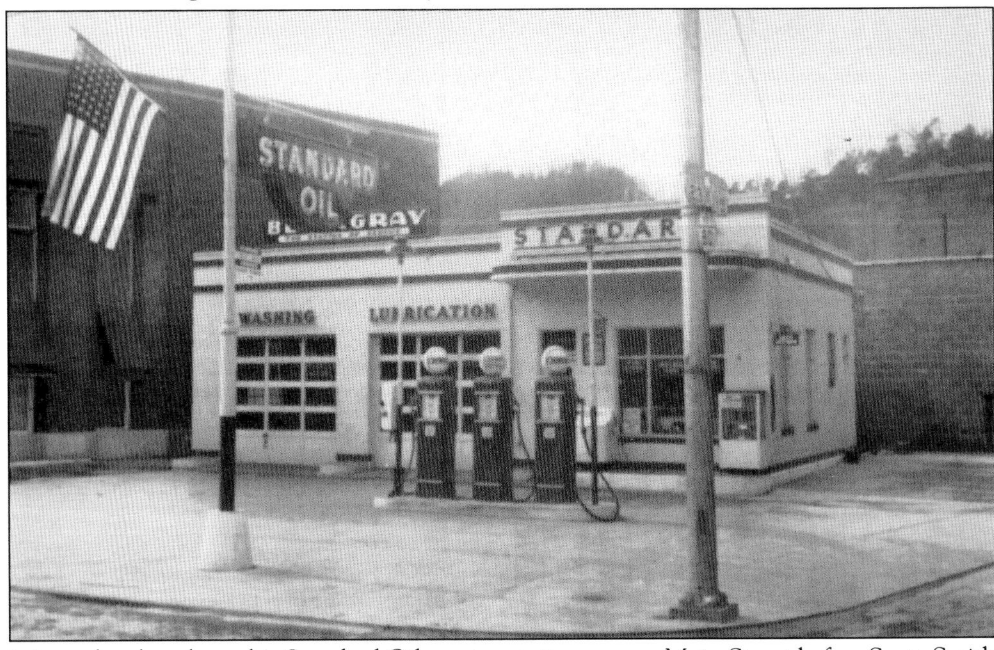

It is unclear how long this Standard Oil service station was on Main Street before Scott Smith purchased it in 1940. After Scott's son Linton returned from World War II, father and son managed the station together until Scott's death in 1969. The station closed in 2004 and the site is now home to Broken Throne Brewing. (Courtesy of Brenda Hays, John Doug Hays collection.)

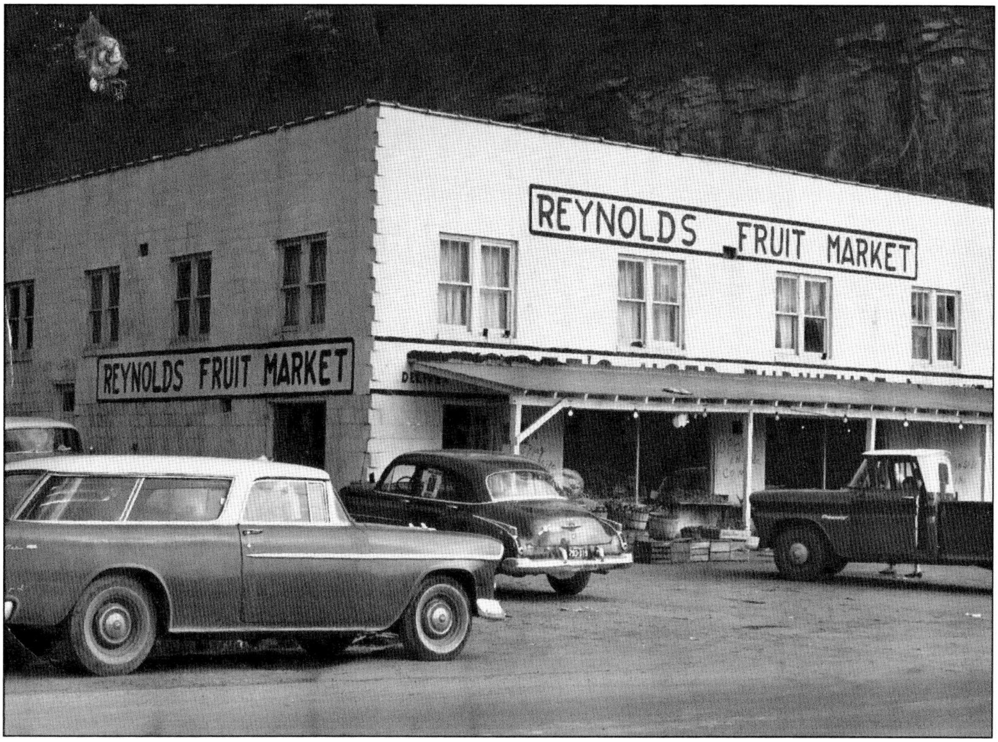

This building originally housed Henry Goff's furniture store, but Clifford Reynolds bought it after his Allen, Kentucky, location flooded in 1957. Reynolds Market opened its doors in Pikeville in 1960, and Dorsie's Dairy Bar—named for his youngest daughter—opened next door two years later. His son joined him in the market and continues the business today in a building built in 1984. (Courtesy of Clifford E. Reynolds.)

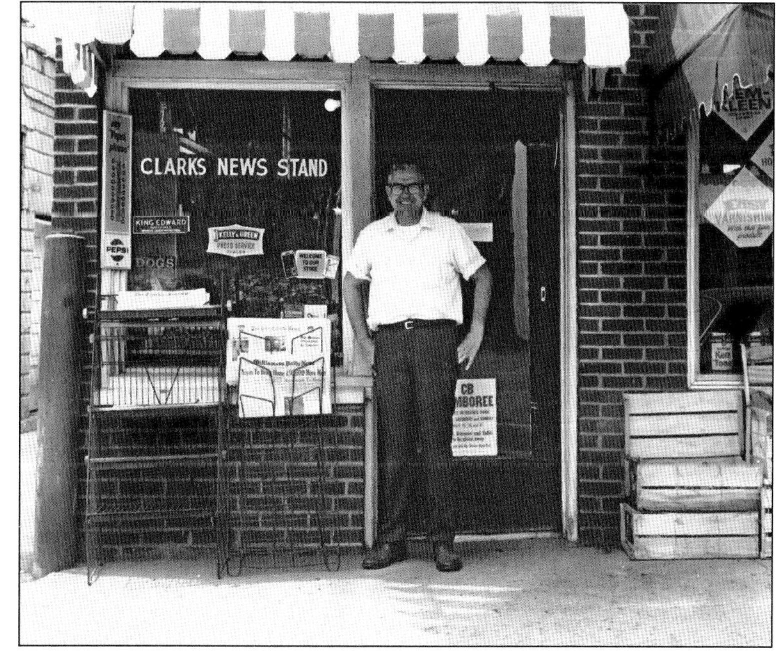

Clarks News Stand was on Main Street from the 1960s through the 1980s next to Gene and Mike's Record Shop on the block where the Pike County Judicial Center now stands. James A. "Butch" Clark, a World War II Navy veteran, owned the newsstand. (Courtesy of the Pike County Public Library.)

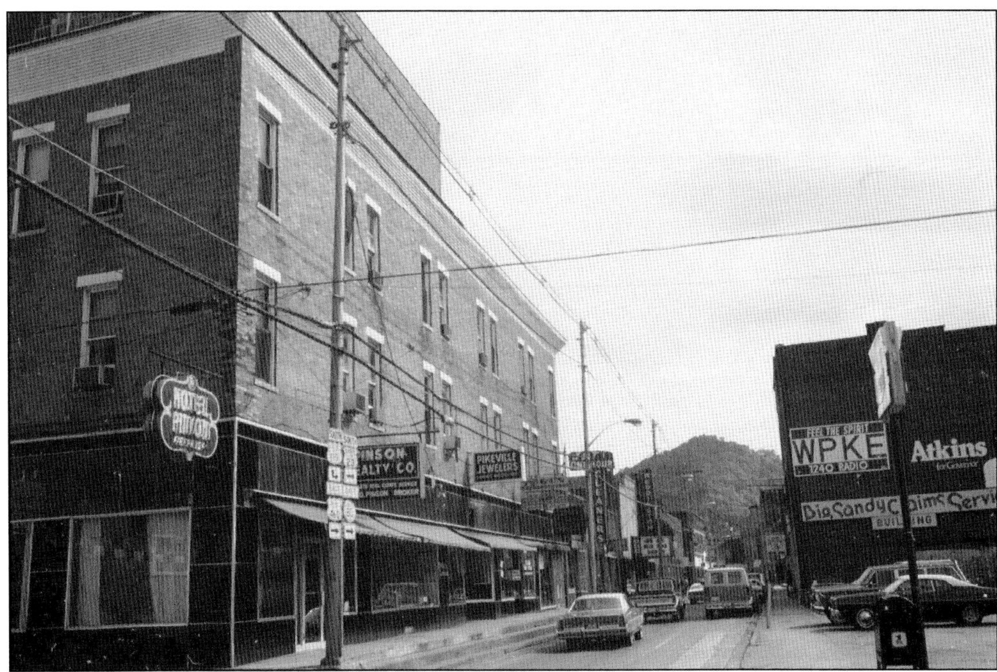

In 1978, the Pinson Hotel stood on the corner of Second and Pike Streets, and several other businesses lined Second Street where the Pike County Judicial Center now stands. The Weddington Theater is the most remembered, seen here showing the Chuck Norris movie *Good Guys Wear Black*. (Courtesy of the University of Kentucky Libraries Special Collections Research Center.)

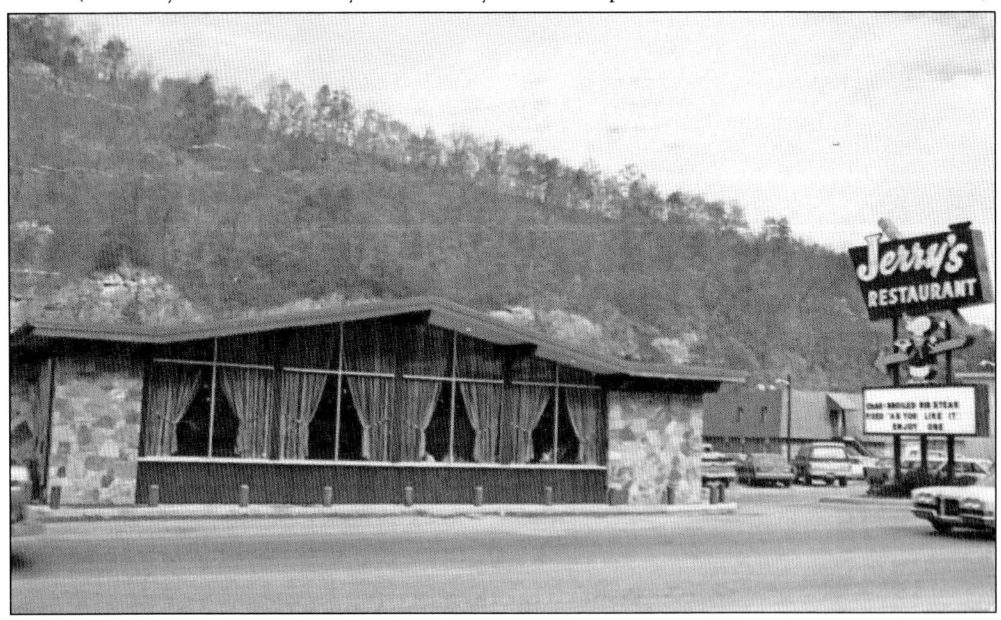

Frank and Mattie Justice bought the Chuck Wagon restaurant in 1958 and converted it into a Jerry's franchise two years later. Three generations of the family owned and operated the restaurant until it closed in December 2013. Virtually everyone born in the Pikeville area during those decades has their own happy childhood memories associated with a trip to Jerry's. (Courtesy of Brenda Hays, John Doug Hays collection.)

Four

Transportation

The steep mountains, narrow valleys, and winding streams found around Pikeville make this one of the most scenic places in the world. Unfortunately, they have also long made transportation exceedingly difficult.

Native Americans who hunted the Big Sandy Valley traveled along the river or followed animal traces, as did the European settlers who began arriving in the 1790s. As the population grew, rudimentary roads suitable for walking or riding horses appeared. The mountains to the east ensured that the best connection to the outside world continued to be the Big Sandy River, which flowed out of Virginia to the Ohio River around 100 miles north of Pikeville.

Beginning in the 1830s, many steamboats made regularly scheduled trips to deliver mail, goods, and people while others towed barges or logs. However, the river was only deep enough for them for about six months of the year. Pikeville was the farthest upriver steamers could reach, which helped make it the area's economic hub.

As the 20th century approached, railroads arrived in Eastern Kentucky bringing men like John D. Rockefeller Jr. to the area to explore business opportunities. The railroad came to Pikeville in 1905, and the last steamboat left around 1921. Early trains hauled passengers, but rail cars carrying freight soon outnumbered them. Highway travel eventually spelled the end of passenger trains in the 1960s, but trains continue to haul coal and other freight to this day.

The first road in Pike County had only a single lane and connected Pikeville to Williamson. Over time, two-lane paved roads crisscrossed the county, and by 1940, four major routes clogged the streets of Pikeville. Passenger buses filled the passenger train gap through the 1970s, until increasing car ownership robbed them of their business. Meanwhile, highway construction continued in fits and starts over the years, and now two limited-access highways connect Pikeville to adjacent states with another set to open soon.

In effect, these transportation improvements have shrunk the county and brought the outside world nearer than it has ever been.

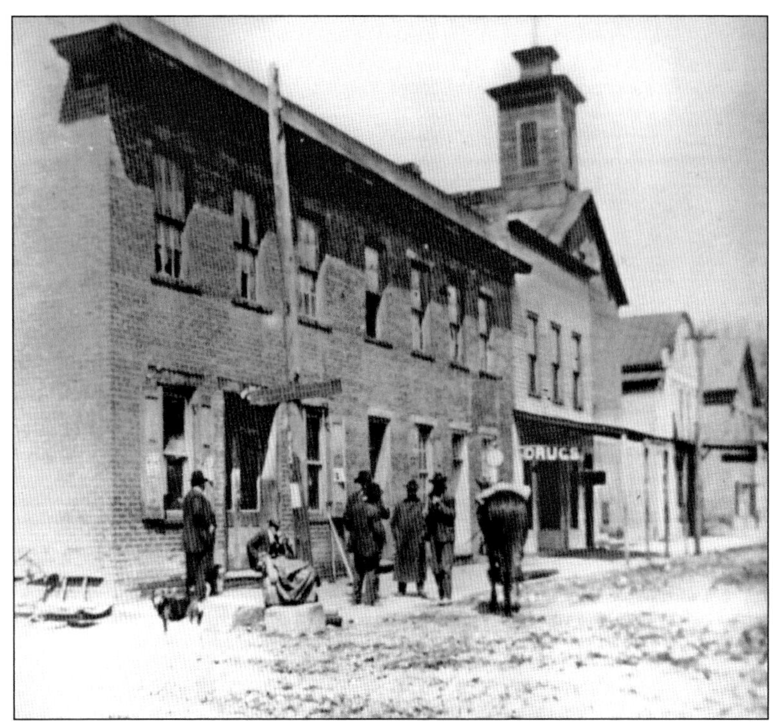

Though this image—with its dirt street, wooden sidewalks, and a horse ready to ride off into the sunset—evokes the old West, it was actually taken near the intersection of Main and Division Streets in 1903. Harrison Bowles is the man standing, and Hi Pauley is seated. (Courtesy of the Pike County Public Library.)

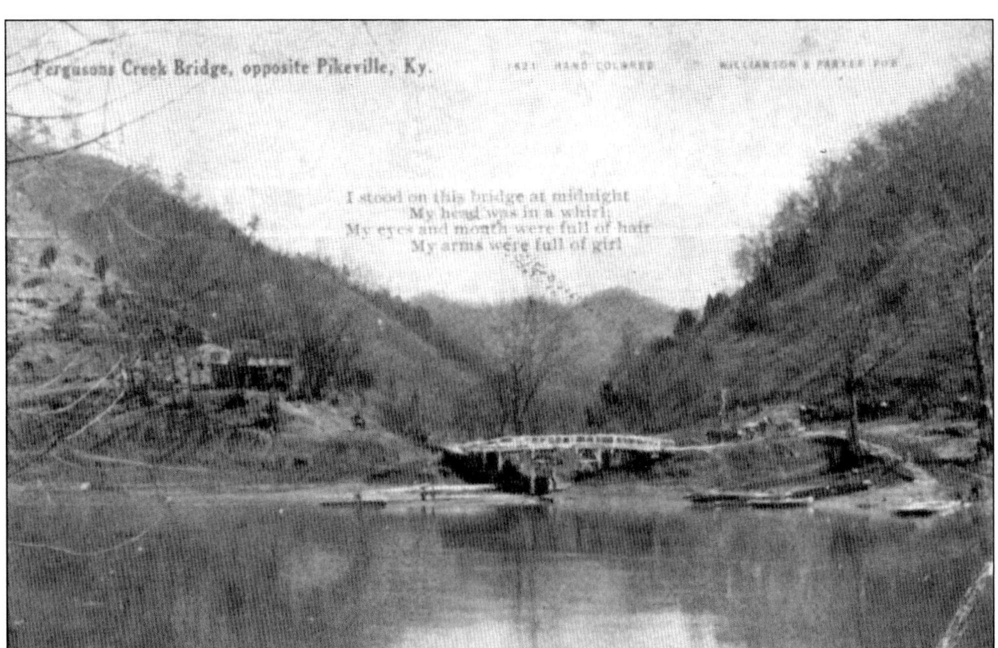

This postcard shows the Ferguson Creek Bridge in 1909. It was less than 1,000 feet below the Middle Bridge. Note the man standing on a flatboat at lower right. Randall McCoy (see page 97) ran a ferry at that location until around 1910, so the photographer may have unknowingly captured an image of the old feudist. (Courtesy of Brenda Hays, John Doug Hays collection.)

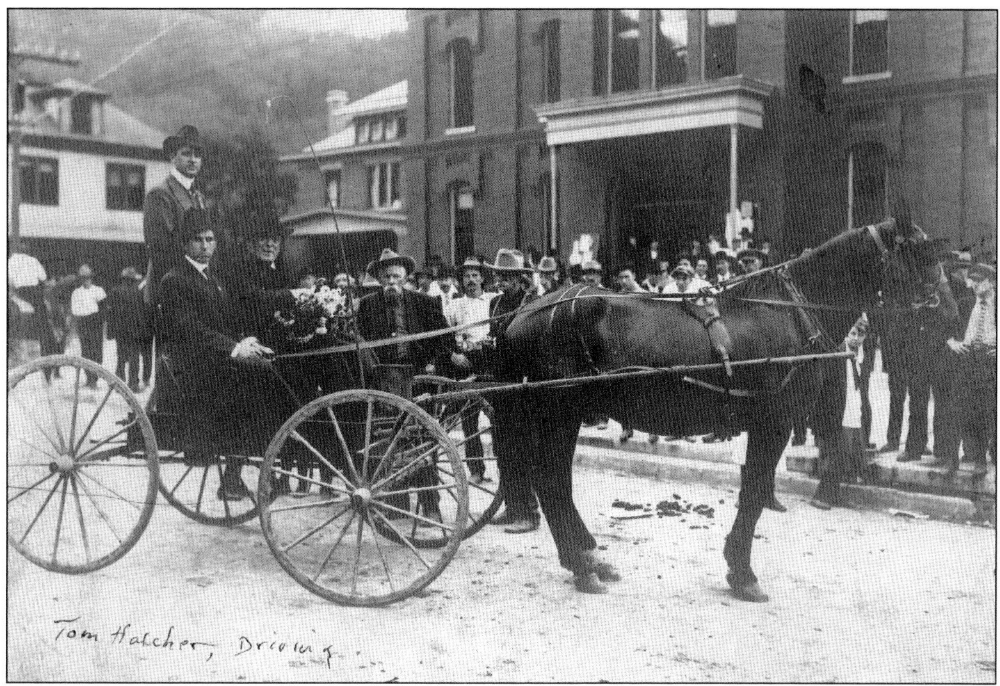

According to the *Louisville Courier-Journal* of October 23, 1915, many Pikeville citizens came out to hear a speech by US senator Ollie Murray James (in carriage at right, with flowers). The driver is Tom Hatcher, a successful businessman and member of various corporate boards in the community. (Courtesy of the Frank M. Allara Library, University of Pikeville.)

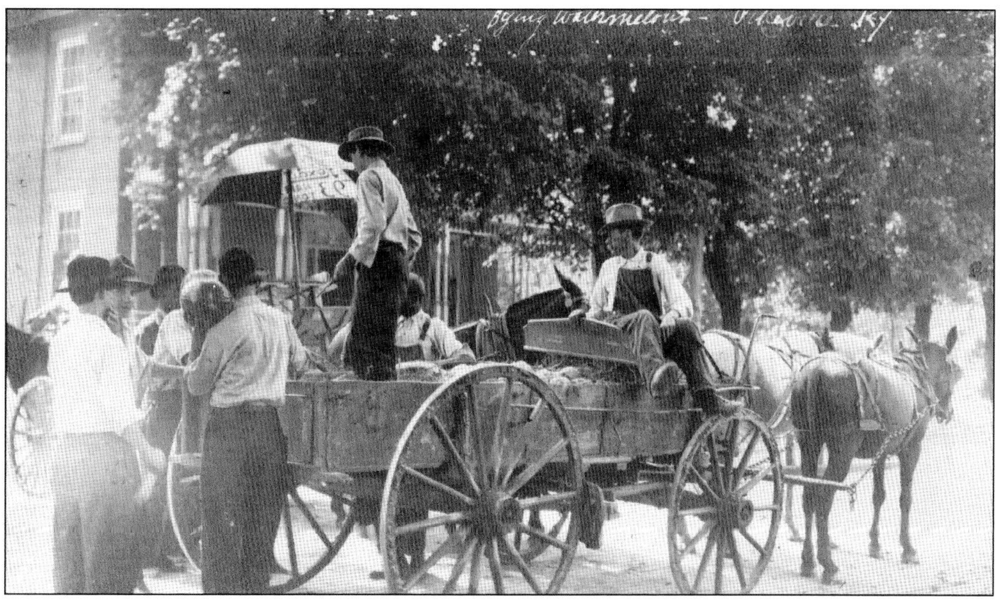

This c. 1910 photograph shows a man selling watermelons from a mule-drawn wagon typical of the time. This is believed to be just below the intersection of Main and Pike Streets across from the Main Street Church of Christ. The home in the background once belonged to Col. John Dils Jr. (Courtesy of Brenda Hays, John Doug Hays collection.)

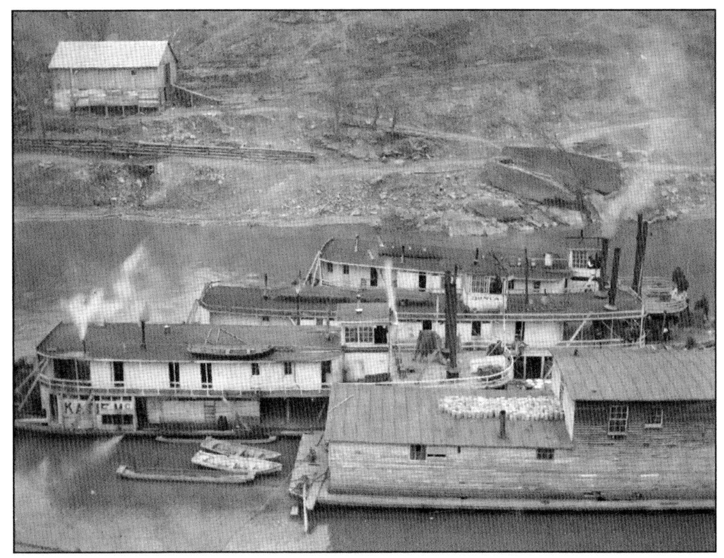

Goods and people disembarked from the river in downtown Pikeville directly behind the county courthouse. Seeing three or four steamboats like these at the wharf would not have been unusual. The wharf boat (foreground) was used instead of a dock so that it could readily rise and fall with the level of the river. (Courtesy of the Frank M. Allara Library, University of Pikeville.)

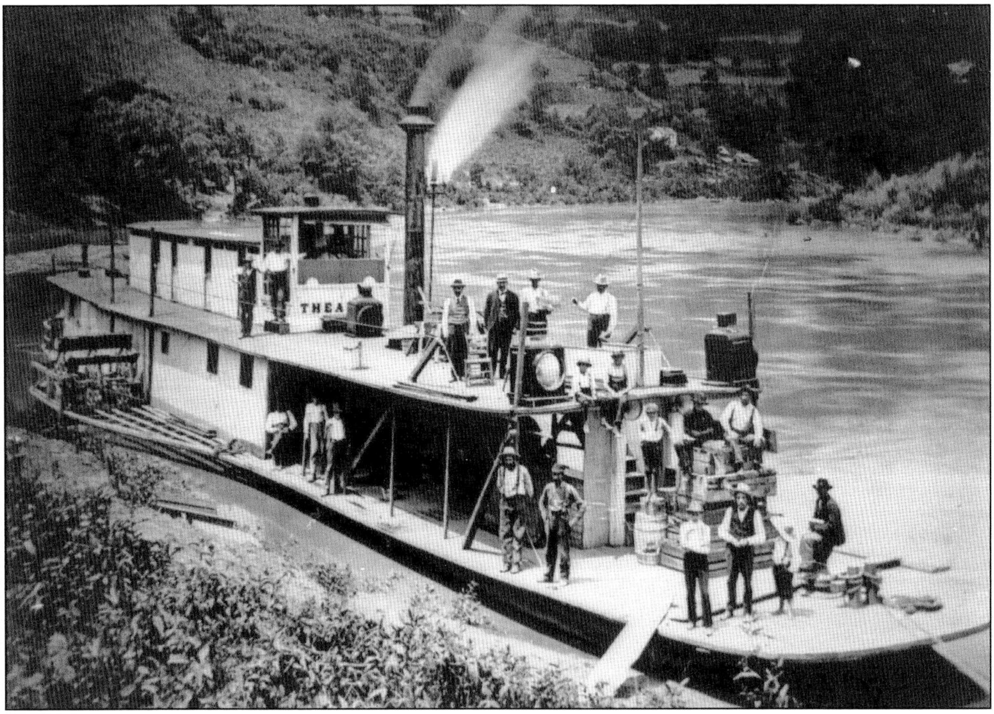

Packet boats like this were steamboats that ran a regular route hauling people and goods between fixed locations. The *Thealka* operated between Catlettsburg and Pikeville, and reportedly set the speed record for the 240-mile round trip at 24 hours in February 1900. It was named for Captain Meek's daughter Alice Jane, whose nickname was Alka. (Courtesy of Murphy Library Special Collections/ARC, University of Wisconsin-La Crosse.)

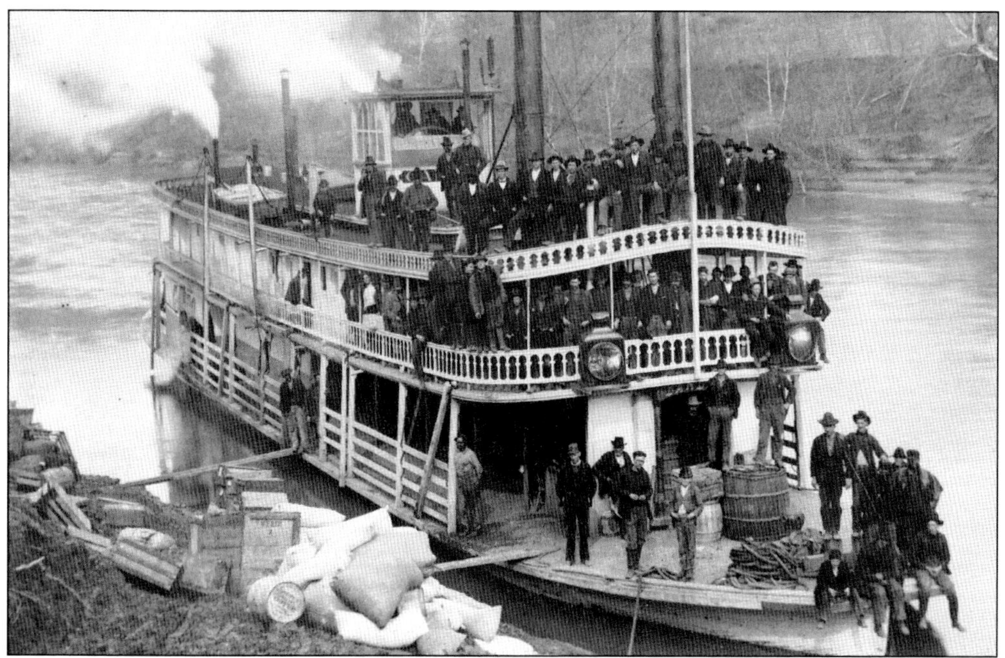

The *Cando* was built in 1899 at Ashland. It was primarily used between Whitehouse in Johnson County and Pikeville during the construction of the C&O Railway into Pikeville. Its name was a mistake on the part of the painter, who thought the name of the railroad on his instructions was a single word instead of initials. (Courtesy of Murphy Library Special Collections/ARC, University of Wisconsin-La Crosse.)

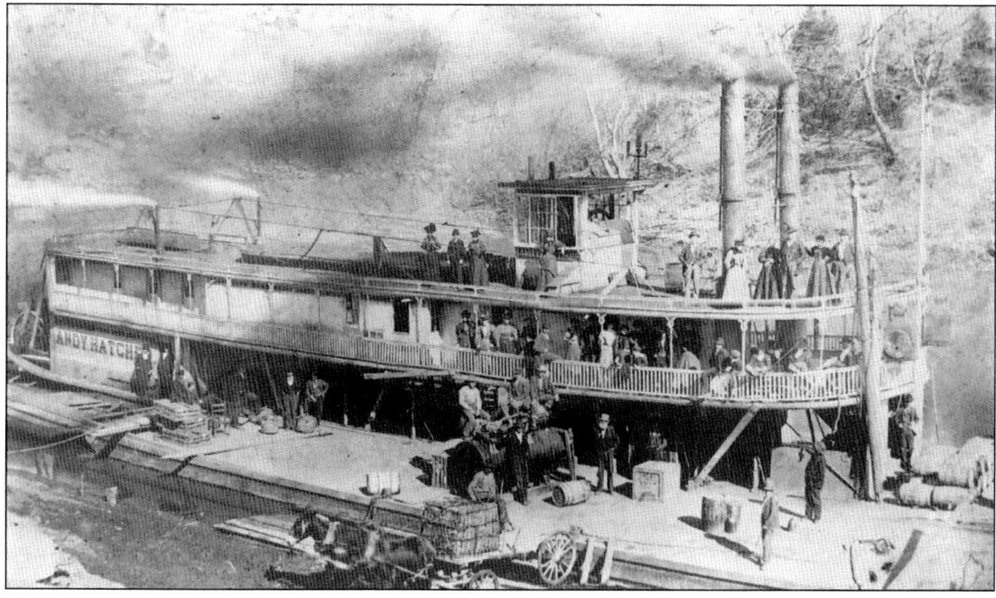

The *Andy Hatcher* was built in 1889 and operated on the Big Sandy until it burned near Paintsville in 1897. It ran in competition with another steamer called the *Frank Preston*, and they often followed one another hauling goods and people. When it burned, its roof bell went to Paintsville High School and its whistle to the *Thealka*. (Courtesy of Murphy Library Special Collections/ARC, University of Wisconsin-La Crosse.)

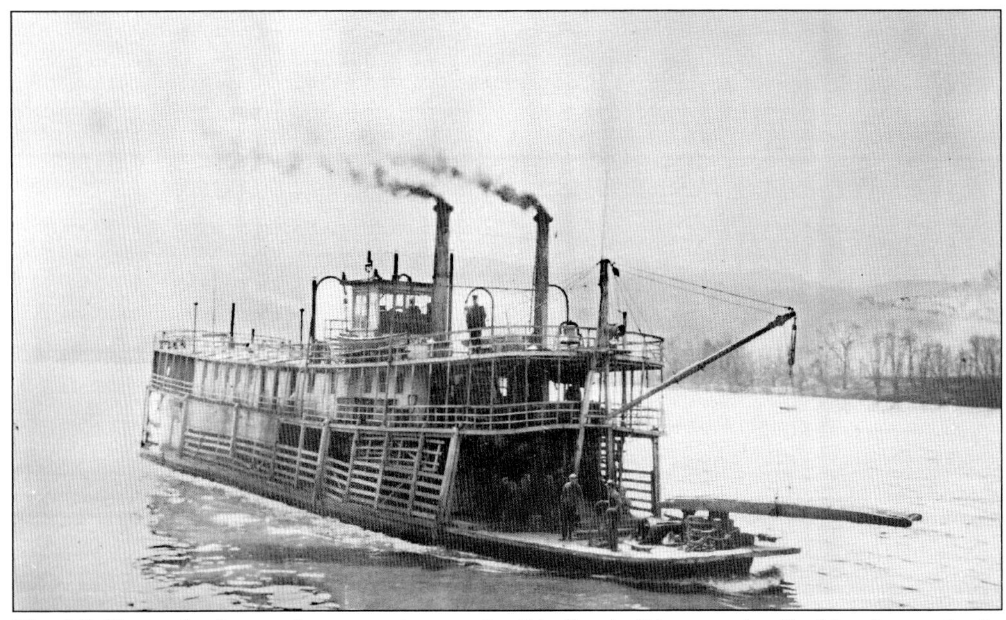

The *J.P. Davis*, the last packet operation on the Big Sandy River, made all of its three trips in 1921. On the last, the 137-foot sternwheeler reportedly became the largest vessel to ever make it to Pikeville, but it sank near Paintsville on its return. Sadly, the role steamboats played in Pikeville's history has been mostly forgotten. (Courtesy of Murphy Library Special Collections/ARC, University of Wisconsin-La Crosse.)

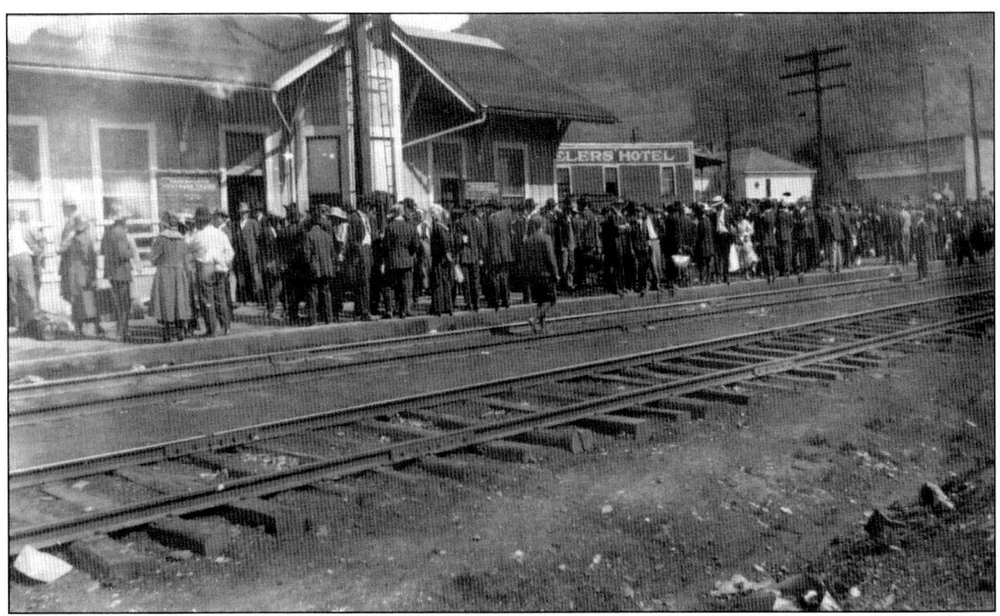

The first passenger train arrived from Ashland on June 5, 1905, with conductor Billy Myers at the controls. Those inaugural passengers disembarked at this first railroad station. It stood close to the present-day location of the Pikeville Police Department between Division and Pike Streets. It is seen here around 1918. (Courtesy of the Filson Historical Society, Louisville, Kentucky.)

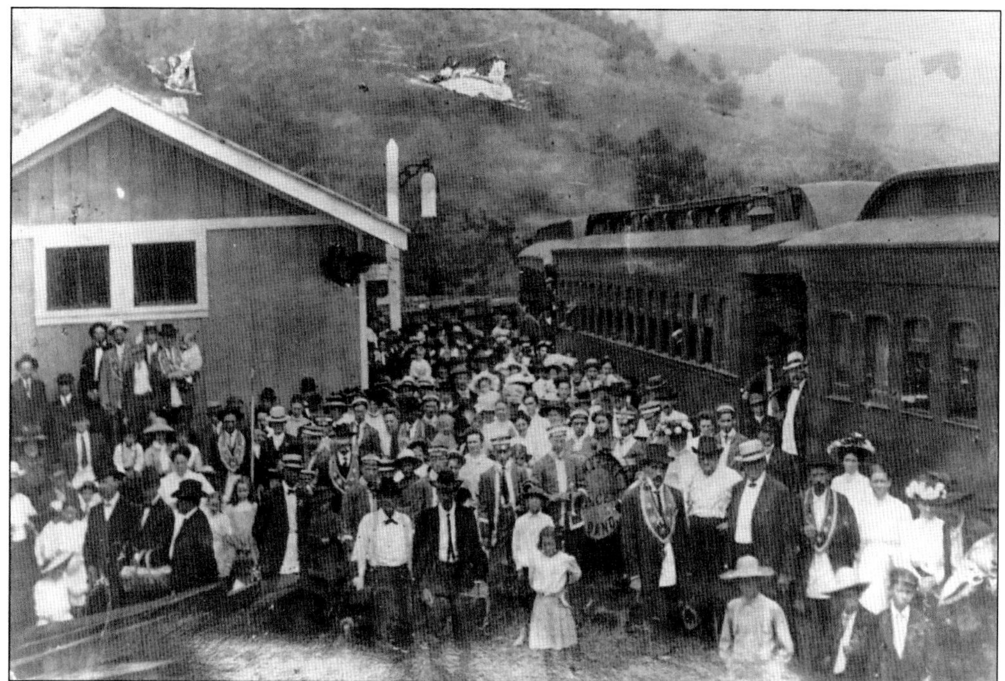

In this photograph, possibly taken in 1919 at the original railroad depot, it appears that a crowd including the Pikeville Concert Band has gathered to celebrate an unknown event. By this time, rail service extended to Elkhorn City and beyond. The last passenger cars—much like the ones pictured here—departed Pikeville in 1963. (Courtesy of the Pike County Public Library.)

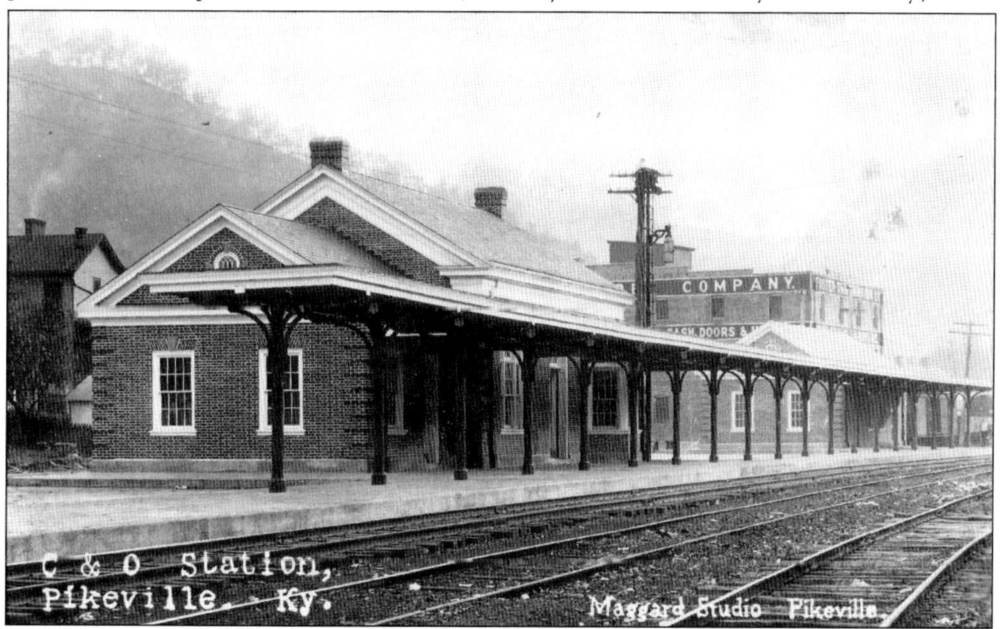

In 1923, the C&O moved its passenger depot onto land donated by Fon Rogers. Passenger service ran out of this complex for 40 years. The nearer building was the passenger terminal; the smaller baggage terminal is on the right. Reportedly, many service members married here just before the 6:30 a.m. train left for Ashland. (Courtesy of the Frank M. Allara Library, University of Pikeville.)

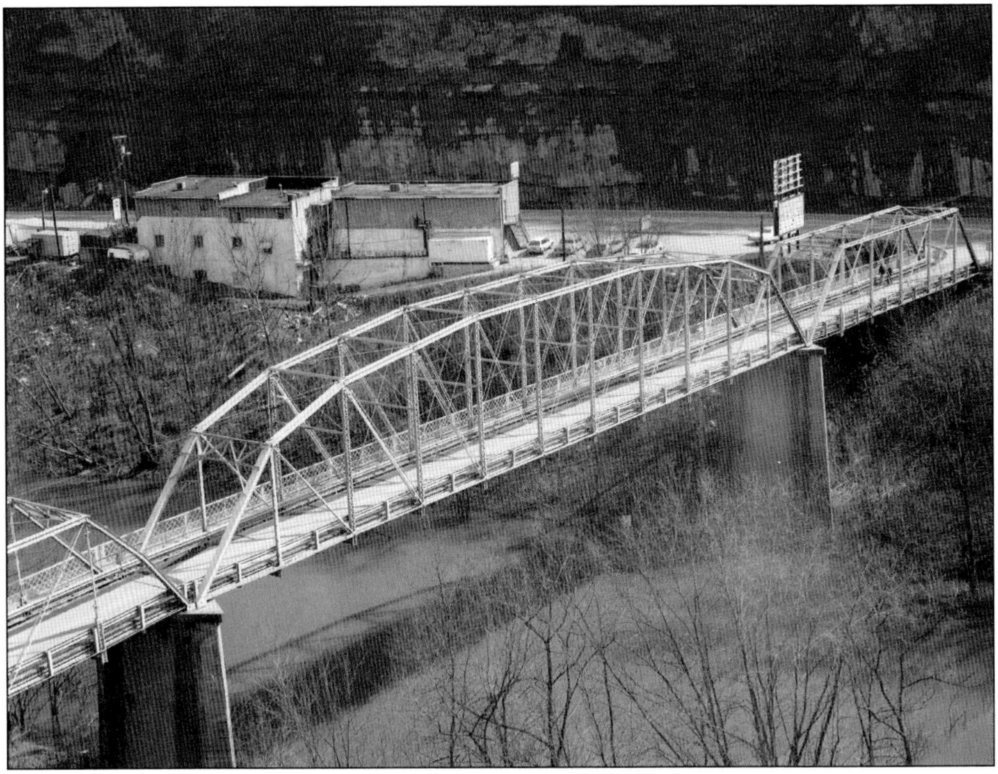

The Middle Bridge crossed the river at the end of Pike Street until it was removed as part of the Cut-Through project around 1986. It was the first bridge crossing the river near Pikeville and was erected by Champion Bridge Company in 1908. It initially operated as a toll bridge for horses and buggies but served automobiles for decades thereafter. (Courtesy of the Library of Congress.)

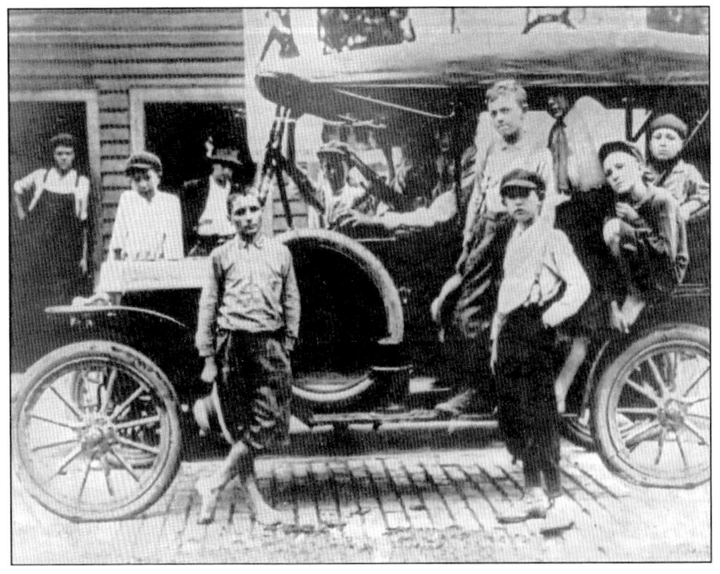

It was not long after the Middle Bridge was constructed that the age of automobiles reached Pikeville. This Ford Model T was the first car driven on the streets of Pikeville around 1915. The only person in the photograph who has been identified is young Harry Robinson of Virgie, standing on the running board. (Courtesy of the Big Sandy Heritage Center Museum.)

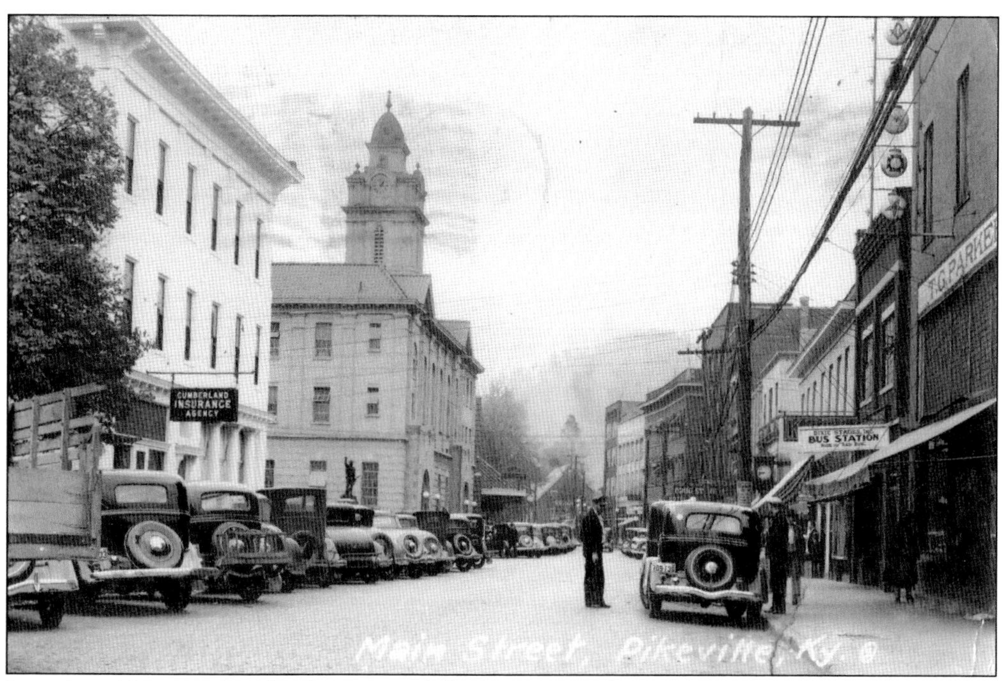

Less than 20 years after the first automobile drove into Pikeville, Main Street was full of them, as seen here in 1934. The direction of traffic flow on Main Street has switched several times over the years, including occasionally allowing two-way traffic. Among the many past businesses in this photograph, the Dixie Stages Bus Station is on the right. (Courtesy of Brenda Hays, John Doug Hays collection.)

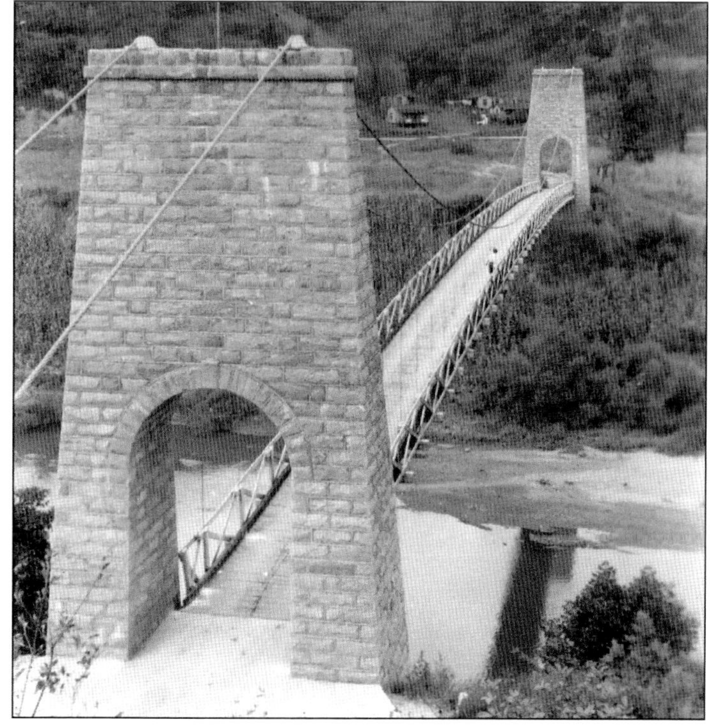

Pauley Bridge was completed in 1940 by local men employed through the Works Progress Administration, part of the government response to the Great Depression. It is thought to be unique as it is the only known swinging suspension bridge with sandstone towers. It supplied vehicular access to Pauley Addition until it was designated pedestrian-only in 2001. (Courtesy of the University of Kentucky Libraries Special Collections Research Center.)

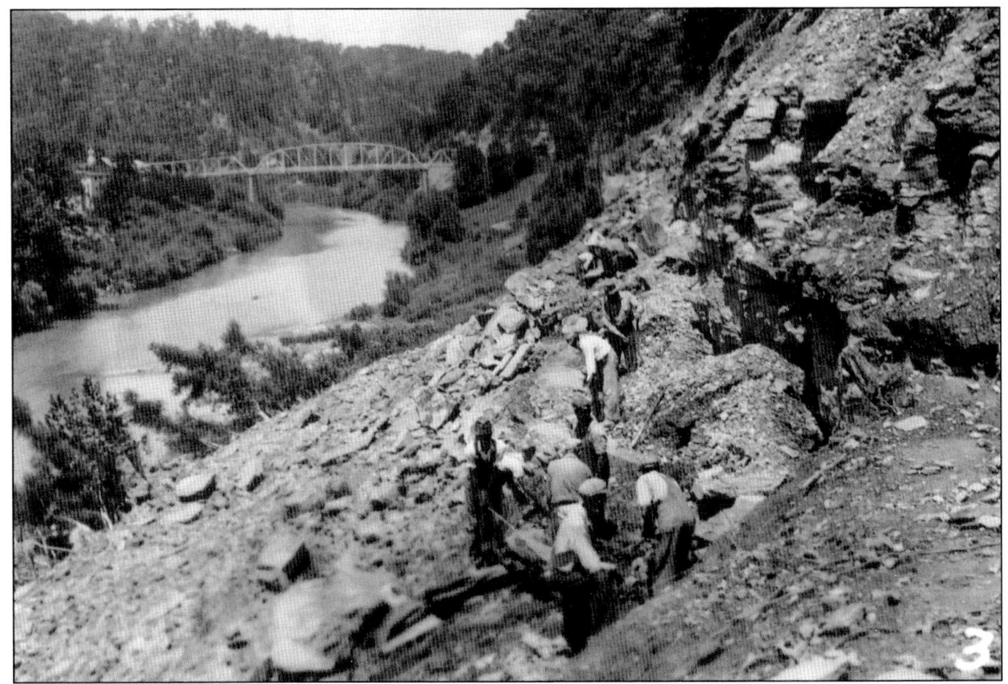

Around the time Pauley Bridge was completed, work began on another Works Progress Administration project. The men seen here were likely standing just to the north of Chloe Creek while engaged in the backbreaking labor of excavating by hand the roadbed for Bypass Road. Middle Bridge can be seen in the background. (Courtesy of the University of Kentucky Libraries Special Collections Research Center.)

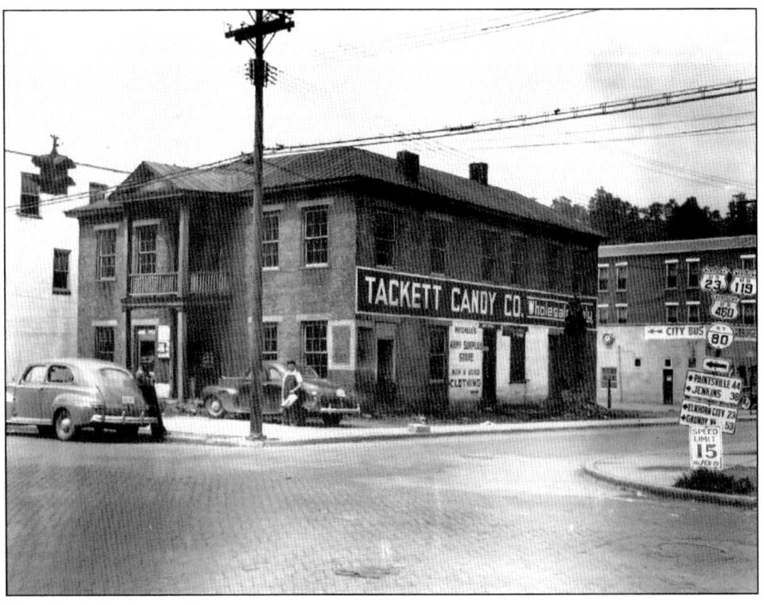

This look at the highway sign that stood at the intersection of Main and Pike Streets in about 1940 goes some way to explaining traffic congestion in Pikeville. Three US highways and Kentucky Route 80 ran through the downtown streets, and there was no practical way to go around the town. (Courtesy of the Pike County Public Library.)

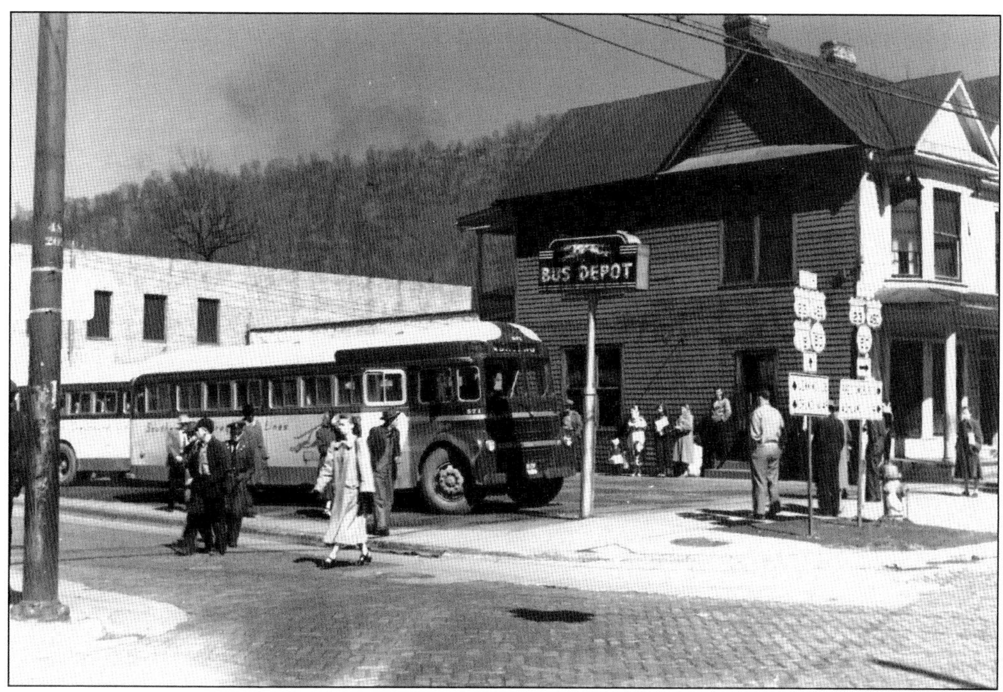

With the expansion of two-lane highways throughout Eastern Kentucky, by 1946, this vacant lot at Main and Pike Streets served as the Pikeville bus depot for Southeastern Greyhound Lines. The Ashland bus appears to be dropping off passengers as others wait to board. The home in the background belonged to Jack Akers. (Courtesy of the Pike County Public Library.)

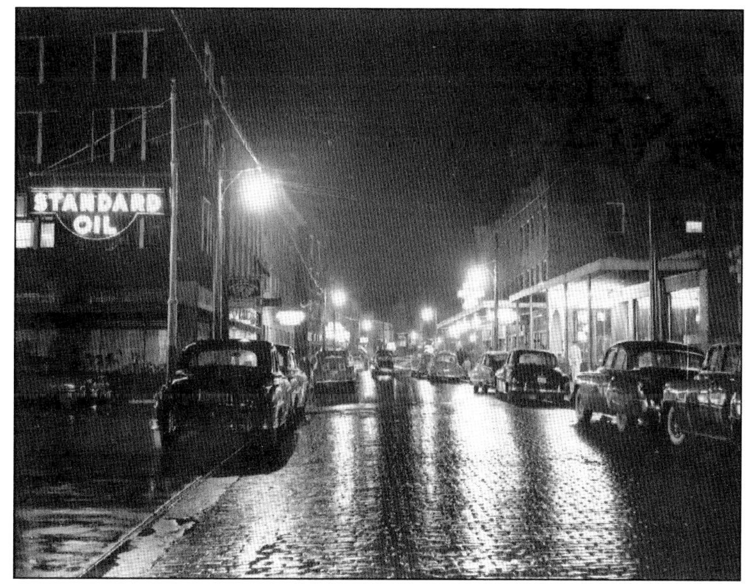

This is a rare night view of Main Street taken around 1954 following a rain shower. The direction of traffic has turned around, likely due to the completion of Bypass Road, allowing southbound traffic an easier road to travel. Caroline Avenue is on the left and the Hatcher Hotel is on the right. (Courtesy of the Big Sandy Heritage Center Museum.)

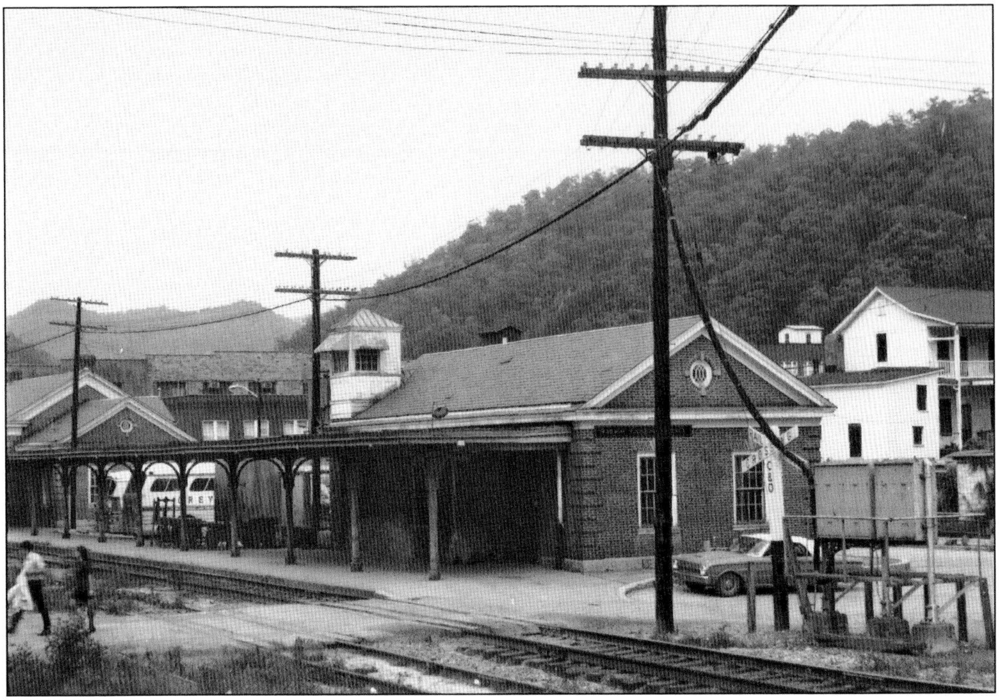

By 1971, passenger trains had long since stopped running out of the railroad depot. However, the C&O continued to use the baggage terminal to manage its freight operations, and Greyhound used the passenger depot as its bus station until service ended around 1980. The City of Pikeville currently uses the building as its Office of Economic Development. (Courtesy of Brenda Hays, John Doug Hays collection.)

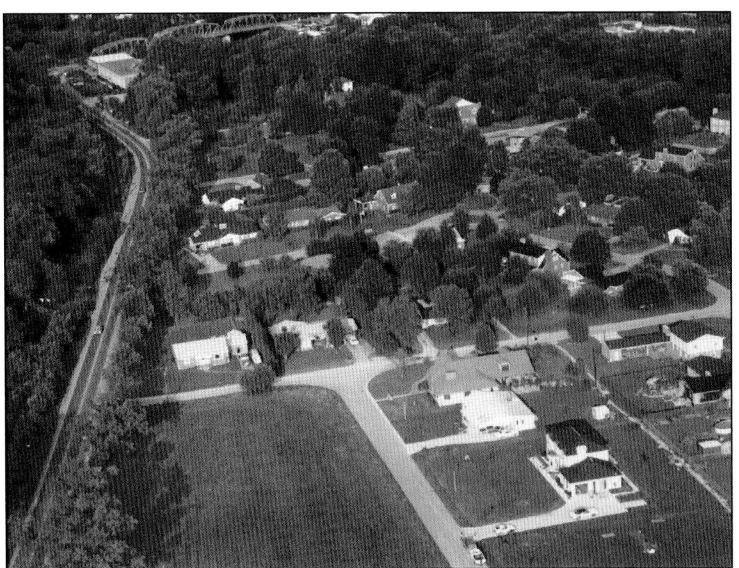

Through the 1960s, there was a steady stream of highway improvements consisting of two-lane roads and steel truss bridges. Seen here on the left, what was then US Route 23 and is still North Mayo Trail runs alongside Bowles Addition before crossing the Lower Bridge at what is now Lorraine Street. (Courtesy of the Pike County Public Library.)

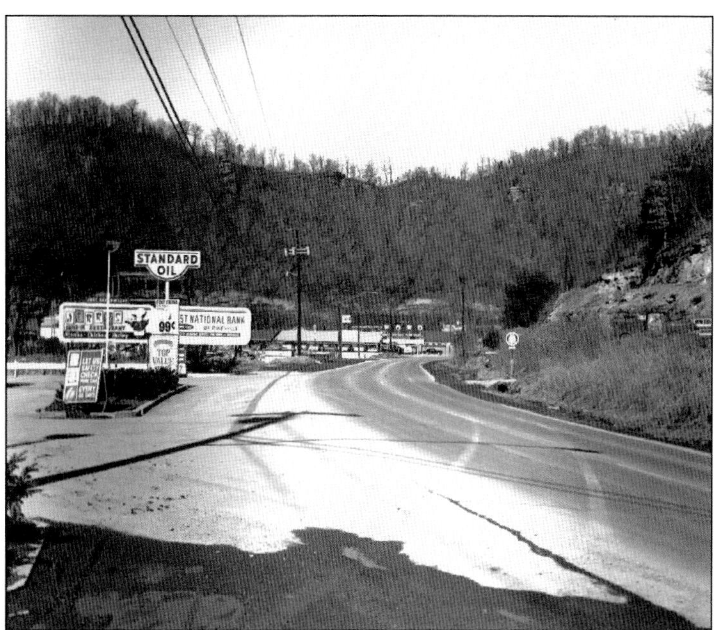

This is South Mayo Trail south of downtown Pikeville prior to the construction of the Cut-Through. These two-lane roads were the best the region had to offer until four-lane highway construction began in the 1970s. Bruce Walters Ford is on the same spot today, but the Cut-Through removed most of the mountain behind it. (Courtesy of the Pike County Public Library.)

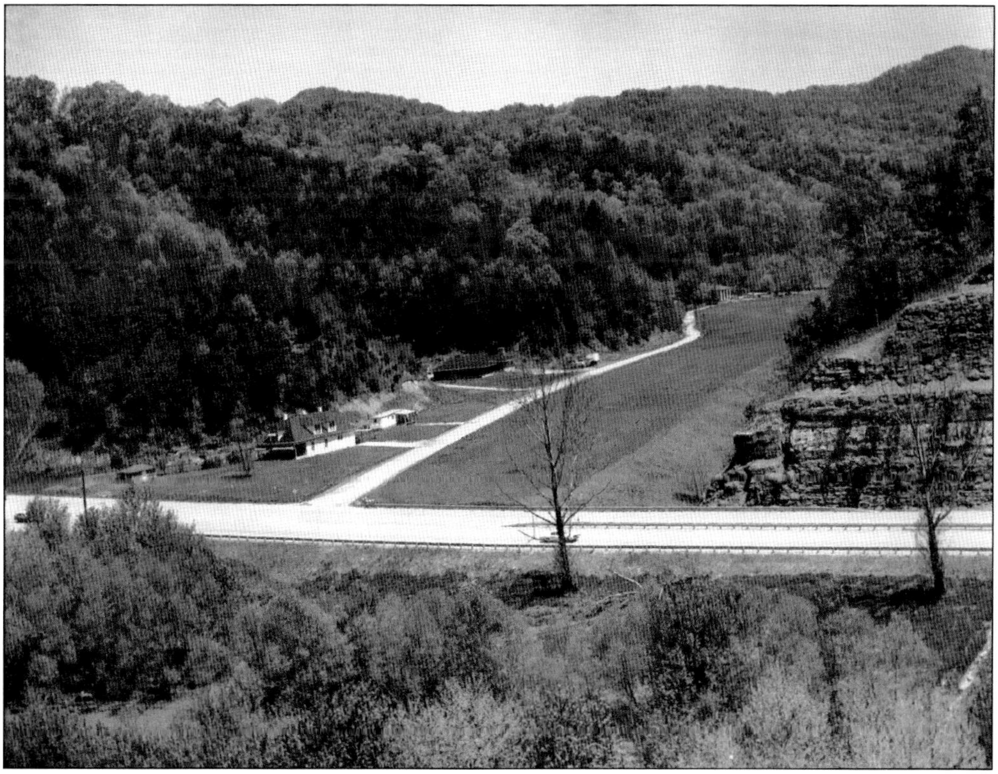

This is US Route 23 near its present-day intersection with US Route 119 at Cassidy Boulevard around 1980. The Appalachian Development Highway System helped fund the construction of both of these four-lane highways, and today each extends across Pike County. US Route 460 is also near completion to the Virginia state line. This improved infrastructure provides untold economic benefits. (Courtesy of the Pike County Public Library.)

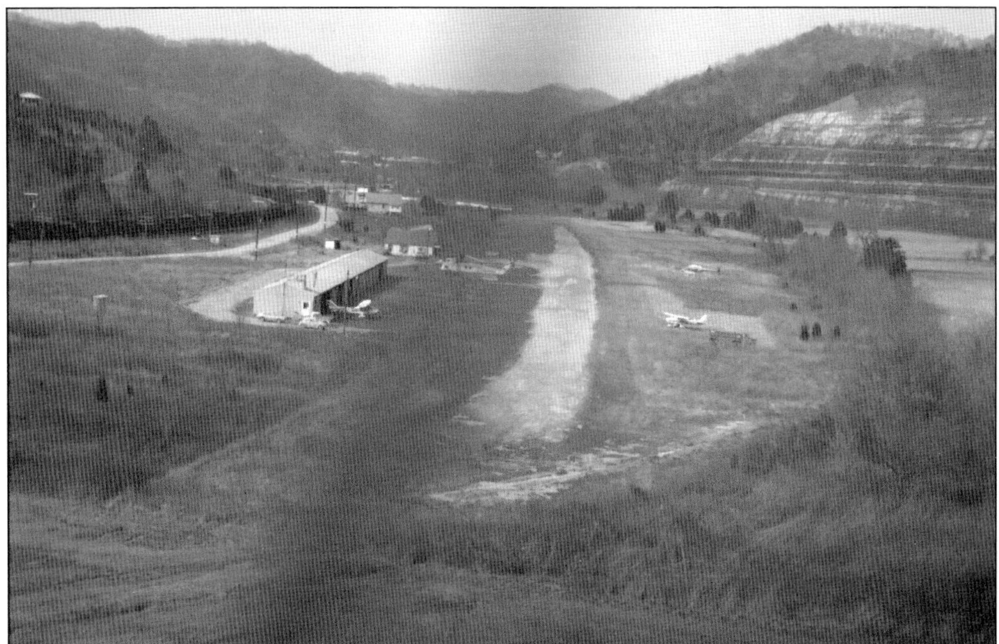

The old Pikeville airport—seen here around 1972—was near the Pauley and Keel Additions and extended nearly to Cassidy Boulevard. Unlike Hatcher Field, it did not offer commercial services, but this is the field that Pikeville native and aviation pioneer John Paul Riddle flew from at the beginning of his career. (Courtesy of the Frank M. Allara Library, University of Pikeville.)

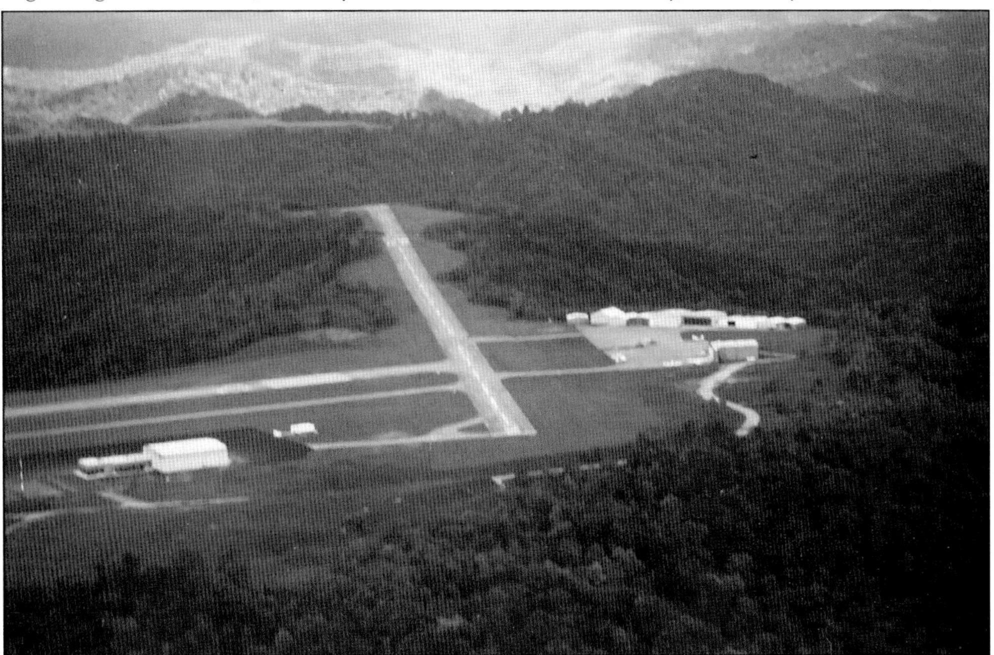

The Pike County Airport (Hatcher Field) opened in 1987 on 46 acres of level land produced by the reclamation of a surface mine. About six miles north of downtown Pikeville, it features one runway around 3,500 feet long and a second mile-long runway. (Courtesy of the University of Kentucky Libraries Special Collections Research Center.)

Five

Healthcare

During the 1891 typhoid outbreak, Dr. I.E. Gray and Dr. W.A. Campbell were the only two doctors in Pikeville. It took until 1896 to form the Pike County Board of Health. Dr. William J. Walters became the first public health officer in 1904, a position he held for about 14 years.

The fiscal court established the Pike County Health Department in 1927, and the Pikeville Woman's Club donated its rooms on Grace Avenue to serve as its first home. In 1953, it moved into a building behind the courthouse where it remained until moving into its current facility in 1991.

Dr. Mary Pauline Fox served as public health officer from 1970 until her retirement in 1993. She previously worked for over 20 years in private practice and public health. Dr. Fox was among the most accomplished public health professionals in Kentucky's history. She revolutionized the department and won a multitude of awards. The health department continues to serve the community on the foundation she built.

Coal companies often employed doctors, but there were still no hospitals in the area until the 1920s. A Methodist minister named Thomas Ashley moved to Pikeville and began urging local doctors to start a hospital. The private venture stalled, but Ashley convinced the Kentucky Conference of the United Methodist Church of the need. Pikeville Methodist Hospital opened in 1924. Ashley was the administrator from 1936 until 1952.

Financial issues arose when the United Mine Workers of America opened its miners' hospital in 1955. The union soon wanted out and Pikeville Methodist Hospital bought the facility in 1966. An eight-story hospital building opened in 1971 at the mouth of Harold's Branch, and the old building was sold to Pikeville College.

Beginning in the 1990s, the variety of specialty services offered continued to increase. In 2004, the relationship with the Methodist Conference ended and the hospital was renamed Pikeville Medical Center. Its facilities have expanded along with the services, and today it has over 3,000 employees, offers more than 400 different services and 340 beds, and is a trauma center.

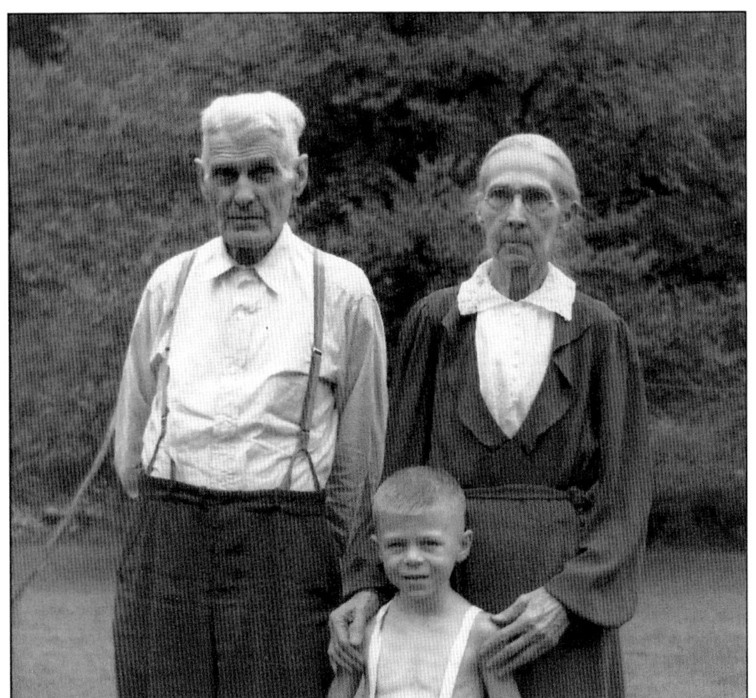

Dr. William Jefferson Walters (left) came to Pikeville in 1900 immediately after earning his medical degree. The nearest hospital at that time was in Ironton, Ohio. He was Pike's first public health officer in 1904, and though he spent many years in private practice, he was periodically called back in times of need and finally left the office in 1955 at age 87. (Courtesy of the Walters family.)

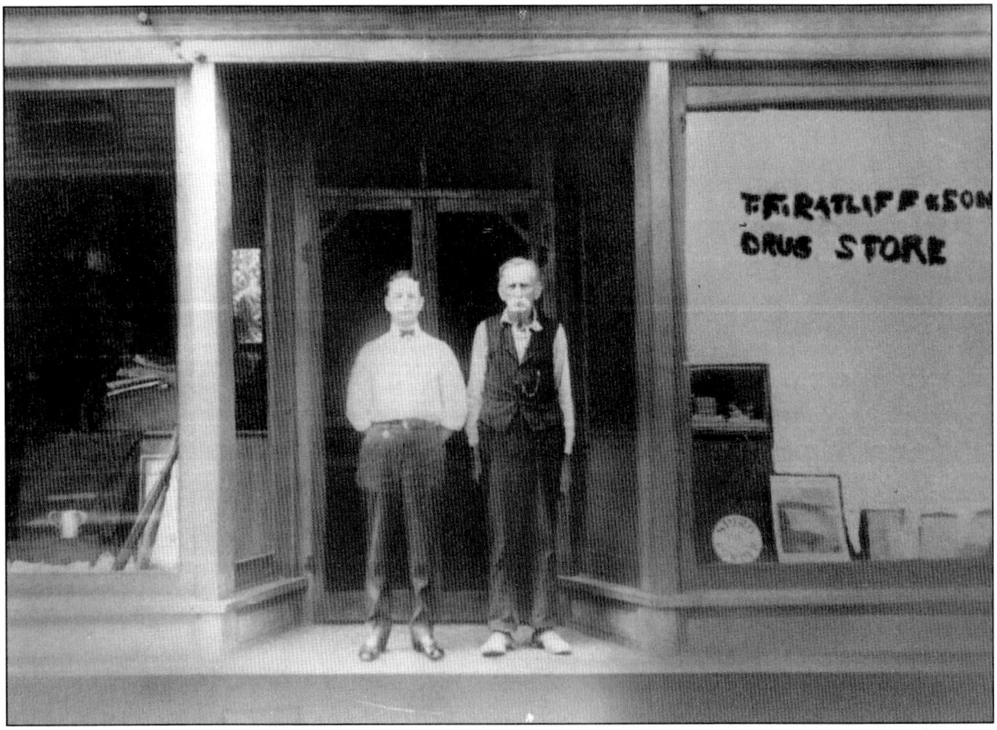

Theodore Freeland "Freejack" Ratliff (right) was born in 1845 and is pictured here with his son Bob in front of the drug store he ran on Division Street from before 1900 until his death in 1920. Freejack's store was open between 4:00 a.m. and 10:00 p.m. each day and served patients arriving on horseback from throughout the county. (Courtesy of the Pike County Public Library.)

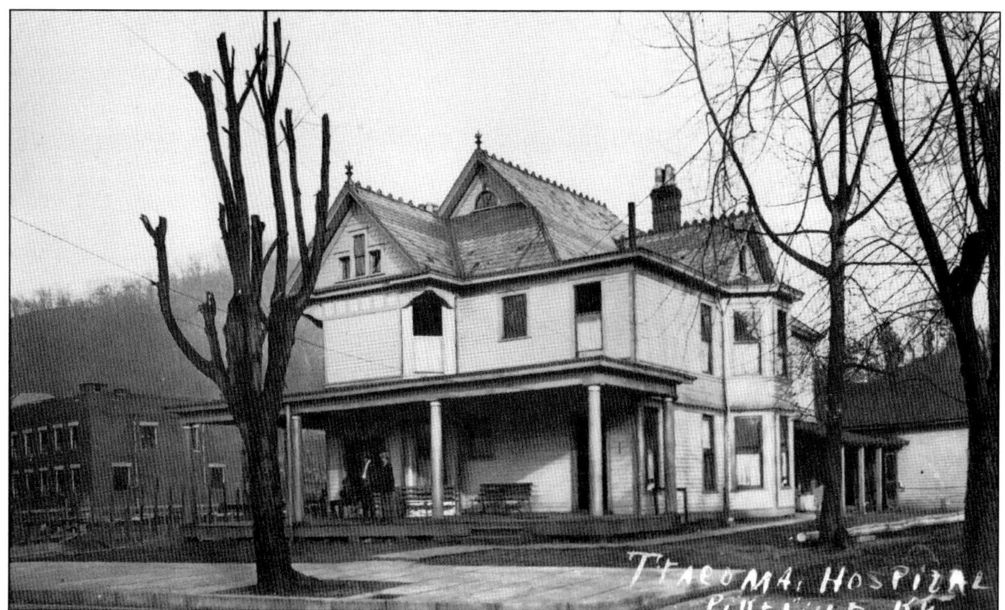

In 1897, trachoma, a disease of the eyes that leads to blindness, was the first disease classified by the US government to be a dangerous contagion. In September 1916, the Kentucky and Pike County boards of health opened a trachoma hospital in this home on Main Street near the present-day location of the post office. (Courtesy of Brenda Hays, John Doug Hays collection.)

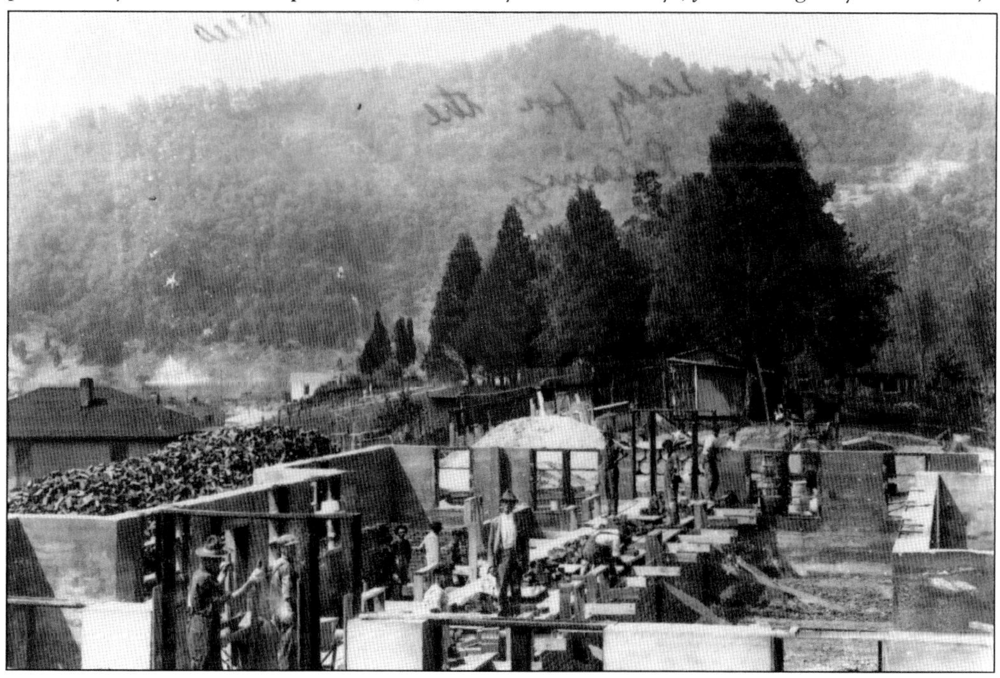

What would become the first Pikeville Methodist Hospital building began construction as a private company called Pikeville General Hospital in 1920. However, construction stalled 18 months later due to cost overruns, and the company's president, Dr. R.S. Johnson, asked Reverend Ashley if he knew "anybody who would like to buy a hospital." (Courtesy of the Frank M. Allara Library, University of Pikeville.)

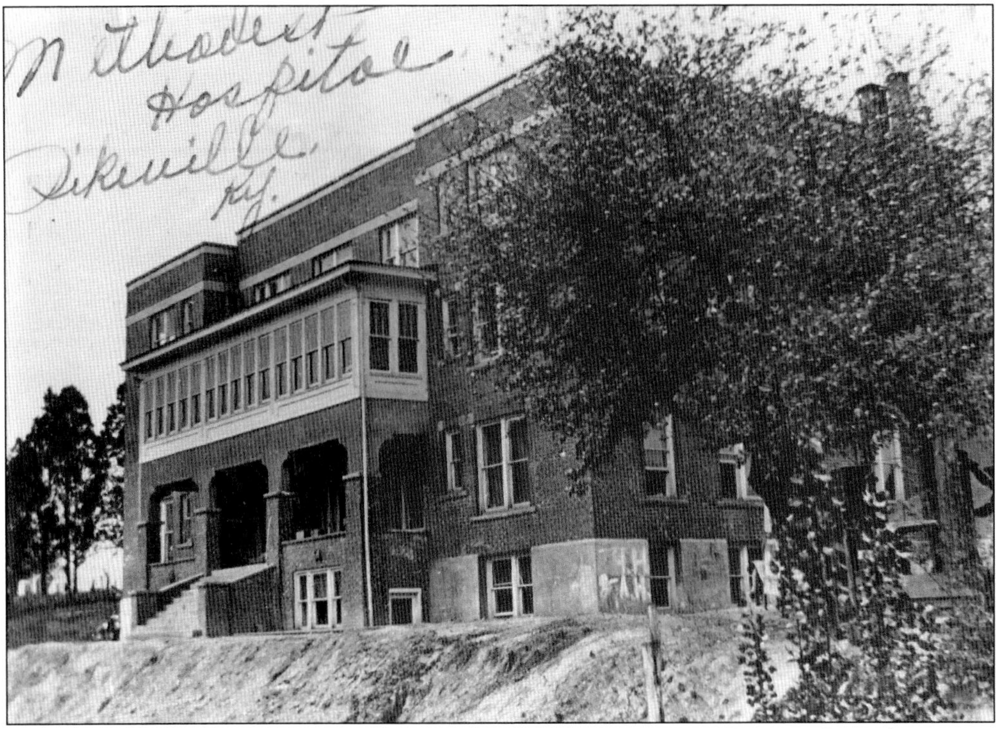

After Reverend Ashley convinced the Methodist Conference to take over from the private company, Pikeville Methodist Hospital opened to the public on Christmas Day 1924 with construction incomplete and only the first two floors of the 50-bed facility available. Dr. W.C. Gardner was chief of staff, and Elsie Sanderson was superintendent of nurses. (Courtesy of the Big Sandy Heritage Center Museum.)

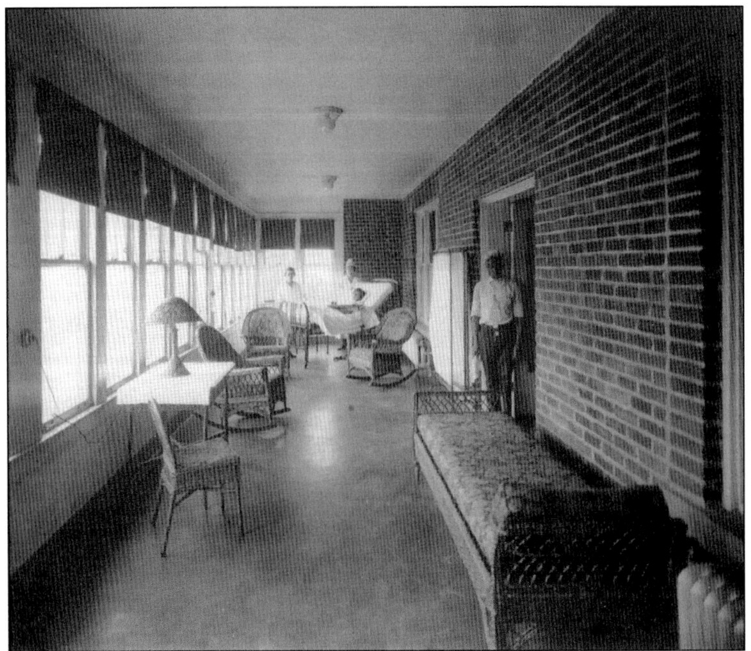

This was the interior of the third-floor solarium that was used to ensure patients were getting enough sunlight. In its earliest days, the hospital was not terribly busy, so its nurses traveled out into the county on goodwill tours to win the confidence of the people in the area. Gradually, these tours succeeded, and more patients arrived. (Courtesy of the Big Sandy Heritage Center Museum.)

The hospital staff around 1930 included Nurse Elnyr Slayton (rear, left) who established a first aid station on Johns Creek in 1928. Next is Dr. S.K. Hunt, the hospital's able administrator from 1925 until 1936. Sally Nolan Baker (front, fourth from left) was one of the nurses who carried frail patients over hills when necessary to get them treatment. (Courtesy of Pikeville Medical Center.)

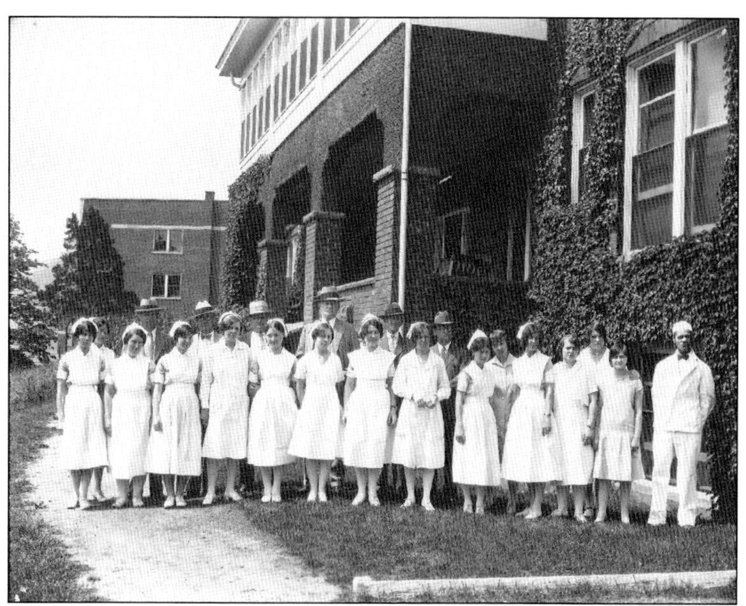

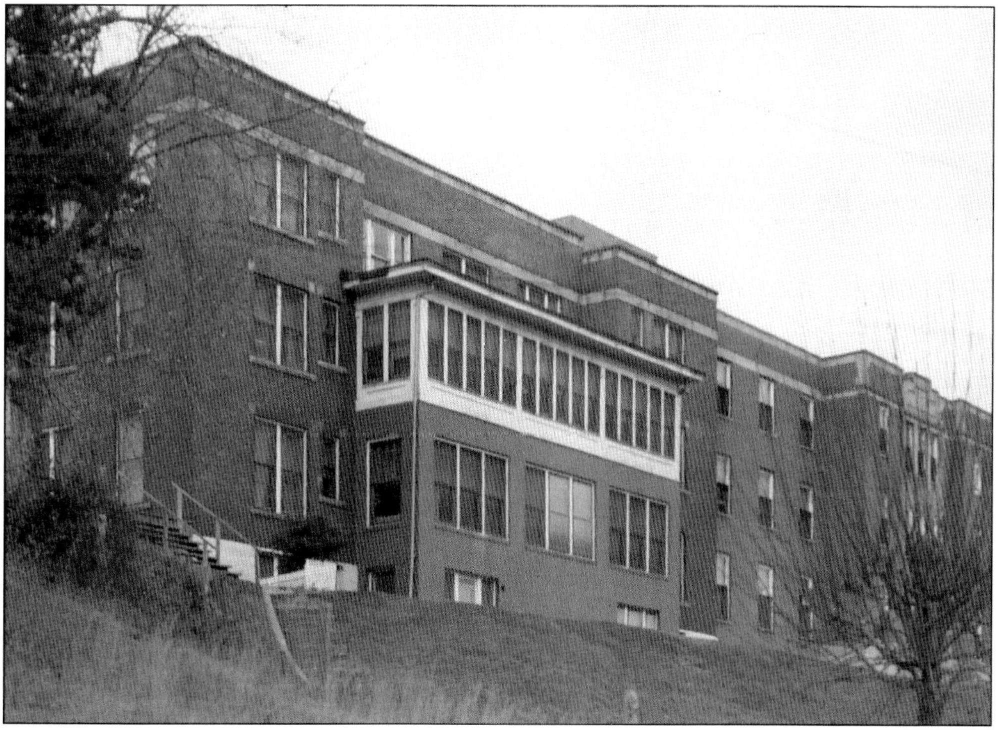

The hospital expanded in 1940 from 50 beds to 90. This expansion included enclosing the porch below the solarium. A second expansion in 1952 increased the capacity to 150 beds. The older section was eventually demolished, but the two additions (right) were renovated and serve as the University of Pikeville's Frank M. Allara Library today. (Courtesy of the Frank M. Allara Library, University of Pikeville.)

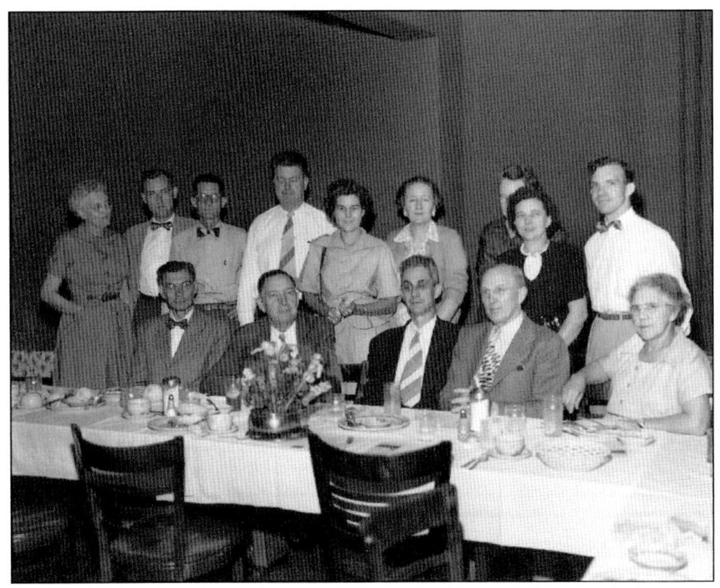

Reverend Ashley (seated second from right), was already called the "father of the Pikeville Methodist Hospital" when he was asked to return as an administrator in 1936. He spurred the building program that resulted in the two expansions and was making his case to the board for the second when this photograph was taken around 1945. (Courtesy of the Pike County Public Library.)

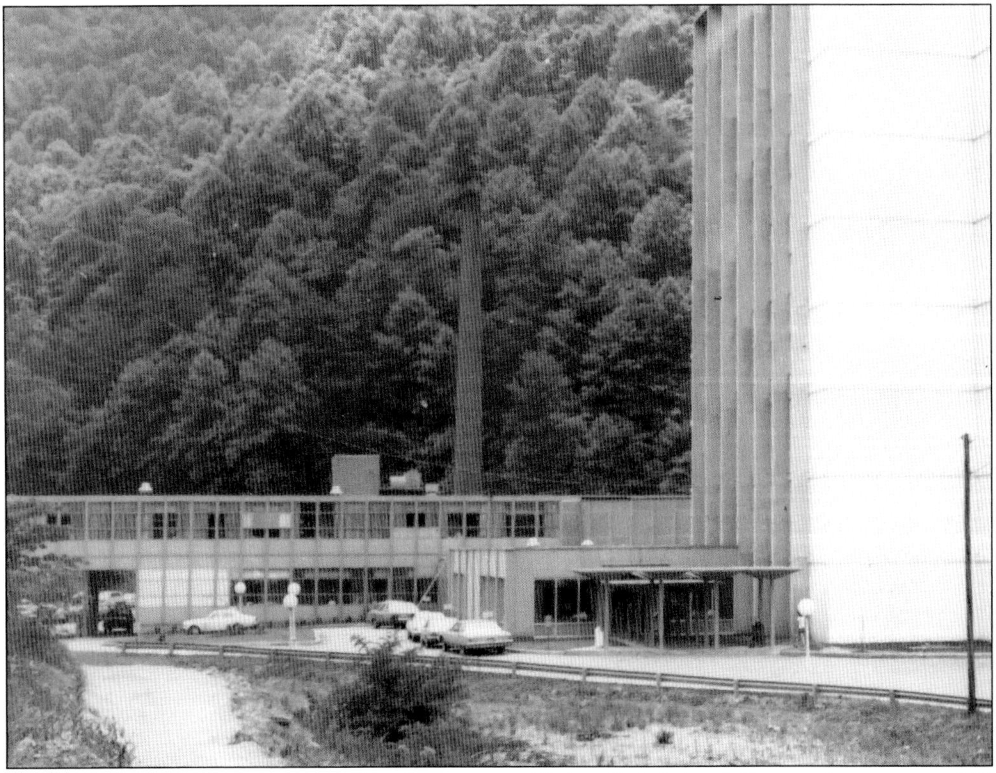

The two-story building at left is the oldest part of Pikeville Medical Center. It was one of 10 hospitals the United Mine Workers of America built in Central Appalachia in the 1950s. It opened as the Miners' Memorial Hospital in 1955, but both hospitals struggled financially until Pikeville Methodist Hospital's administrator, Eugene Lopez, arranged to buy the other. (Courtesy of the Big Sandy Heritage Center Museum.)

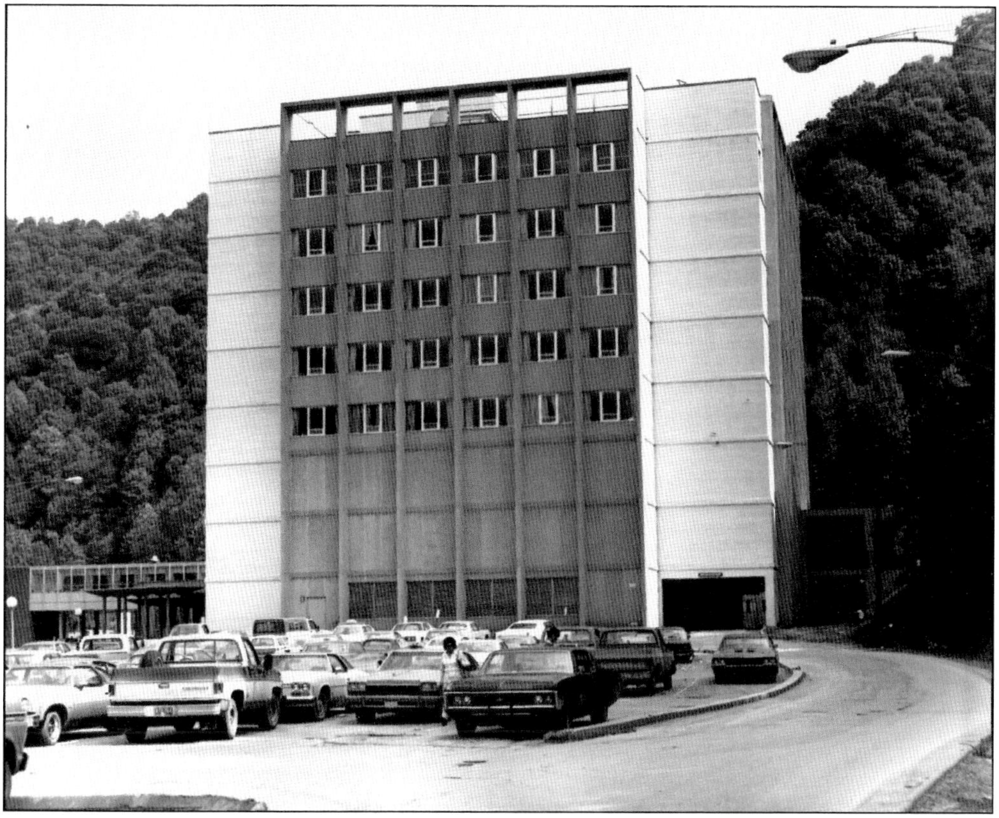

Eugene Lopez recognized the limitations of the old hospital on the hill and dreamed of a large new facility that would connect to a remodeled miners' hospital. Unfortunately, he passed before his dream could come to fruition. The new hospital opened in December 1971 at a cost of $7.3 million with 225 beds and 382 employees. (Courtesy of the Pike County Public Library.)

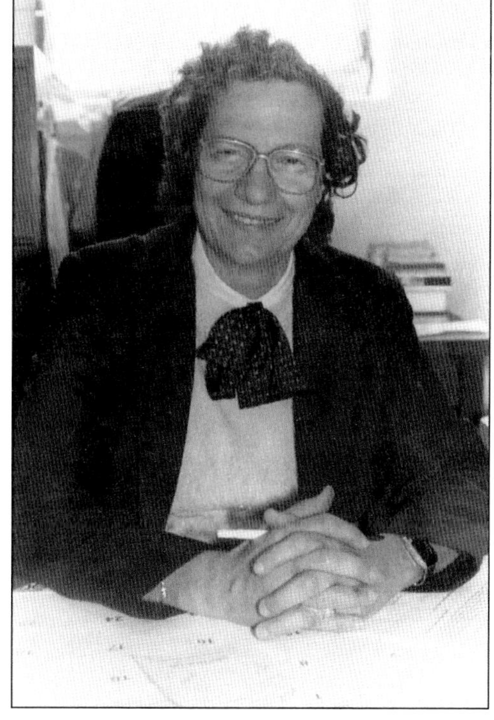

Dr. Mary Fox was a nationally recognized public health expert and a tireless advocate for women's and children's health and for preventive healthcare in general. She earned dozens of awards for her medical and charitable work, including being named a Local Legend of Medicine through the National Institutes of Health. (Courtesy of the Frank M. Allara Library, University of Pikeville.)

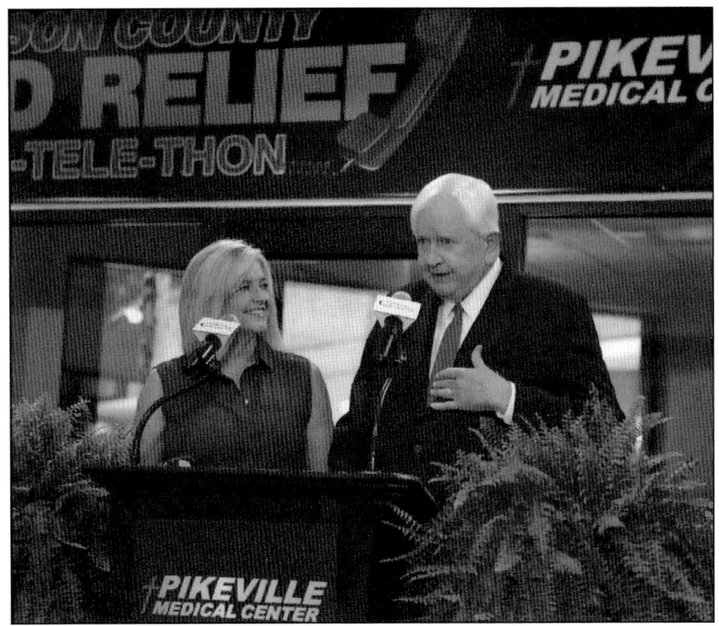

Walter E. May, pictured here with daughter Cindy May Johnson, was mayor of Pikeville from 1989 through 1993. After 40 years as a board member, May served as president and chief executive officer of Pikeville Methodist Hospital from 2000 through 2018. His vision, tenacity, and leadership, along with the dedication of hundreds of others, transformed the hospital into a world-class regional healthcare network. (Courtesy of Cindy May Johnson.)

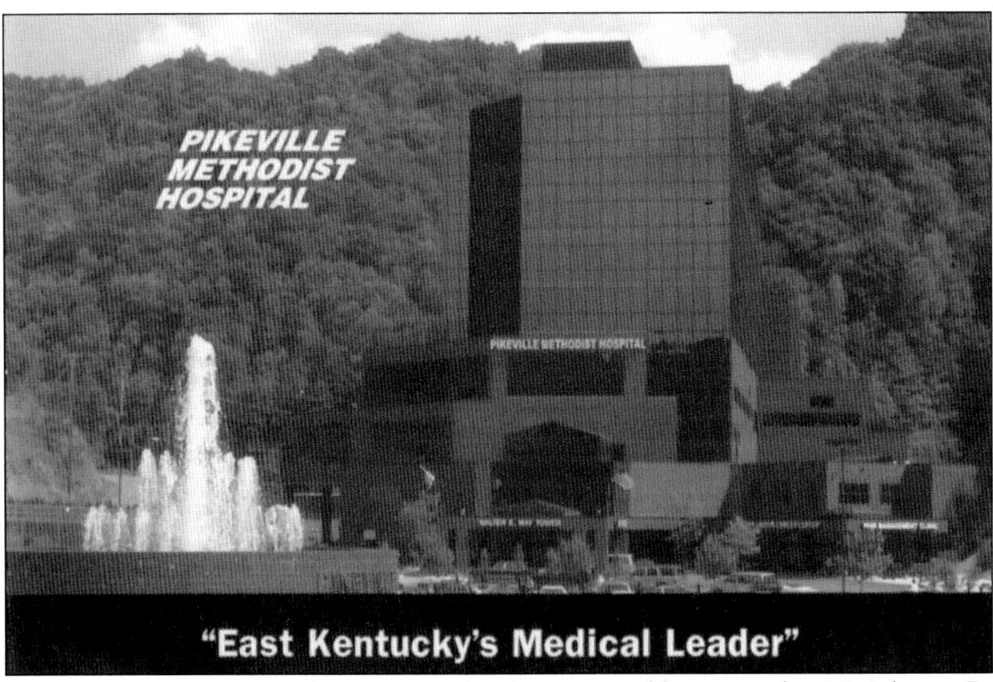

The 11-story expansion seen here was completed in 2000 and later named in May's honor. By 2010, Pikeville Medical Center had 1,700 employees. Millions of dollars in construction continued under May, bringing services into the city and increasing employment until the hospital reached 3,000 employees in 2016. The hospital is the greatest driver of the physical and economic health of the region. (Courtesy of Sam Hatcher.)

Six

Arts and Entertainment

Pikeville's preferred means of entertainment has, in some ways, remained fairly constant over the years. Music and athletics have always supplied entertainment to our people.

While informal playing of instruments has undoubtedly been ever-present, Pikeville also had a more formal musical outlet in its past. The Pikeville Concert Band began playing at gatherings around town in 1907 and continued to do so through 1922.

Renowned musical artists born or raised in Pikeville include Patty Loveless, Dwight Yoakam, and members of the Continental Five. Pikeville is home to Appalachian Wireless Arena, a 7,000-seat multi-purpose facility that features national musical acts on a regular basis. The plaza outside hosts free concerts featuring local artists twice each month during the summer.

The Appalachian Center for the Arts presents theater, music, and visual arts in addition to educational opportunities in the performing arts.

By the early 1900s, baseball was the nation's pastime, and this was no different in the coal fields. Towns throughout Appalachia had teams, with local talent often supplemented by paid semi-professionals. Pikeville played host to the first Kentucky Semi-Pro State Tournament in 1946 and won the state title the following year.

Pikeville also had a tennis team, and regional tournaments were held in the city. Support for the high school teams is extremely high, and the city has also occasionally hosted professional sports, including a minor league baseball team in the 1980s and professional basketball and indoor football teams in the 2000s.

Perhaps the most significant artist to come from Pikeville was Effie Waller Smith. Born to former slaves in 1879, she was a teacher but also published books of poetry. She was the first Black woman to publish poetry in national magazines and was elected to the Kentucky Writers Hall of Fame in 2015.

Festivals and parades offer another form of entertainment for our community. Hillbilly Days is one of the largest and most famous festivals in the state and raises money for the local chamber of commerce and for Shriners Children's Hospitals.

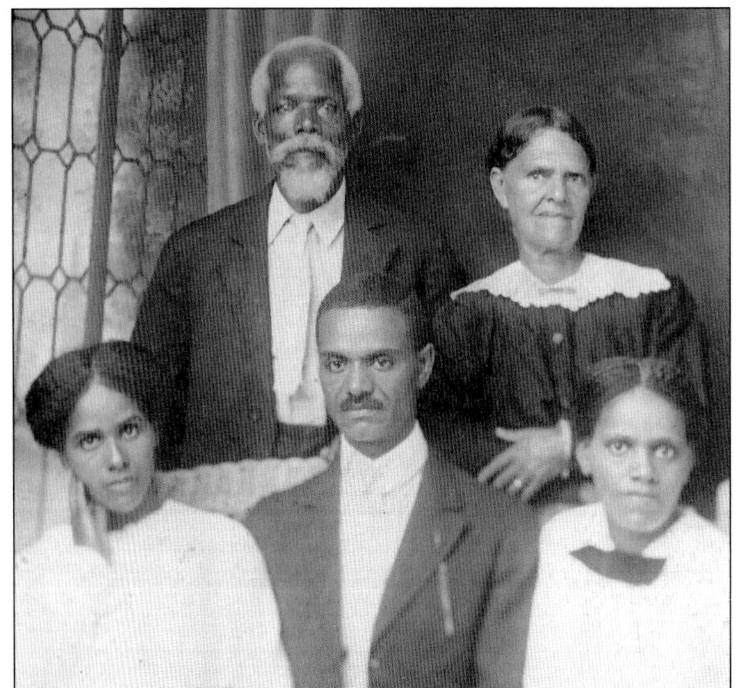

Frank and "Sibbie" Waller (second row) were married in Pikeville in 1873 shortly after the Civil War. Frank worked as a wharfmaster, farmer, and blacksmith. Their children (from left to right)—Rosa, Alfred, and Effie—were all educated to be teachers at what is now Kentucky State University. (Courtesy of the Frank M. Allara Library, University of Pikeville.)

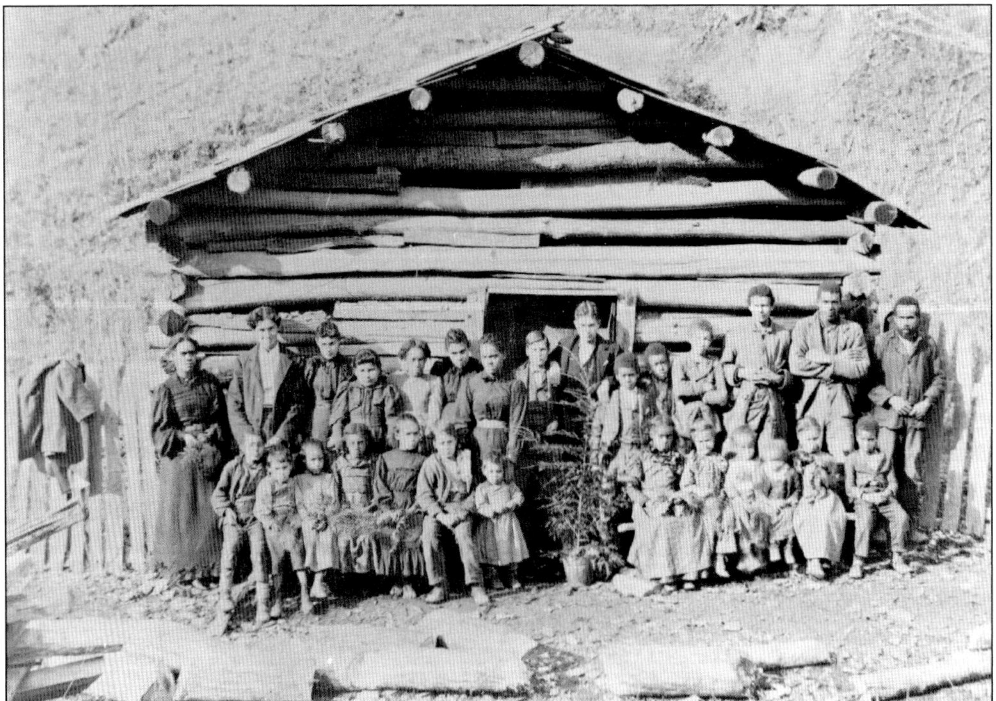

"Miss Effie" Waller, as she was known, had a short marriage to a local deputy sheriff named Charles Smith who was killed in the line of duty. Seen here on the left around 1898, she was the teacher at this school on Biggs Branch in Pike County. It was supposed to be a segregated school, but also included white children. (Courtesy of David Deskins.)

Effie Waller Smith's poems display a deep love of her home—particularly the natural beauty, mountains, and local culture—and she became known as the "Singing Poet of the Cumberlands." She moved to Wisconsin, but had promised a sick friend, Polly Ratliff (left), that she would raise Polly's daughter Ruth should Polly die. Ruth was Effie's only child. (Courtesy of the Pike County Public Library.)

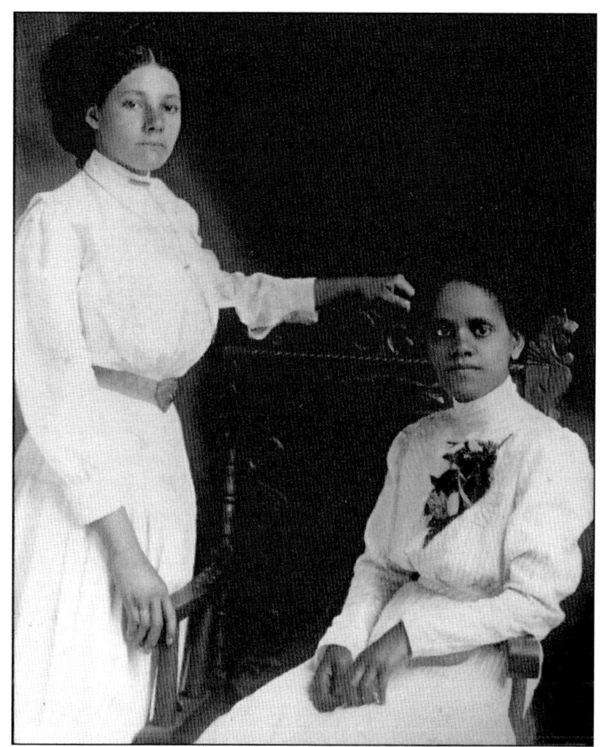

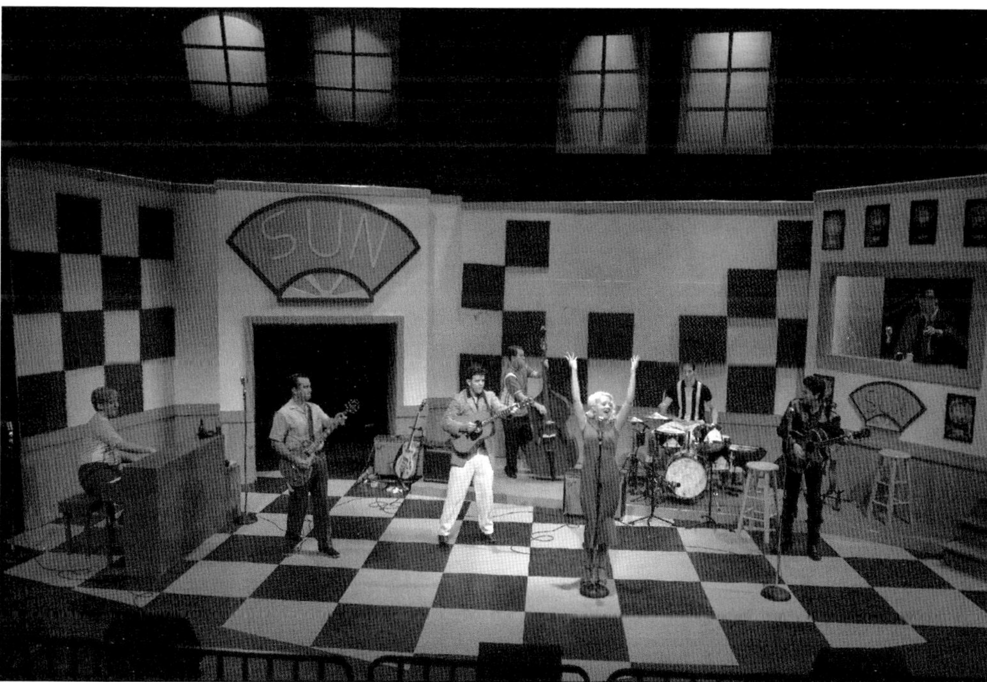

Recently, a theatrical performance about Smith's life called the *Effie Waller Smith Monologue* was produced by the Appalachian Center for the Arts. "The App," as it is known, is a center for visual and performing arts in downtown Pikeville that often features productions such as this one of *Million Dollar Quartet* in 2019. (Courtesy of Dusty Layne, City of Pikeville.)

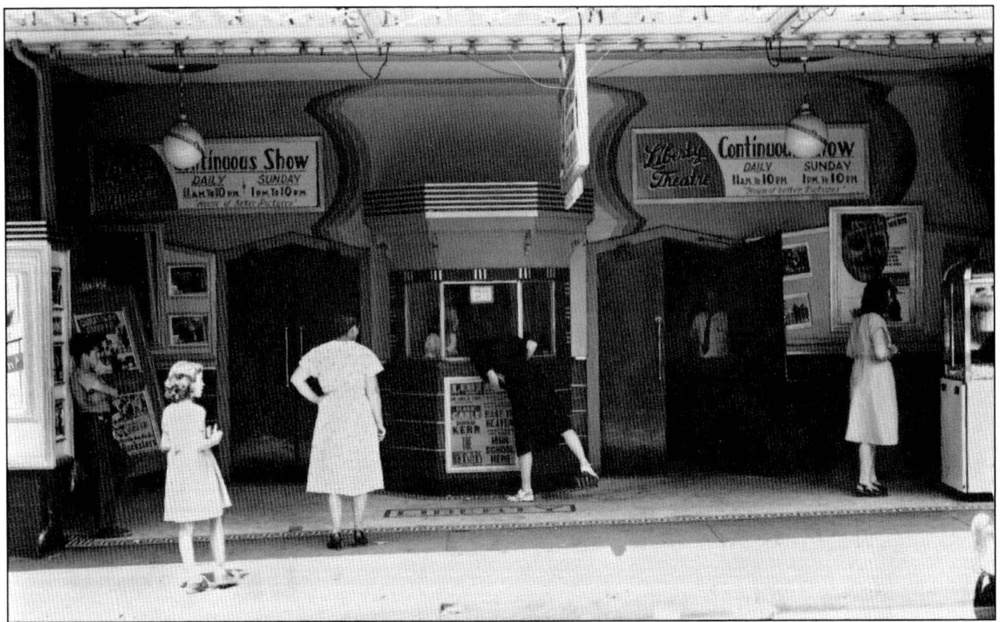

Liberty Theatre was a one-screen cinema that opened with around 600 seats on Main Street in the 1930s. Here, the poster beneath the ticket stand is advertising *The Hucksters*, a 1947 movie starring Clark Gable and Deborah Kerr. The theater is thought to have closed in the 1960s. (Courtesy of the Pike County Public Library.)

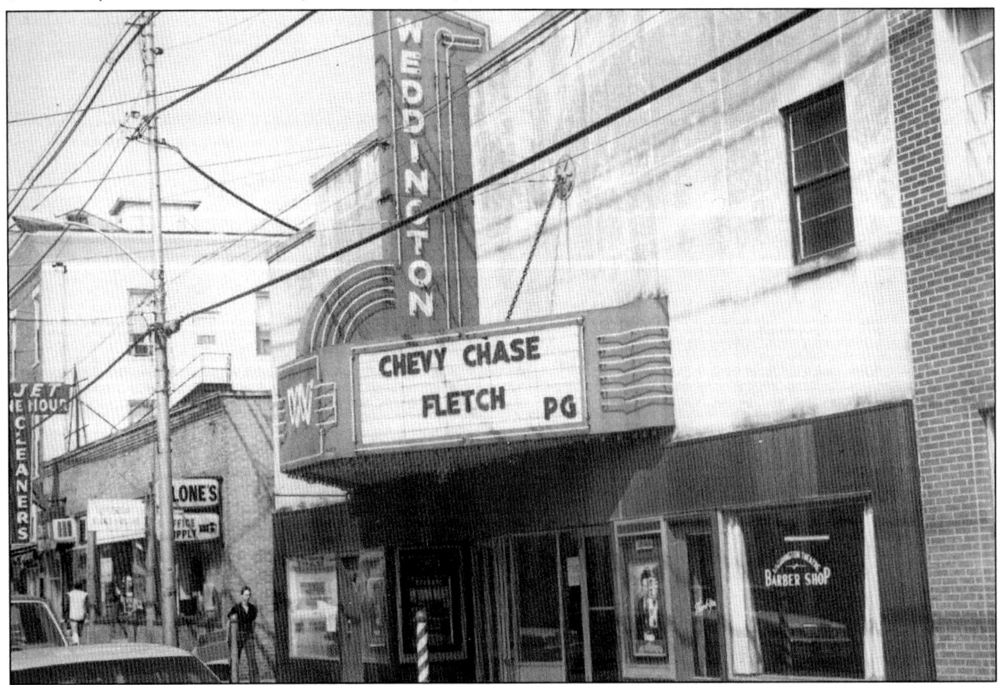

Weddington Theater opened on July 13, 1921, on Second Street with over 800 seats under the management of Jasper Saad. It was extensively damaged by fire in February 1946 and remained closed for two years. It closed for good in the early 1990s and was demolished in 2010 to make way for the Pike County Judicial Center. (Courtesy of the Frank M. Allara Library, University of Pikeville.)

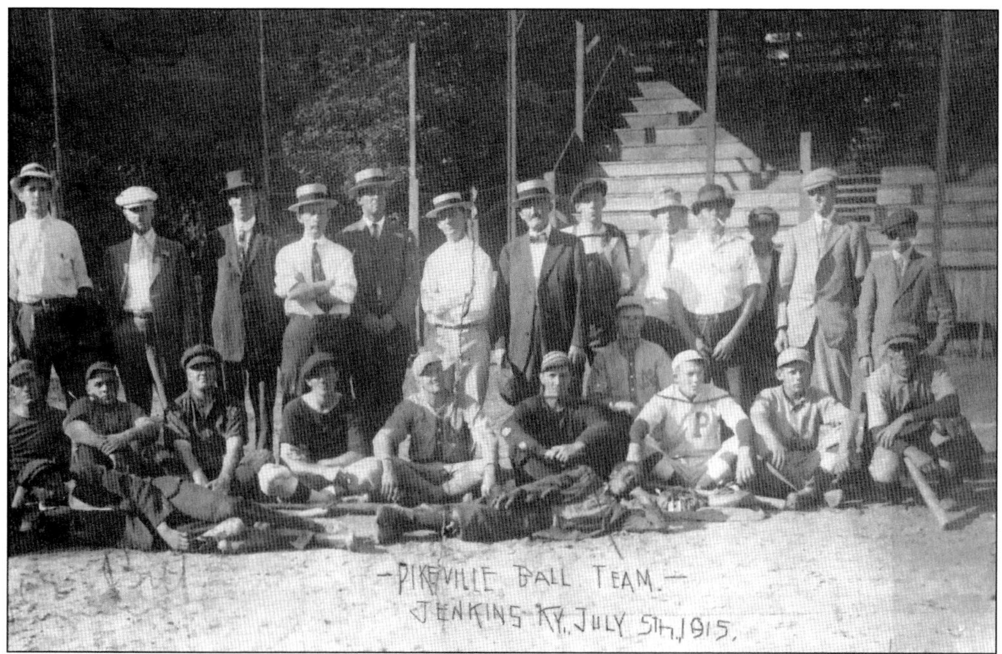

This is the Pikeville semi-professional baseball team at Jenkins in 1915. Virtually every coal company and town in the area had a team, with more than 20 in the Big Sandy Valley at one time. In Pikeville, the field was near what is now Myra Barnes Avenue, part of the old Perry Cline farm. (Courtesy of the Big Sandy Heritage Center Museum.)

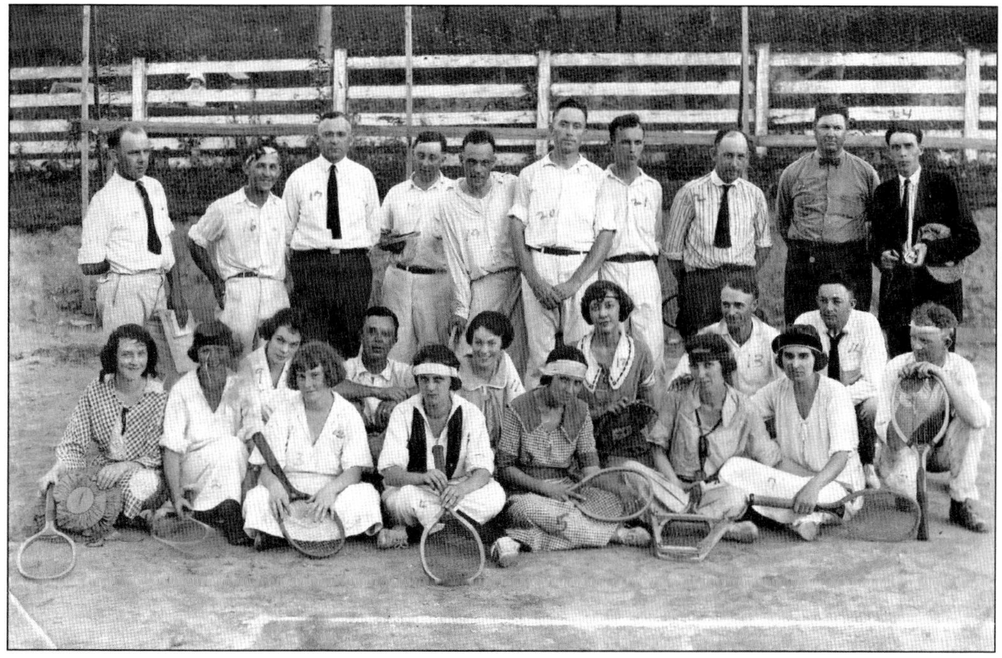

In 1922, the Pikeville Tennis Club hosted the third Eastern Kentucky Open tennis championships, which had been held in Jenkins the previous two years. Some of the contestants are shown here, including the women's and men's singles champions, Margaret Perkins (seated, far right) and C.E. Brandon (standing, far right). (Courtesy of the Frank M. Allara Library, University of Pikeville.)

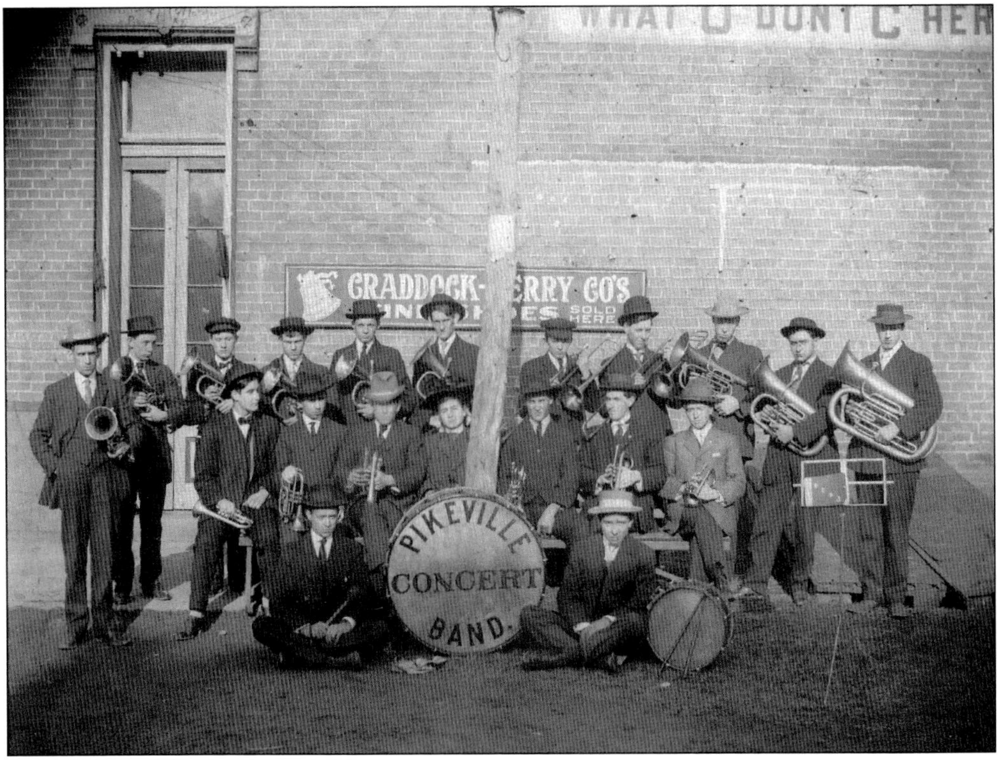

Frank Forsyth (second row, second from left) was a local historian and member of the Pikeville Concert Band for the entirety of its 15 years. The band had a rotating membership of dozens from all walks of life. Every political event, parade, or public gathering of that time included entertainment by this band. (Courtesy of the Frank M. Allara Library, University of Pikeville.)

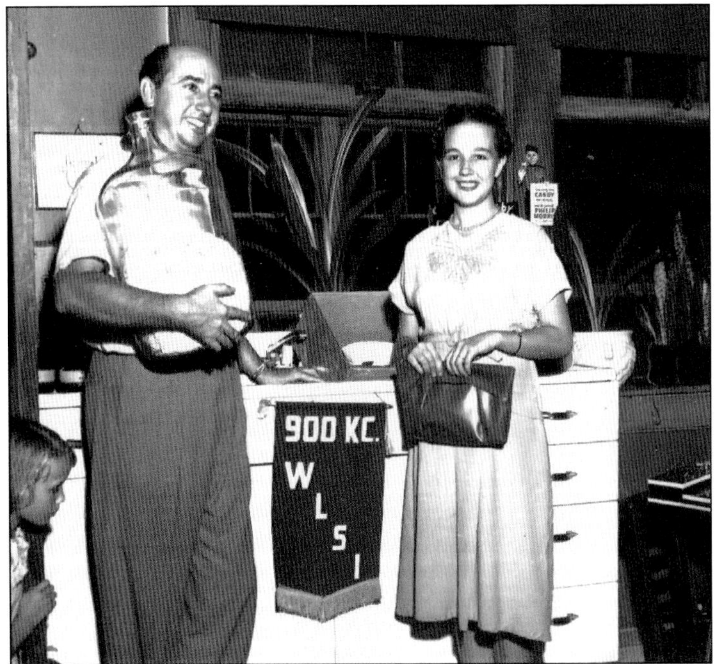

Mike Laymon (left) was the first manager of Pikeville's first radio station, WLSI, which began broadcasting in January 1949 under the ownership of Cumberland Publishing Company. Layman would later be president of the Kentucky Broadcasters Association. A second station, WPKE, began broadcasting in July 1949. Both stations are now part of Mountain Top Media. (Courtesy of the Pike County Public Library.)

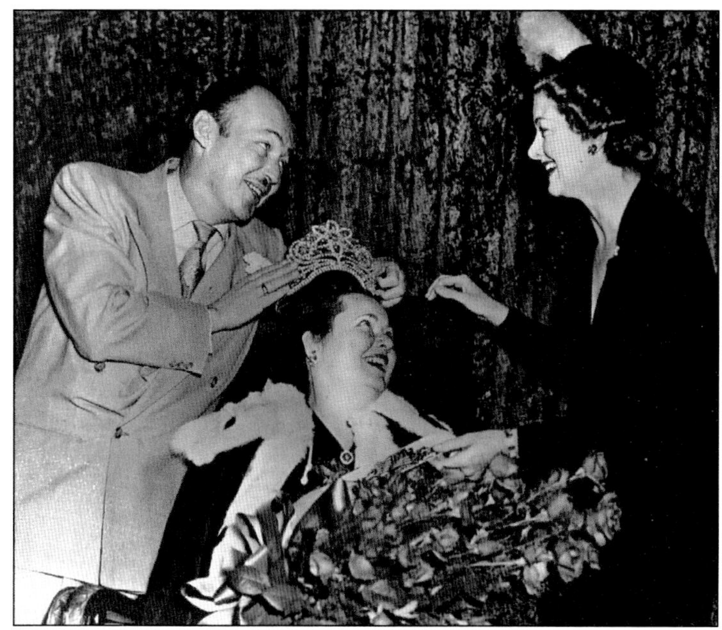

In October 1949, the popular radio show *Queen for a Day* ran a contest with 450 radio stations, including WPKE, to name a woman "Queen of America" based on her good works. Pikeville's own Sally Nolan Baker (center) was chosen from among 15,000 applicants based on her extensive charitable deeds. She was crowned by host Jack Bailey and Myrna Loy. (Courtesy of the Pike County Public Library.)

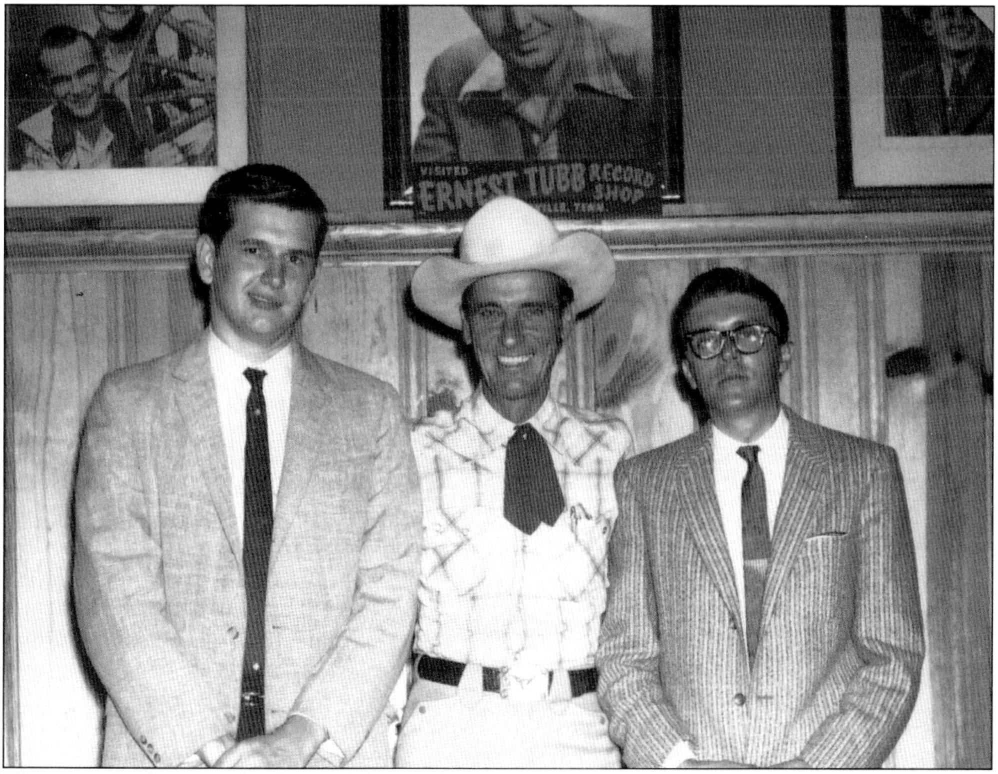

This c. 1959 photograph of, from left to right, Walter E. May, country music pioneer Ernest Tubb, and David Stephens was taken in Nashville six years after May became Pikeville's first rock-and-roll disc jockey at age 16. In 1962, he became part owner of East Kentucky Broadcasting and general manager of WPKE. May grew the company into a multi-million-dollar business with nine stations spread throughout Eastern Kentucky. (Courtesy of Cindy May Johnson.)

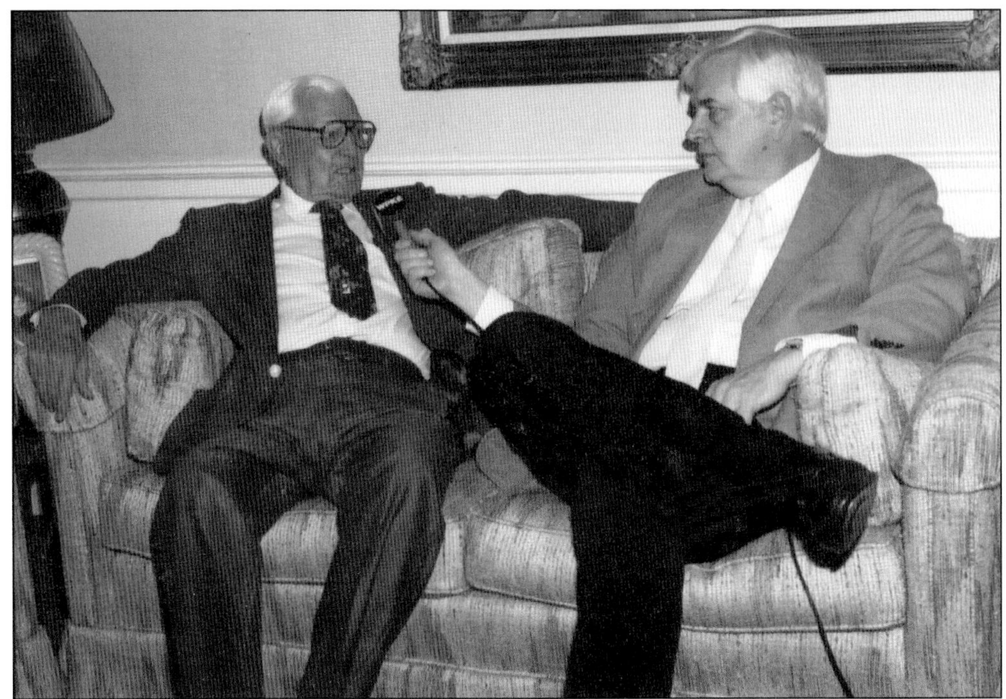

Walter May (right) interviews Pikeville businessman Walter P. Walters in the 1980s. May's broadcasting talents won him opportunities such as live coverage of the launch of Apollo 11 in 1969 and interviewing five former presidents. He served as president of the Kentucky Broadcasters Association and was the first Kentuckian named chairman of the Radio Board of the National Association of Broadcasters. (Courtesy of Cindy May Johnson.)

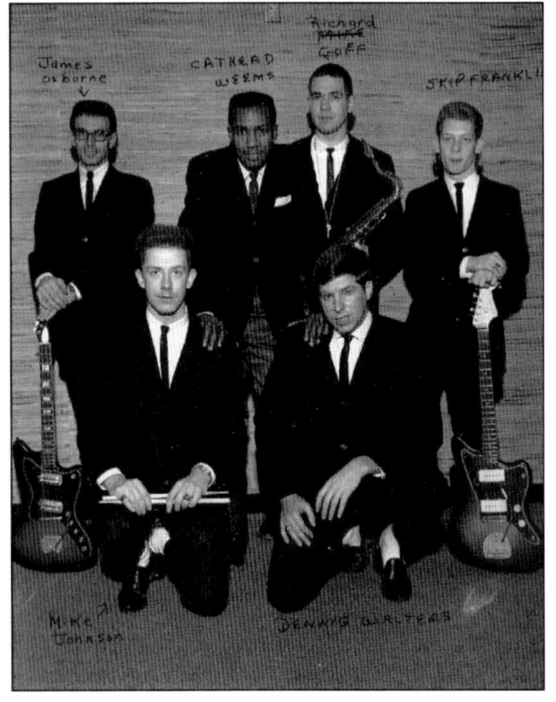

Pikeville's first rock-and-roll band, Ritchie Weems and the Continental Five, debuted in 1962, and Walter May soon began featuring them on WPKE. The next year, the band signed a record deal with Spot Records, a subsidiary of RCA, and released a song called *Natural Born Man* that reached No. 52 on *Billboard's* top-100 chart. (Courtesy of the Pike County Public Library.)

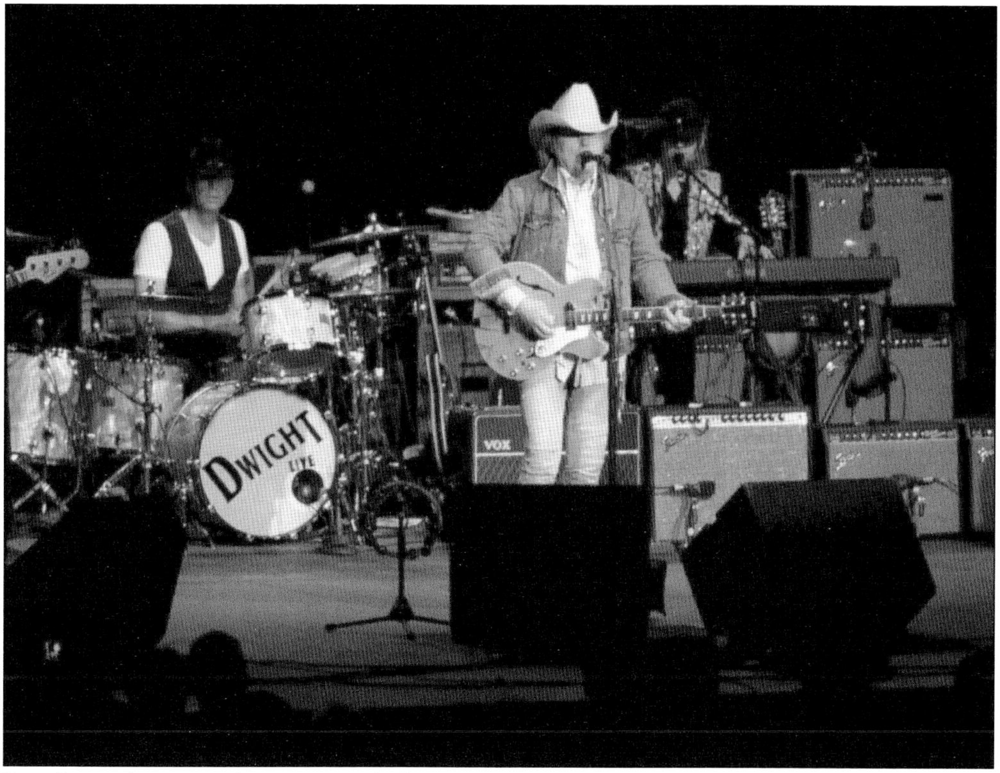

Dwight Yoakam, seen here at Appalachian Wireless Arena in 2016, was born in Pikeville in 1956. His first home was in nearby Betsy Layne, but the family moved to Columbus, Ohio, a few years after his birth. Yoakam has sold more than 30 million records and recorded twelve gold and nine platinum albums. He has also enjoyed a successful film career. (Courtesy of Dusty Layne.)

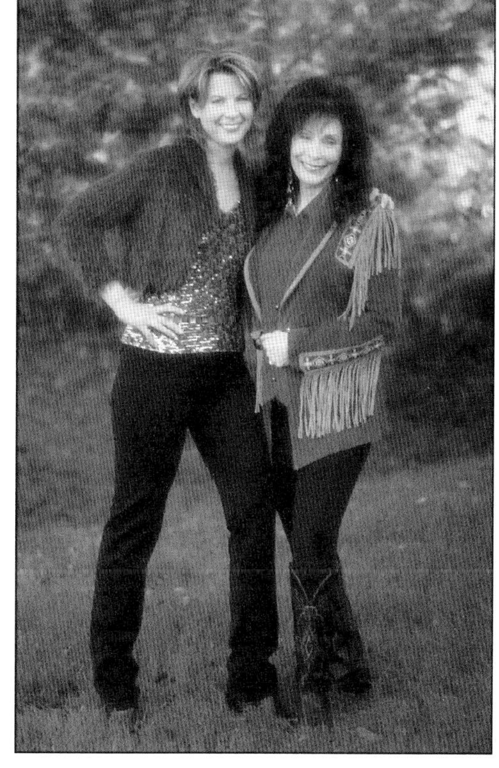

Pictured with Loretta Lynn (right) from nearby Johnson County, Patty Loveless was born in Pikeville in 1957 and lived near Elkhorn City until moving to Louisville in 1969. The Grand Ole Opry star has released three gold and four platinum albums and received five Country Music Association, three Academy of Country Music, and two Grammy awards. (Courtesy of the Country Music Hall of Fame and Museum.)

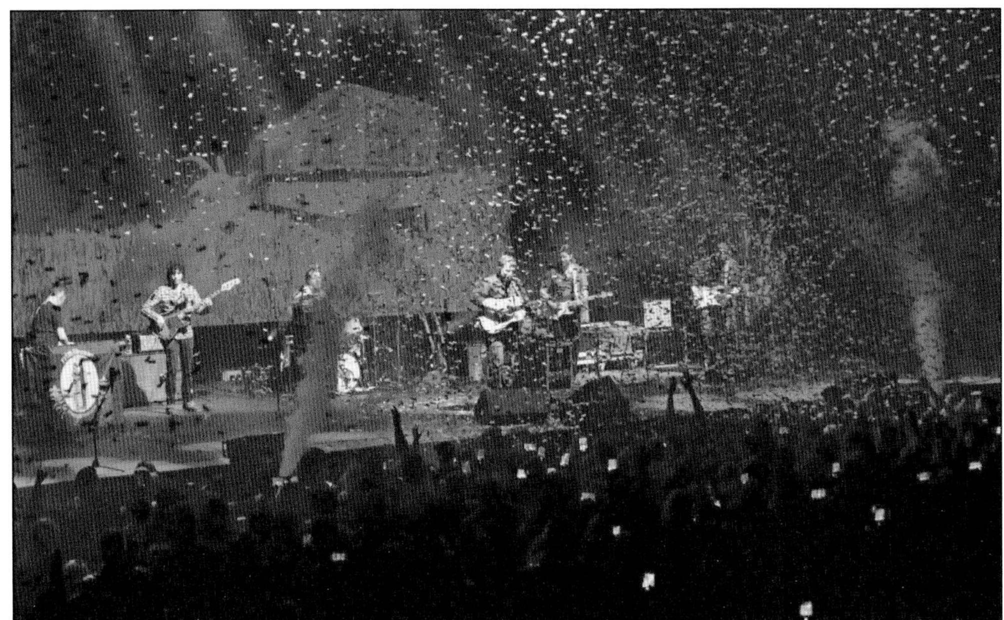

While Appalachian Wireless Arena has presented many successful concerts over the years, none have matched the crowds that Eastern Kentucky native Tyler Childers brought in December 2019. Childers brought in the new year with three sellout crowds, making him the highest-grossing act to ever play the arena. Mayor James A. Carter presented Childers with a key to the city. (Courtesy of Dusty Layne, City of Pikeville.)

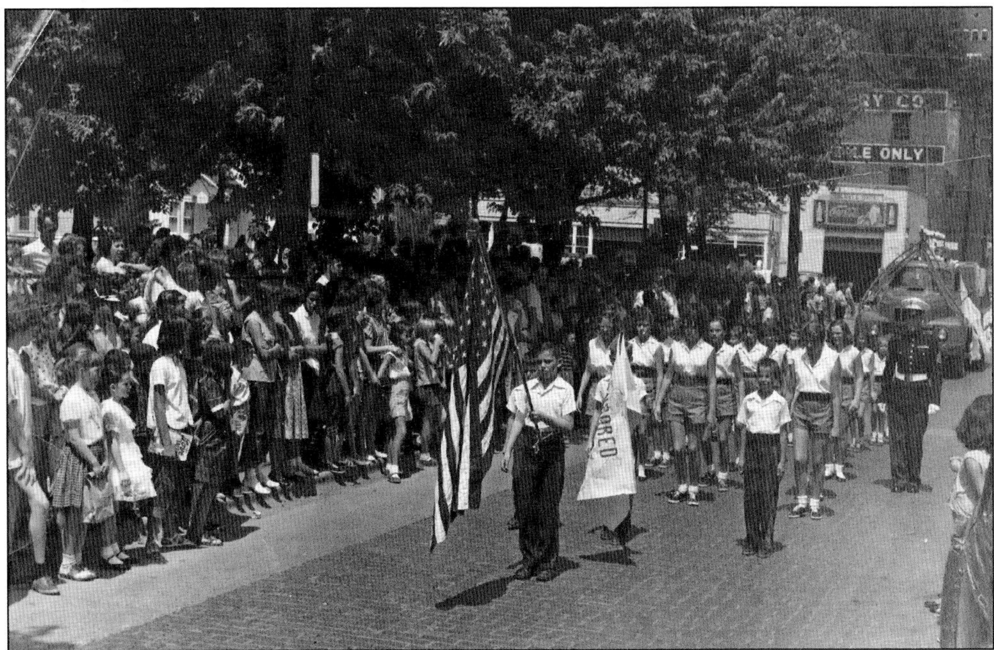

This Independence Day parade in the 1950s was led by flag bearer Buddy Forsyth. Parade participants marched along Huffman Avenue next to the City Park. The warehouse in the background stood where the downtown parking garage is now. (Courtesy of the Frank M. Allara Library, University of Pikeville.)

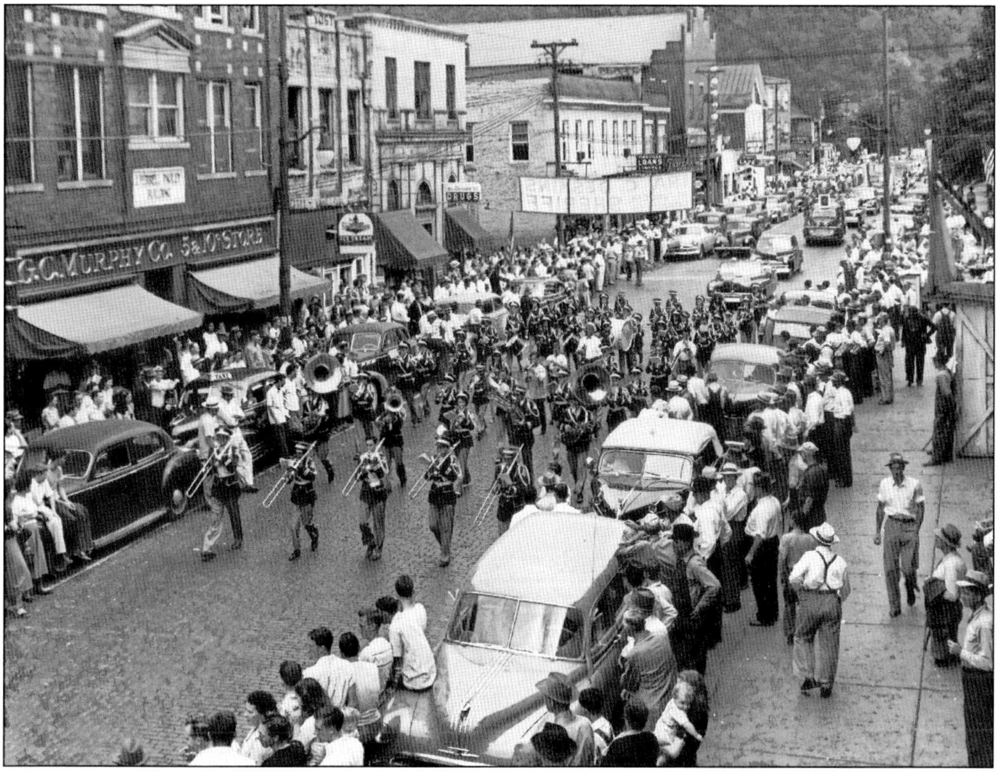

This c. 1949 parade featured the Pikeville High School band marching on Main Street toward the City Park. The banner crossing Main Street is advertising the candidacy of Ira C. Deskins for Pike County sheriff. In a quirk of timing, Deskins once served as chief deputy sheriff, sheriff, and tax commissioner in less than 40 hours. (Courtesy of the Big Sandy Heritage Center Museum.)

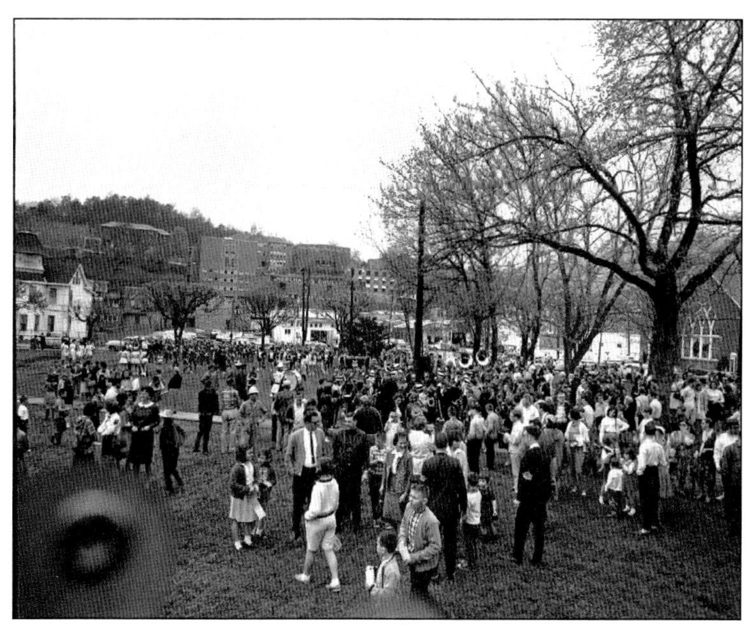

In about 1968, various high school bands from the area gathered in the City Park for what may have been a marching band competition or the beginning of a parade. Parades for Christmas, Independence Day, or the occasional visiting dignitary often included bands from area schools. (Courtesy of the Pike County Public Library.)

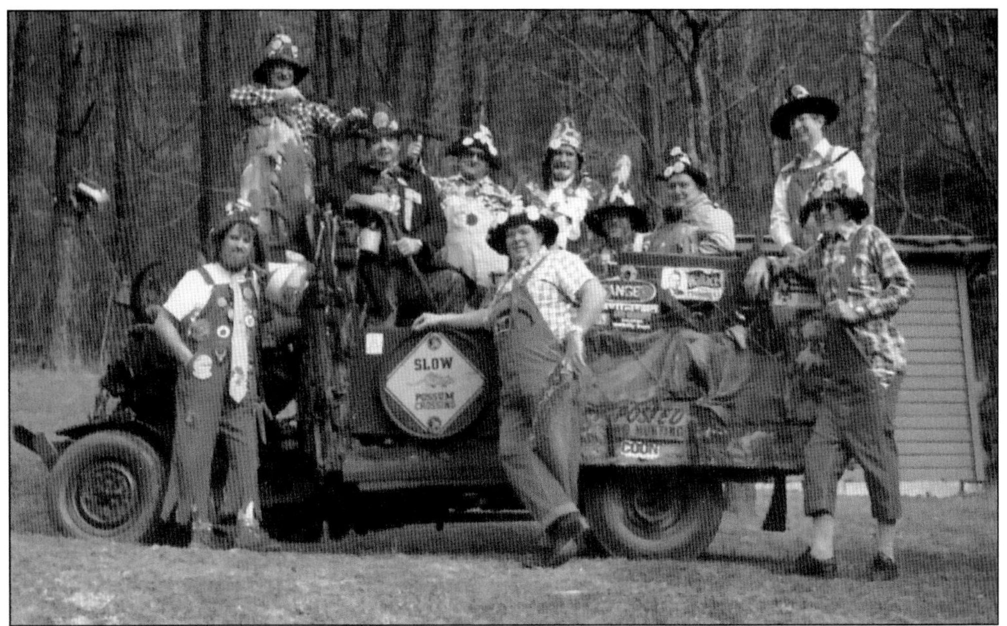

Pikeville's most famous festival is Hillbilly Days, held each April. Howard Stratton and Grady Kinney started the event with a local chapter of Shriners International to raise money for children receiving treatment at Shriners hospitals in Lexington, Kentucky, and Cincinnati, Ohio. The festival was intended to combine a light-hearted take on false stereotypes with authentic Appalachian food and entertainment. (Courtesy of Brenda Hays, John Doug Hays collection.)

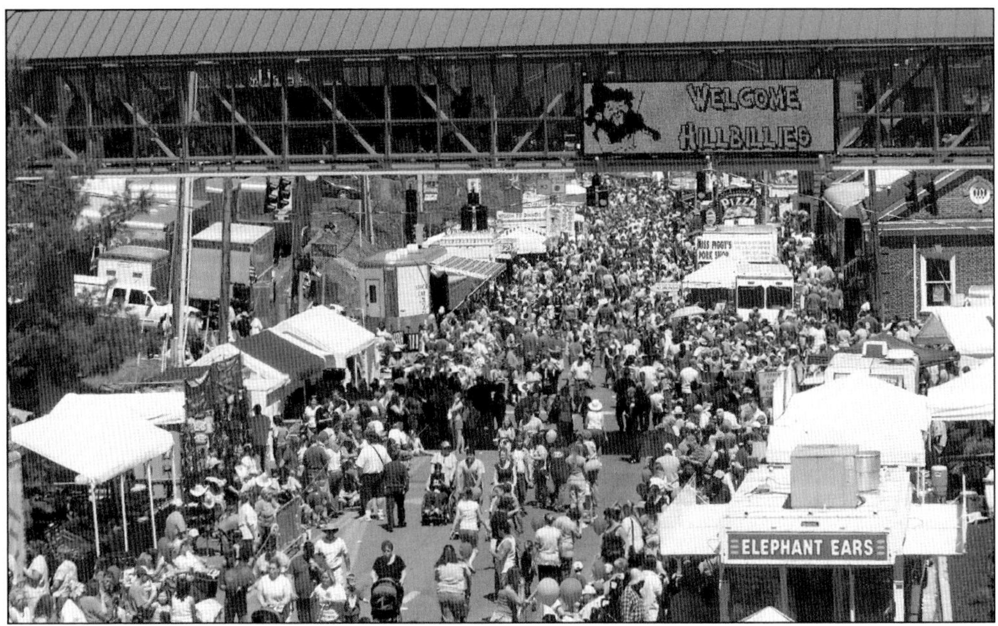

The festival has grown tremendously, with over 100,000 attendees each year. The Shriners partner with the Southeast Kentucky Chamber of Commerce while the city supplies workers and logistics. The event includes a carnival, over 100 vendors, live music on three stages, and a concert in Appalachian Wireless Arena. To date, Hillbilly Days has raised over $4 million for the Shriners hospitals. (Courtesy of Dusty Layne, City of Pikeville.)

Seven

Service and Religion

Many of Pike County's original settlers received land grants for their service in the Revolutionary War or the War of 1812.

The Civil War almost certainly had the largest wartime effect on Pikeville. James Garfield's presence is well known, but the turmoil Pikeville and Pike County experienced is underappreciated. Control of Pikeville alternated between Union and Confederate forces. The Confederates arrived first in October 1861 and quickly arrested Union supporter John Dils and transported him to Libby Prison. Upon his release, he returned to Kentucky and formed the 39th Kentucky Mounted Infantry.

Judge William Cecil, a Confederate supporter, adjourned Pike County's court in December 1861 just before Union troops arrived and arrested him. He was shot dead on Main Street by Union scout and Pikeville citizen T.J. Sowards without trial. It was February 1865 before the court went back into session. The absence of real law enforcement in Pike County meant raids, thievery, and the risk of starvation.

Pikeville's citizens continued to answer when called to defend their country, and they have fought and died in every major American war.

The Pikeville Police Department was established before 1913 but after the 1893 appointment of its first town marshal. Two officers have been lost in the line of duty: Alonzo Robinson in 1929 and Scotty Hamilton in 2018.

The Pikeville Fire Department began with three hose carts and six ladders around 1910. Capt. James McKenzie was lost in the line of duty in 1970.

Pikeville's first known church was the Methodist Church South, built in 1845. Soon after, the rival First Methodist Episcopal Church opened down the street. Beginning around 1851, a Christian church featuring traveling preachers met and was formally organized as the First Christian Church in 1883. The Presbyterian church also arrived in 1883. As the years have gone by, the variety of Christian denominations has expanded.

Finally, civic organizations such as the Masons, the Woman's Club, the Rotary Club, the chamber of commerce, and Kiwanis have each been helping citizens for more than a century.

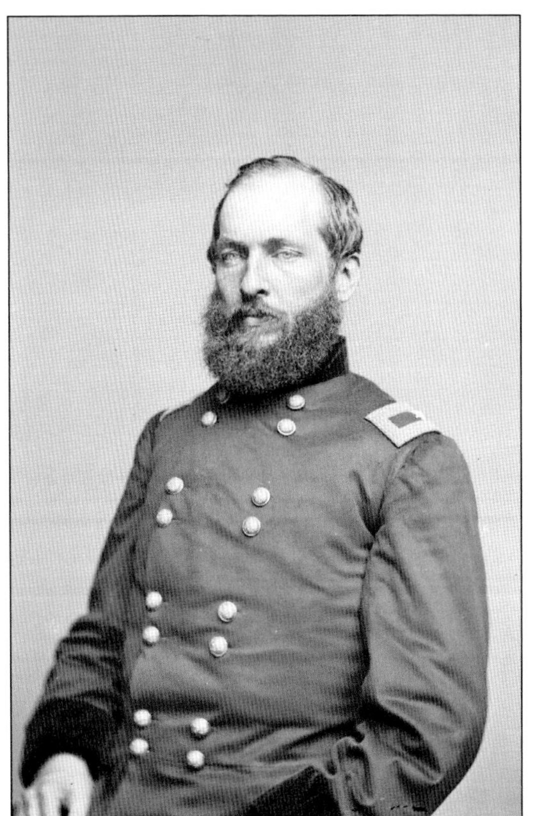

James Garfield was a newly appointed colonel in January 1862 when he led Union troops to victory at the Battle of Middle Creek near Prestonsburg. His camp in today's City Park suffered from dwindling supplies. This led Garfield to take one man and a skiff downriver to Catlettsburg, where he commandeered a steamboat to resupply his men. (Courtesy of the Library of Congress.)

In March 1862, Garfield became the youngest brigadier general in the Union with Squire John Charles administering his oath in today's City Park. This title likely meant that Charles was an elected justice of the peace. Garfield led 700 men to Pound Gap on March 14 and pushed the Confederate forces out of Pike County. (Courtesy of the Pike County Public Library.)

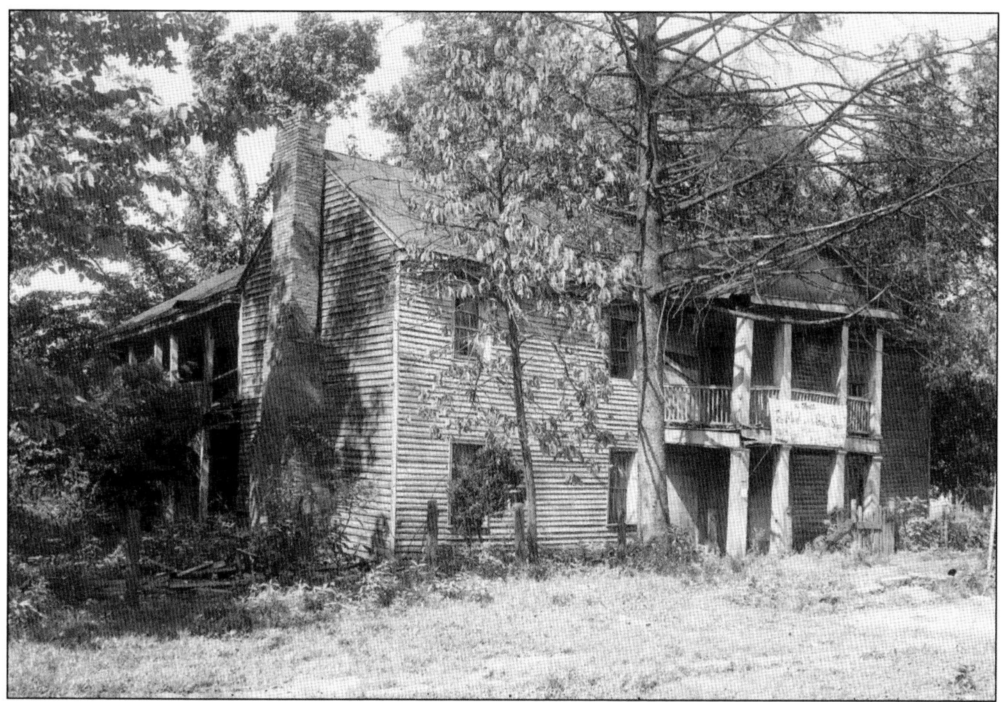

This home, built in 1856 by Judge William Cecil and located in today's City Park, was used as Colonel Garfield's quarters in 1862. Some reports say Garfield took his oath there. It was called Ratliff's Tavern or the Bowles House at various times, the latter because Capt. Orlando C. Bowles and his wife later made this property their home. (Courtesy of the Filson Historical Society, Louisville, Kentucky.)

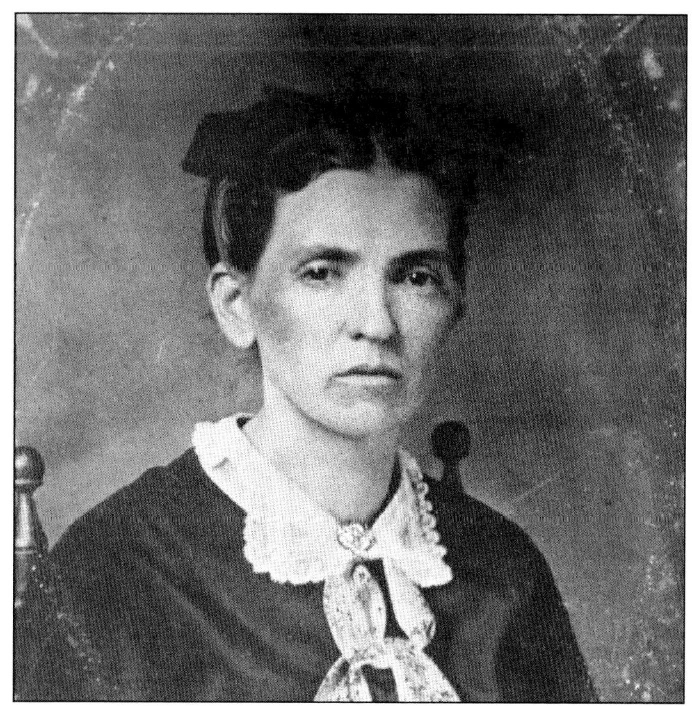

Pauline Cecil Bowles, pictured here in the late 1800s, was the daughter of Judge William Cecil, a Confederate sympathizer shot and killed in Pikeville by a Union soldier in January 1862. Yet just six months later, she married Union soldier Orlando C. Bowles, who had arrived with Garfield from Ohio. The couple became among Pikeville's most influential. (Courtesy of the Frank M. Allara Library, University of Pikeville.)

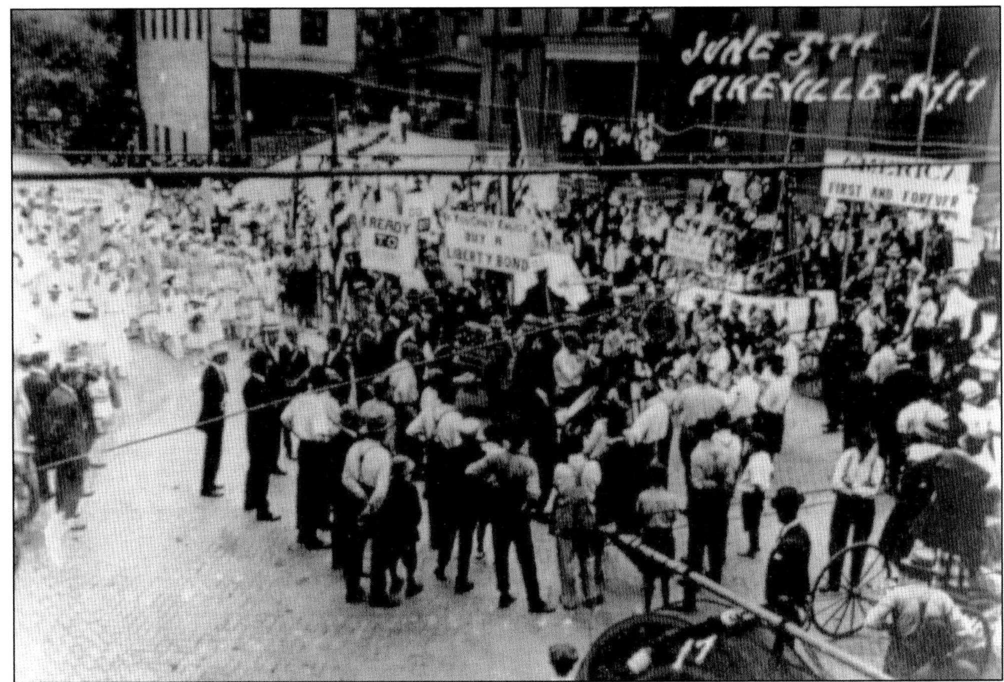

The US Congress declared war on Germany in April 1917, and within a few months, communities across the country were holding parades to encourage the purchase of Liberty Bonds. Many local men enlisted, and Pikeville showed its support with this Liberty Bond Parade in June 1917. (Courtesy of the Pike County Public Library.)

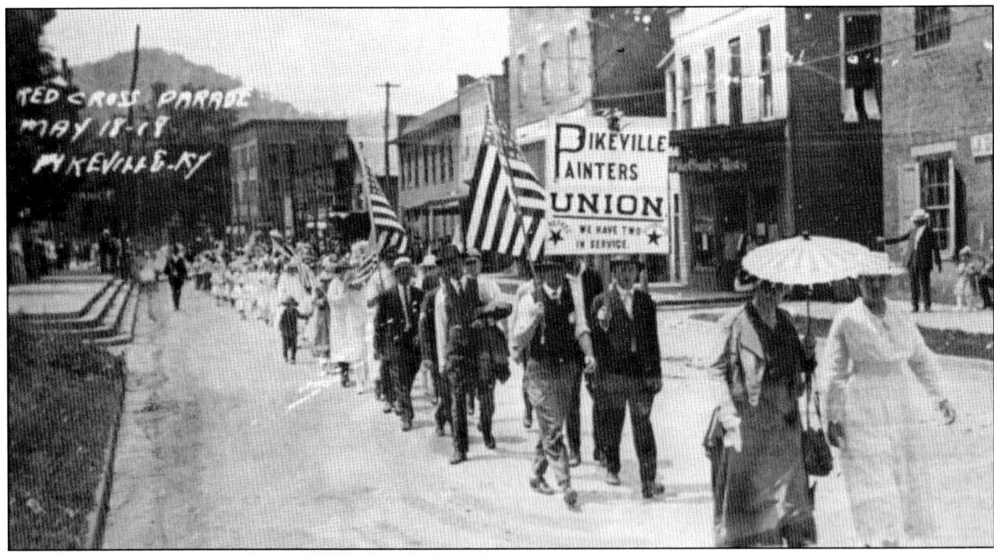

World War I also saw the Red Cross grow dramatically as need for its services increased. A fundraising drive began in May 1918, and Pikeville's parade in support was lauded as a success by the *Big Sandy News*, which reported that Gov. Augustus Stanley and two soldiers from France led the half-mile-long procession. (Courtesy of the Pike County Public Library.)

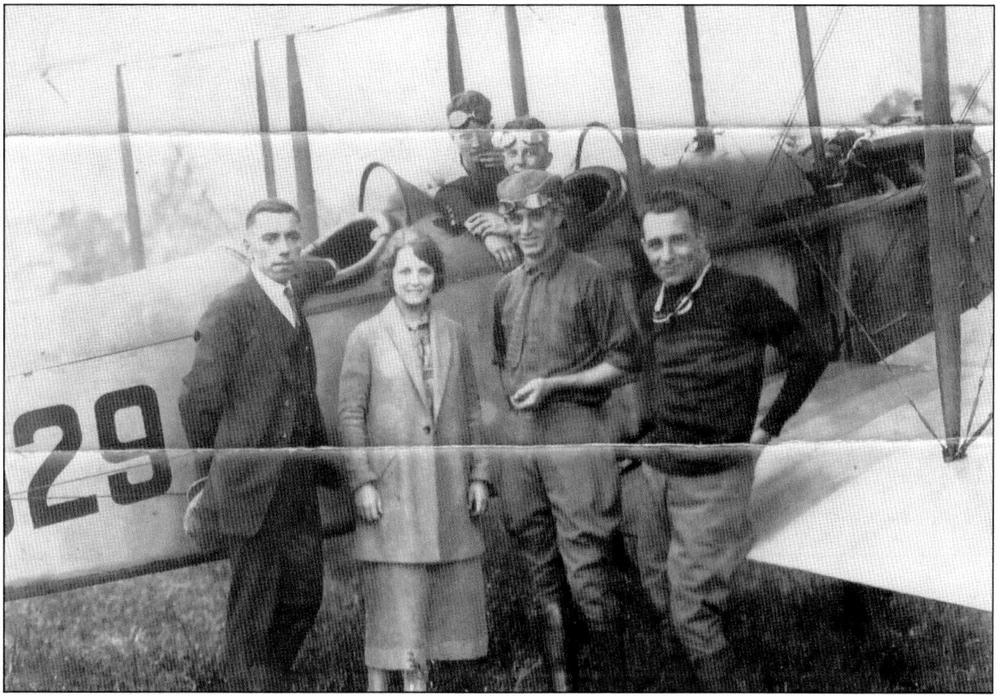

On Independence Day 1923, John Paul Riddle (second from right) wowed a crowd by flying under Pikeville's Middle Bridge. Two months later, he was in Cincinnati with, from left to right, Charles Rentrop, Olga Emrick, and others. Riddle trained to be a pilot in the US Army, then returned to Pikeville to work for Lewis Stone. (Courtesy of Embry-Riddle University Archives.)

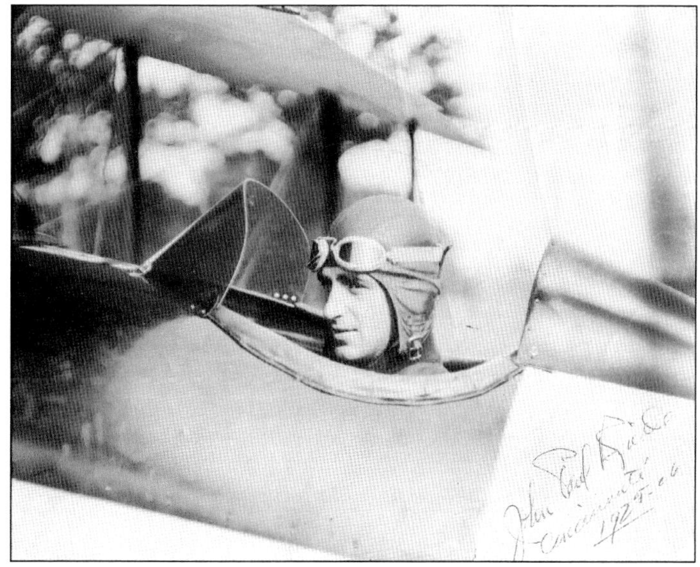

Stone was a local airplane dealer and taught flying lessons in Pikeville. By 1925, Riddle and T. Higbee Embry were based in Cincinnati's Logan Airport operating a flight school and airmail delivery company that later became part of American Airlines. Riddle and his pilots spent their weekends doing aerial acrobatics and entertaining crowds as Riddle's Flying Circus. (Courtesy of Embry-Riddle University Archives.)

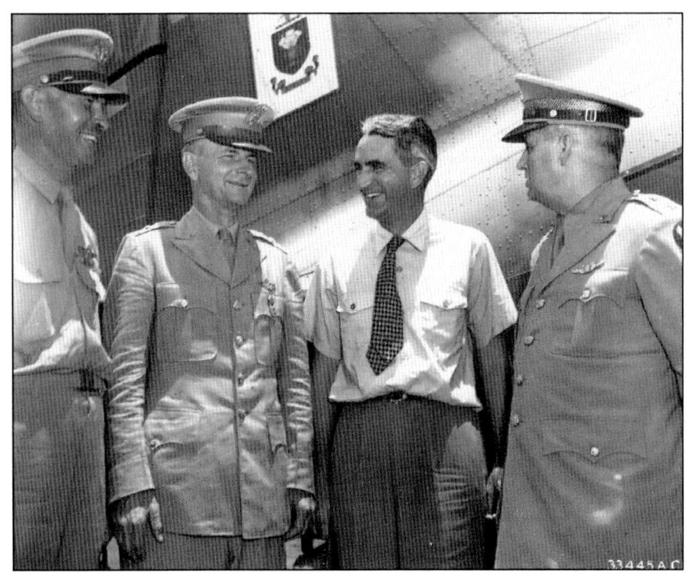

In July 1942, Riddle was with high-ranking officers in the US Army Air Forces Technical Training Command. During World War II, his flight schools trained over 26,000 pilots, mechanics, and air support personnel. The effort proved critical to Allied victory, and the British government awarded him the British Empire Medal in 1945. In peacetime, the school became Embry-Riddle University in Daytona Beach, Florida. (Courtesy of Embry-Riddle University Archives.)

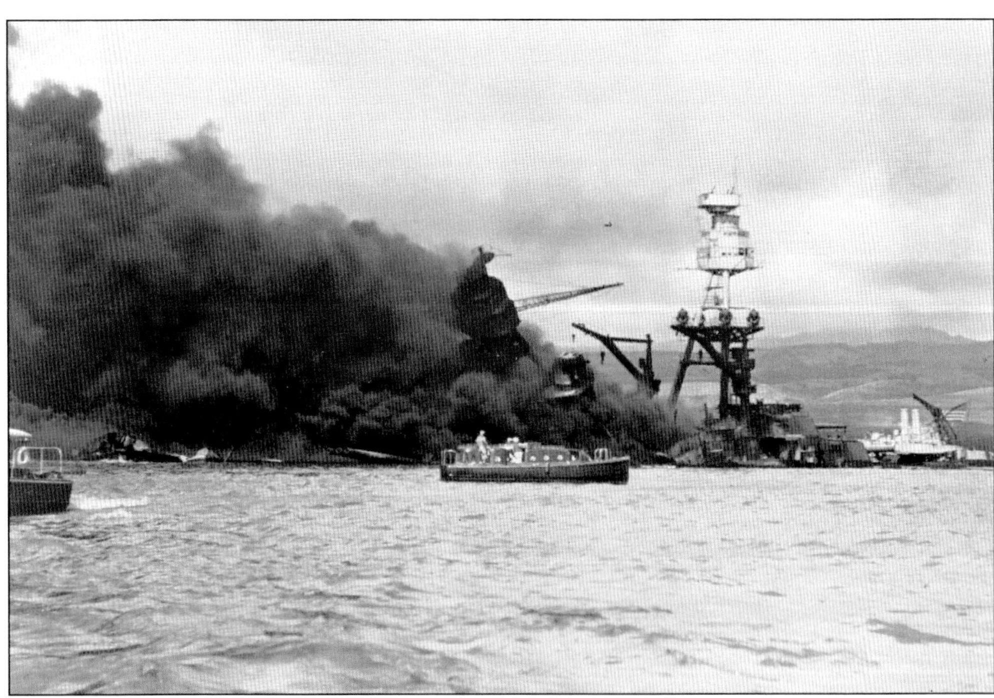

The Japanese attack on Pearl Harbor on December 7, 1941, was the catalyst that brought the United States into World War II. The attack left over 2,400 dead and seven ships sunk. Four Pike County men—Harding Blackburn, Jack Buckley, Millard Burke Jr., and Homer Robinson—were there, and only Robinson survived. Buckley was aboard the USS *Arizona* (pictured), which exploded and sank. (Courtesy of the Library of Congress.)

Men from Pikeville and Pike County fought in the most famous and consequential battles in World War II. Reed Potter Sr., for example, fought as part of the 82nd Airborne in the Battle of the Bulge, Operation Market Garden, and the battle for Berlin. Twice wounded in battle, Potter finished as Gen. James Gavin's personal assistant in Headquarters Company. (Courtesy of Reed Potter Jr.)

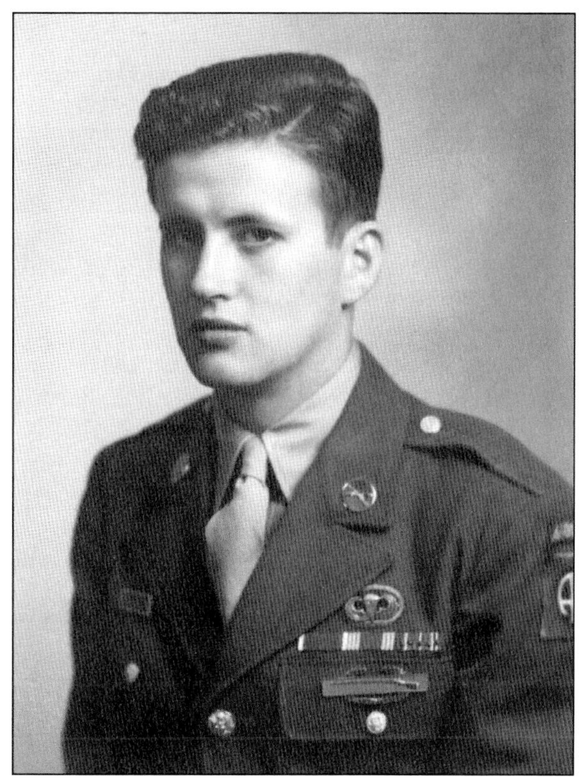

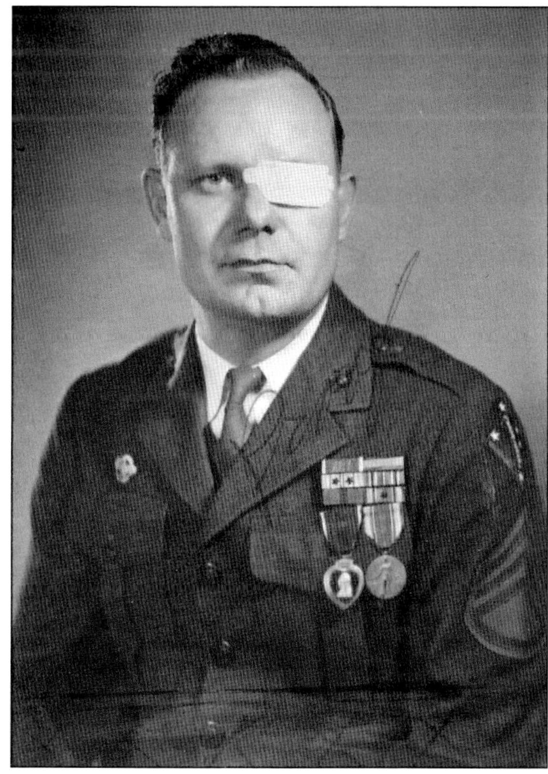

Pikeville and Pike County men also fought in the Pacific Theater. Charles Lowe, later a Pike Circuit judge, was among the US Marines who fought the Battle of Okinawa from April through June 1945. On June 14, at Kunishi Ridge, a mortar attack cost Lowe his left eye. Okinawa fell eight days later, and Japan surrendered in September. (Courtesy of Charles E. Lowe Jr.)

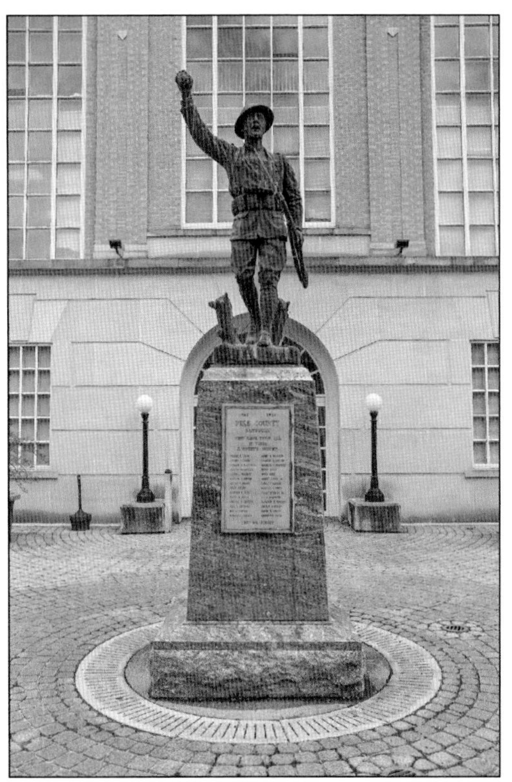

Statues of *The Spirit of the American Doughboy* by E.M. Viquesney were produced to honor World War I veterans. Pikeville's bronze statue stands 14 feet, and was erected near Main Street in 1932 and relocated in 1992. Plaques around the marble base list the 302 Pike Countians known to have given their lives in the two world wars, Korea, and Vietnam. (Courtesy of Dusty Layne, City of Pikeville.)

Pikeville's oldest civic organization is the Thomas C. Cecil Lodge No. 375 F&AM, a Masonic lodge formed in 1860 and named for a prominent citizen. Members met in the courthouse for decades, then in various downtown buildings, as seen here around 1940, likely on Main Street. The lodge's current home on Pike Street opened in 1974. (Courtesy of the Pike County Public Library.)

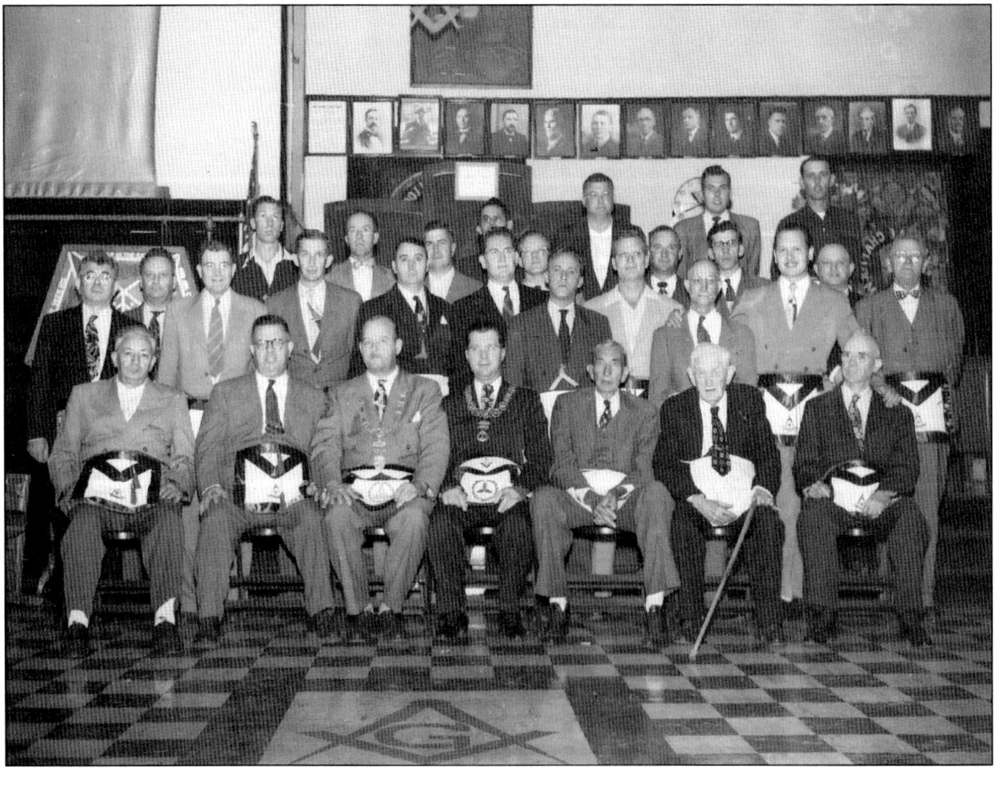

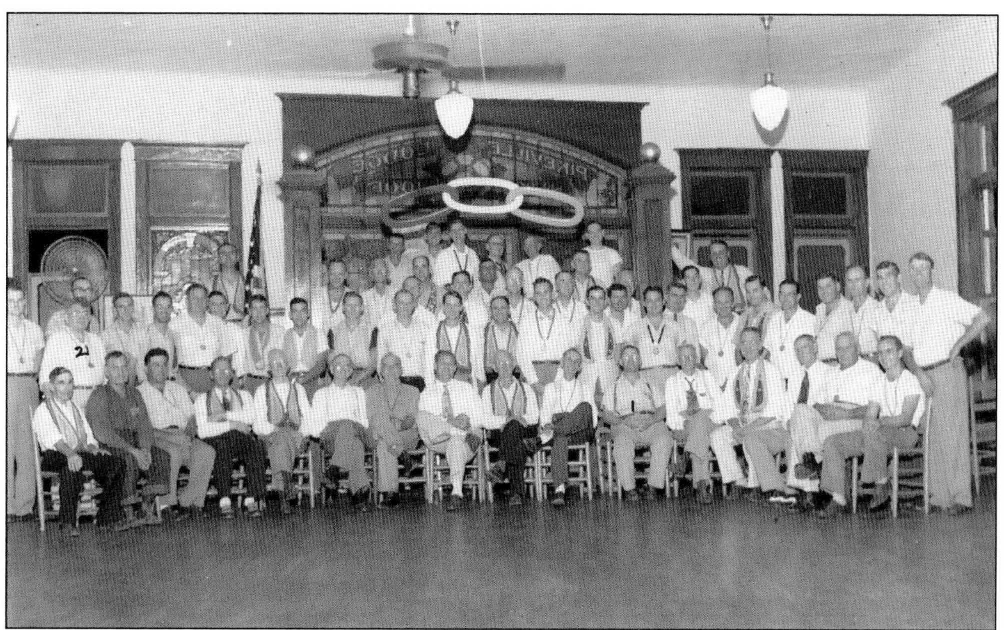

This photograph of the Odd Fellows of Pikeville, a fraternal organization dedicated to helping those in need, was taken around 1950. The Pikeville lodge started in 1890 and has been located in its Second Street building since 1915. Other civic organizations include the Pikeville Woman's Club, founded in 1919, and the Pikeville Rotary Club, organized in April 1922. (Courtesy of the Pike County Public Library.)

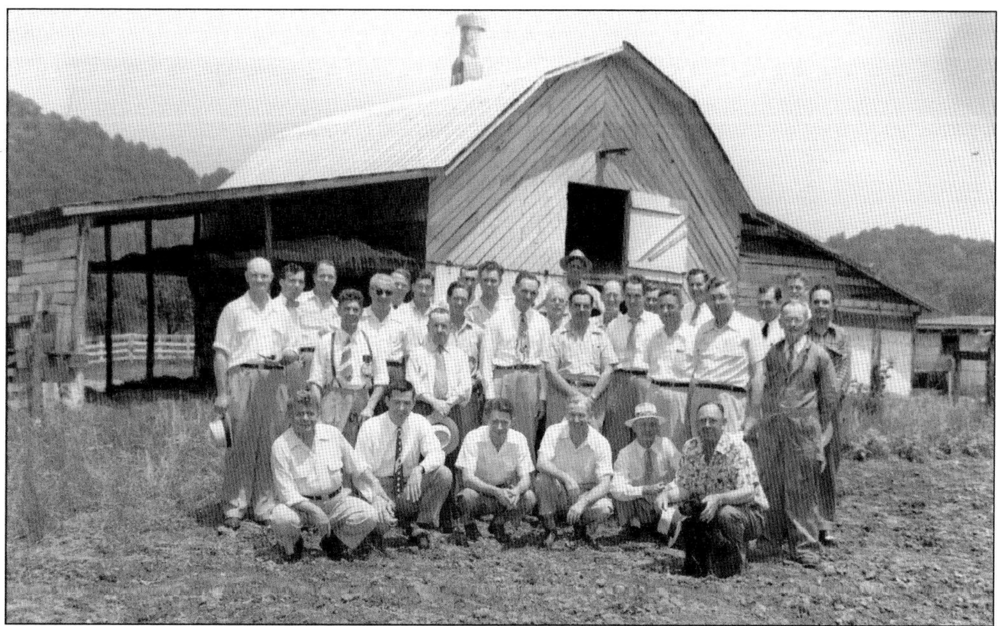

The Kiwanis Club of Pikeville was established in the early 1920s less than a decade after the national organization started in 1915. From its founding through the 1950s, when this photograph was taken, until today, local men, including George Thornbury (fifth from left), and women have contributed their time, money, and energy to serving the children of Pikeville and Pike County. (Courtesy of the Pike County Public Library.)

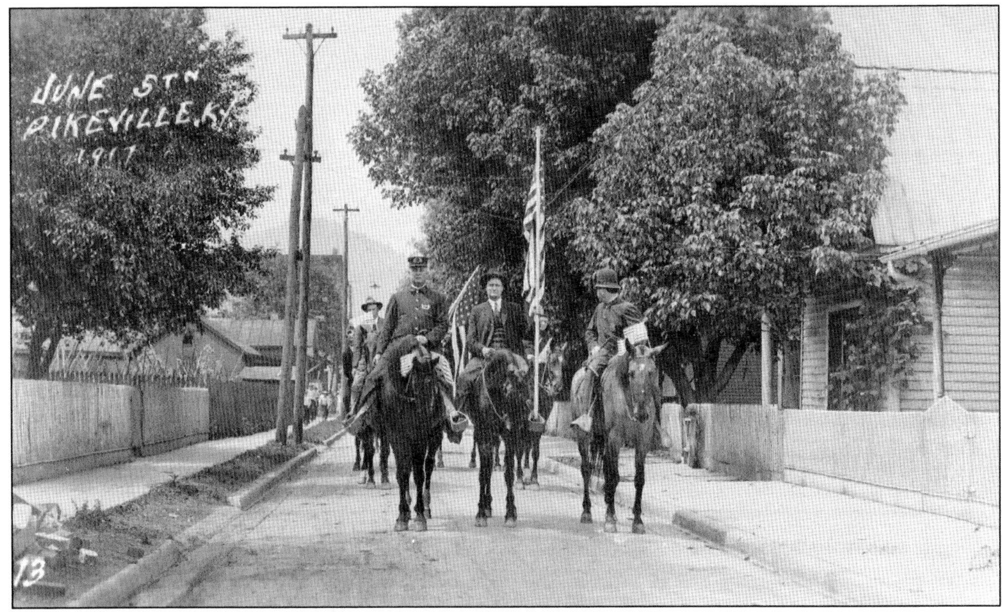

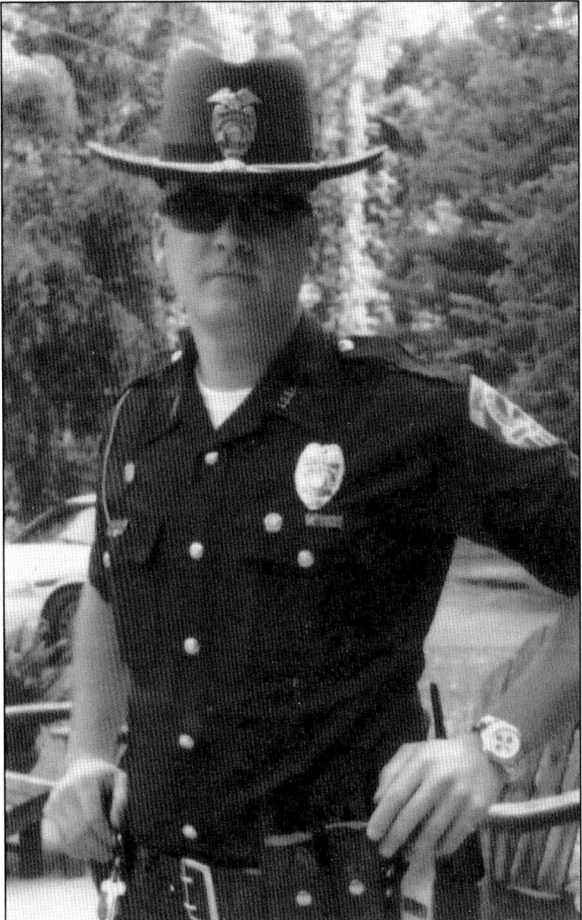

Perhaps the earliest photograph of Pikeville city police officers includes, from left to right, Chief Elexioius Coleman, Mayor Arch Jackson, and officer Herman Redd leading a 1917 parade. Coleman was elected Pikeville's police chief in 1915 and continued to serve through the 1932 ordinance formally establishing the Pikeville Police Department, then at least until 1940. Jackson was a teacher and merchant. (Courtesy of the Pike County Historical Society.)

Officer Scotty Hamilton joined the Pikeville Police Department in 2006 and earned three awards during training. Hamilton's police work quickly earned his fellow officers' respect; he was an enthusiastic part of the department's many public service activities and was named Officer of the Year in 2014. His watch ended tragically on March 13, 2018, and the community still mourns his loss. (Courtesy of Wayne and Patricia Hamilton.)

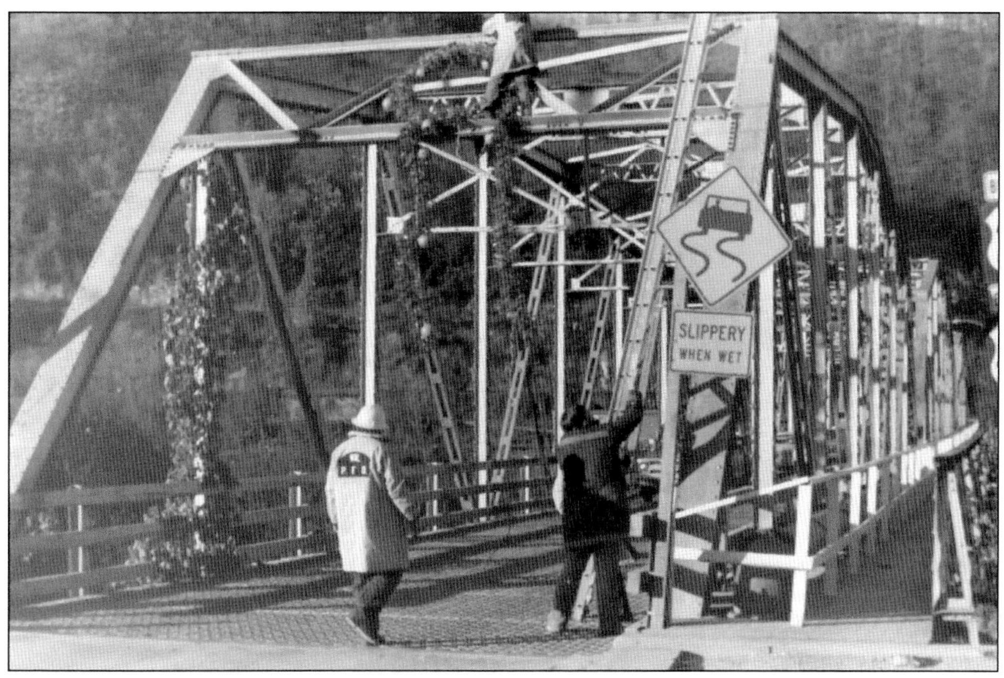

The Pikeville Fire Department's primary role involves life-saving duties such as operating the city's ambulance and firefighting services, but it also takes on a wide range of tasks that make the community a better place to live. Here, firefighters are placing Christmas decorations on the Upper Bridge around 1976, a tradition they continue as they install seasonal decorations throughout the downtown area. (Courtesy of Mayor James A. Carter.)

The city bought its first fire engine from the American LaFrance Fire Engine Company in 1920. Around 30 years later, Pikeville's firefighters were combating this blaze that destroyed the Old Regular Baptist Church that stood on the site of today's Reynold's Market. That church was organized in 1912, and after the fire moved to Ferguson Lane. (Courtesy of the Pike County Public Library.)

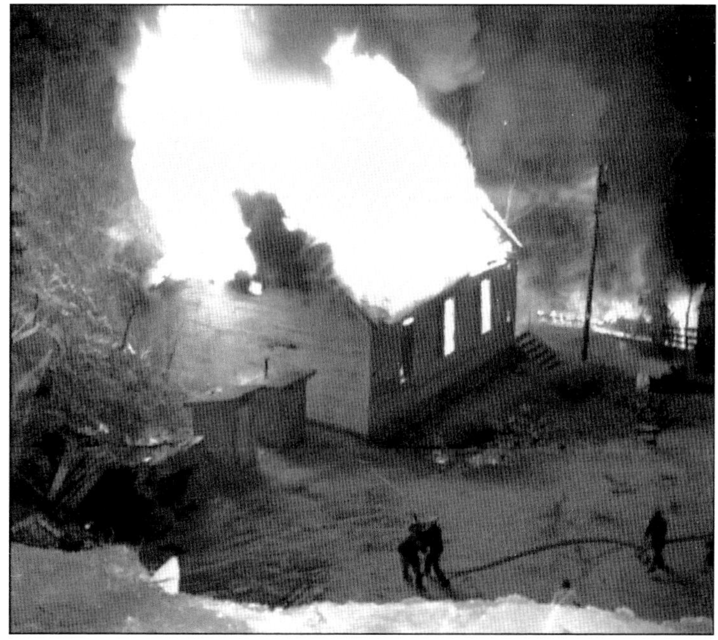

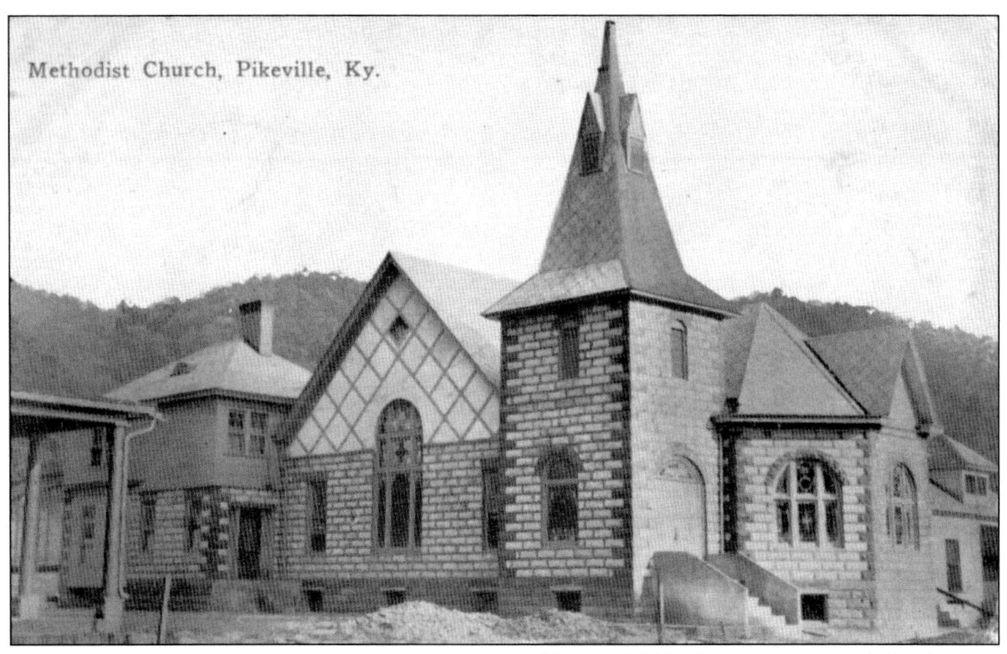

Prior to 1939, there were two Methodist churches in Pikeville, both formed in the mid-1800s. This is a c. 1915 photograph of the First Methodist Episcopal Church. The Main Street Church of Christ formed in 1935 and bought this building in 1943, demolishing it to construct a new church on the site in 1982. (Courtesy of Brenda Hays, John Doug Hays collection.)

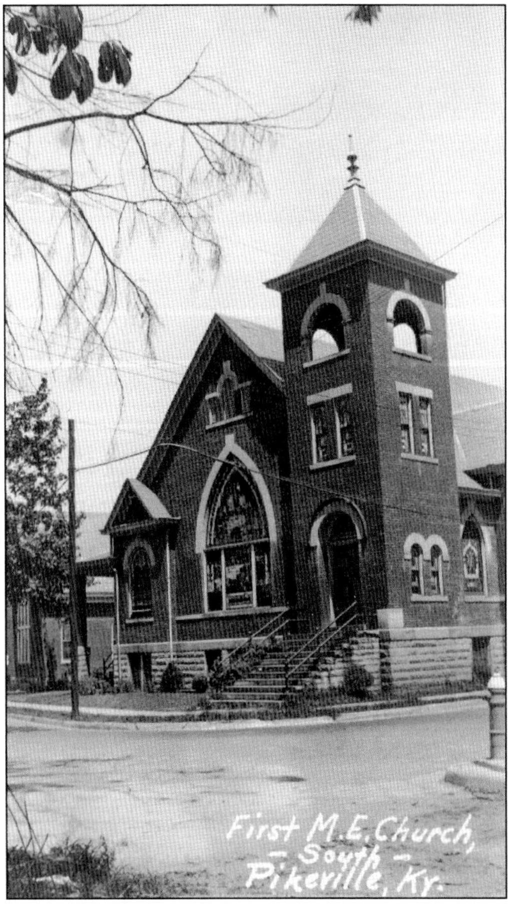

The other Methodist church in Pikeville, the Methodist Episcopal Church South, is today's United Methodist Church that stands at the corner of Main Street and Huffman Avenue. The cornerstone of this building was placed in 1912 and notes that the church was formed in 1845. (Courtesy of Brenda Hays, John Doug Hays collection.)

The First Presbyterian Church of Pikeville was founded in 1883 with Rev. A.C. Stewart as the first pastor. This building stood across from the City Park on Huffman Avenue, and Dr. W.C. Condit preached the dedication sermon on December 10, 1910. The congregation constructed its new building on Cedar Creek in 1998, and this building was demolished in 2004. (Courtesy of Brenda Hays, John Doug Hays collection.)

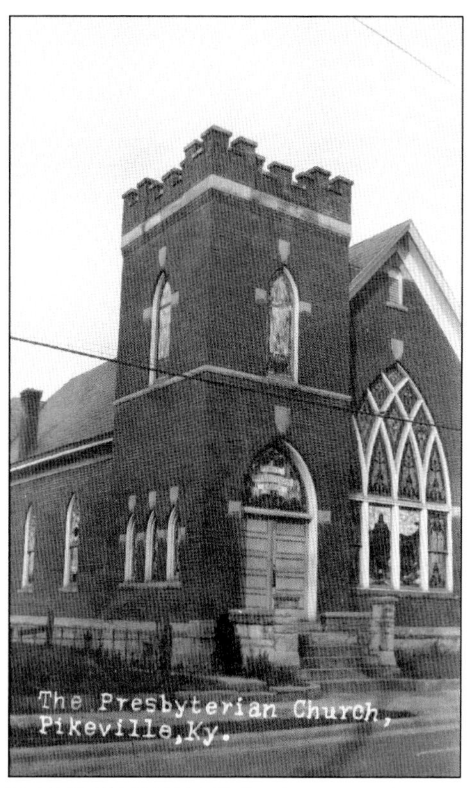

The First Baptist Church of Pikeville began when Reverend Baker gathered a dozen souls in Joe and Jemima Meade's home in 1904. Their first church building opened on Third Street in about 1911. Rev. Harold Wainscott's (left) flock was nearing 800 at the time of this joyous groundbreaking for the current church, and the dedication was held on March 9, 1958. (Courtesy of the First Baptist Church of Pikeville.)

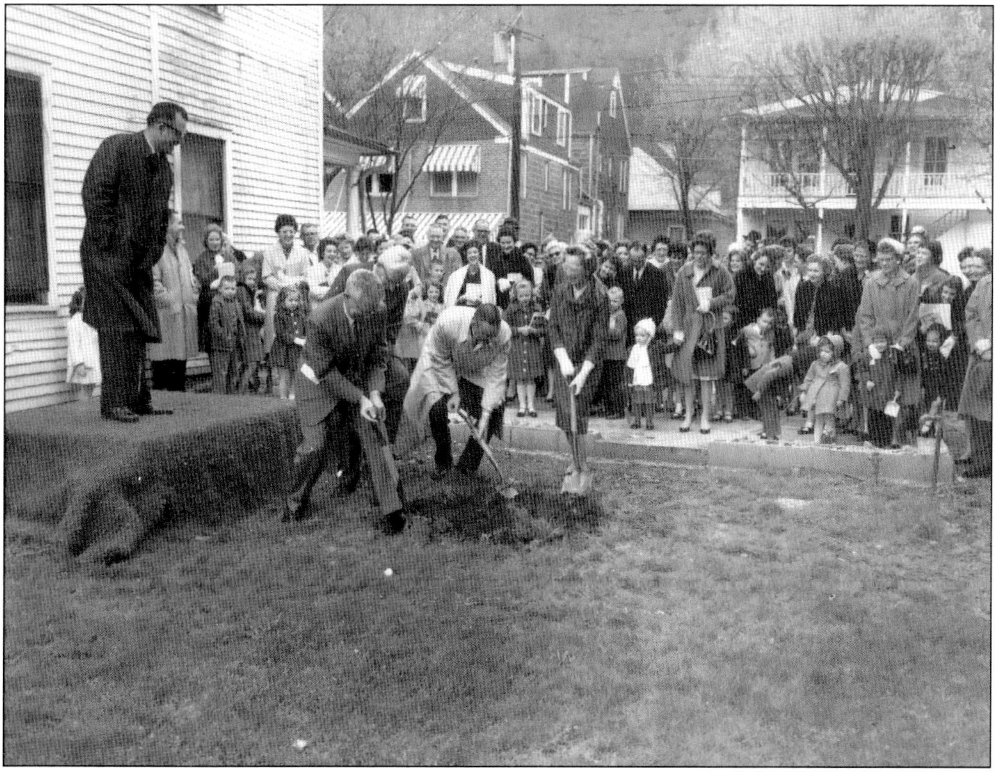

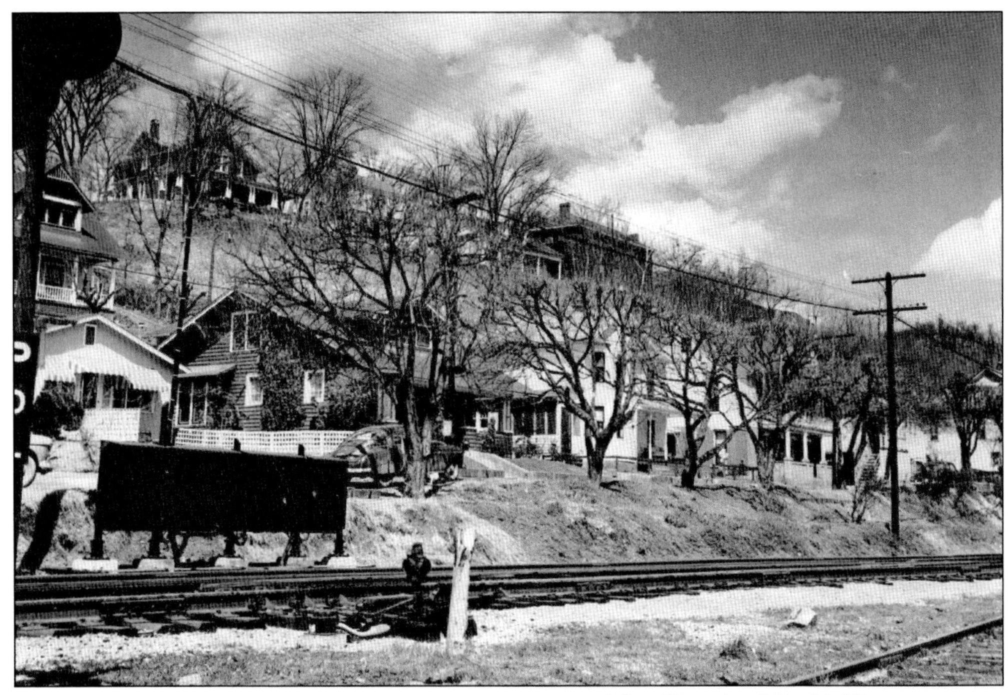

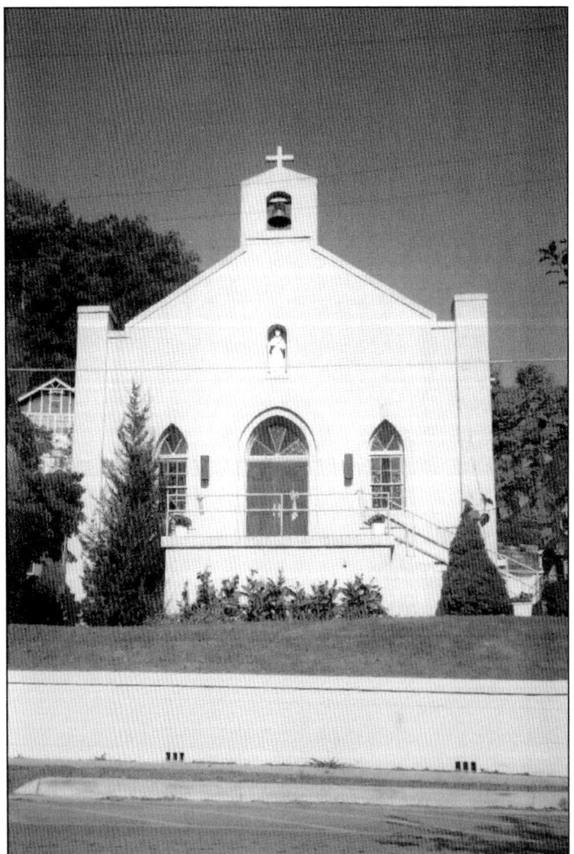

The Church of God Militant Pillar and Ground of Truth is an Apostolic church on Redale Road, but it began in the two-story white house on Hellier Street pictured here (right of center) in about 1940. The home was a boardinghouse run by the first pastor, Amanda Lark. Mayor Hambley said she made the best pies in Pikeville. (Courtesy of the Pike County Public Library.)

There were only two Catholics in Pikeville in 1926, but the congregation grew, and Mass was said once a month in private homes or at Call Funeral Home by 1938. This church was dedicated under the patronage of Saint Francis of Assisi by Bishop William Mulloy and Fr. William Schreder on October 7, 1949, and remained in use until 2015. (Courtesy of Saint Francis of Assisi Catholic Church.)

Eight

The Hatfield-McCoy Feud

The feud between the Hatfields and the McCoys is world-famous, and Pikeville played a key role. Dozens of books have been written about the feud—each filled with disputed facts and most including outright myths. That story is too large to tell here, but the history of Pikeville is incomplete without discussing it.

William Anderson "Devil Anse" Hatfield and Randall McCoy each led families that lived along the Tug Fork of the Big Sandy River, the Kentucky–West Virginia border. Some say the cause goes back to the Civil War, while others blame a stolen hog, timber rights, or forbidden love. A dalliance between two of the patriarchs' children, Roseanna McCoy and Johnse Hatfield, did cause friction. Then in 1882, three of McCoy's sons murdered Devil Anse's brother Ellison, and within two days, the three McCoys were killed by a Hatfield firing squad.

Warrants were issued, but no arrests followed. Then another Hatfield son brutally beat two McCoy women who were Pikeville attorney Perry Cline's nieces. Cline convinced Gov. Simon Buckner to issue warrants and to appoint "Bad" Frank Phillips as a special deputy to serve them. Phillips and over 20 men raided into West Virginia. The Hatfields retaliated by burning down McCoy's home on New Year's Day in 1888—shooting son Calvin and daughter Alifair dead in the process. McCoy moved his family to Pikeville.

Bad Frank Phillips killed two Hatfield men on another raid and brought eight others back to Pikeville to stand trial. It took a decision from the US Supreme Court before they could be tried. Seven convictions resulted in life sentences, but Ellison "Cottontop" Mounts had confessed to killing Alifair McCoy, so he was hanged near the city cemetery.

Before the trials, Perry Cline switched to representing the Hatfields. He, Randall McCoy, and another Pikeville attorney named James York negotiated an end to the feud. The Hatfields sold their land along the Tug Fork, and McCoy remained in Pikeville. He ran a ferry here for 20 years before his death after falling into a fire in his grandson Marvin's home on Harold's Branch.

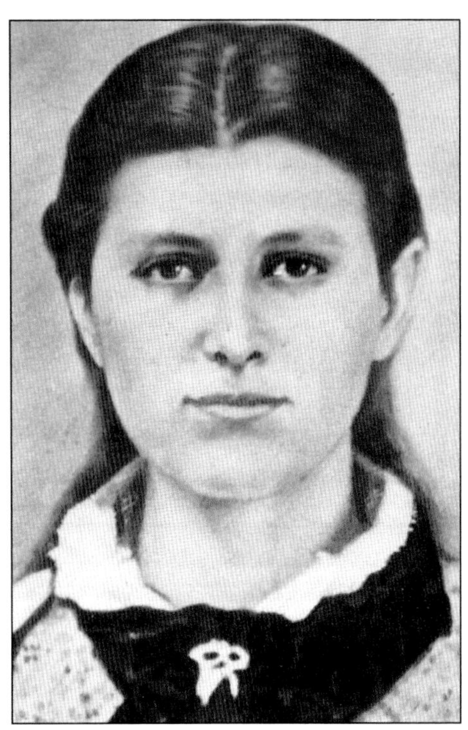

Though the feud was by no means Roseanna McCoy's fault, she is said to have blamed herself for the rest of her life. Her affair with Johnse Hatfield began in 1880 and ended when her brothers arrested Johnse. Roseanna warned the Hatfields, who then ambushed the McCoy brothers. No shots were fired, but Devil Anse taunted the McCoys before retrieving his son. (Courtesy of the Big Sandy Heritage Center Museum.)

Among the McCoys who Devil Anse Hatfield had humiliated during Johnse's rescue was the recently deputized Tolbert McCoy. Later, on election day in August 1882, Tolbert started a fight that ended when he and two of his brothers murdered Ellison Hatfield. Devil Anse Hatfield—seen here around 1900—led a group of around 20 men to capture the three McCoys. Days later, the brothers were tied up and shot to death. (Courtesy of the Library of Congress.)

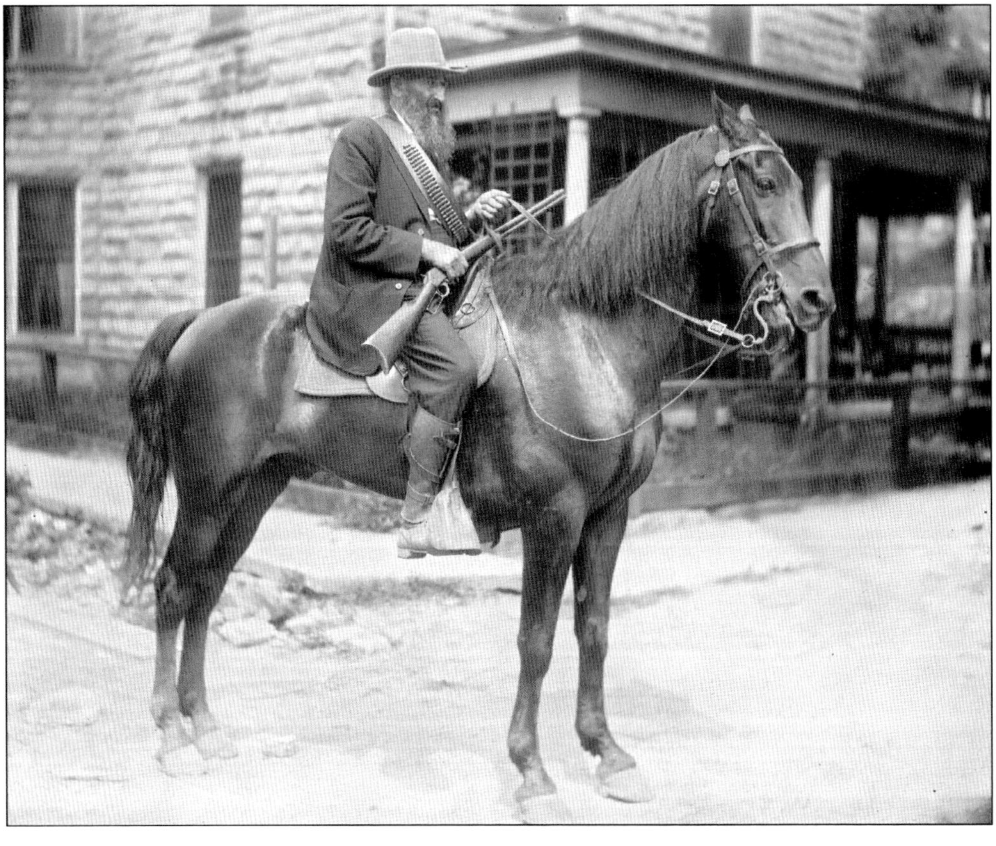

Mary Daniels was the daughter of Asa Harmon McCoy, and the niece, by marriage, of Perry Cline. The feud was mostly quiet from 1882 until the fall of 1886, when Cap Hatfield and Tom Wallace whipped Mary and her daughter because of suspected spying. Mary's brother sought vengeance but was arrested, attempted escape, and was shot by Cap or Tom. (Courtesy of the Big Sandy Heritage Center Museum.)

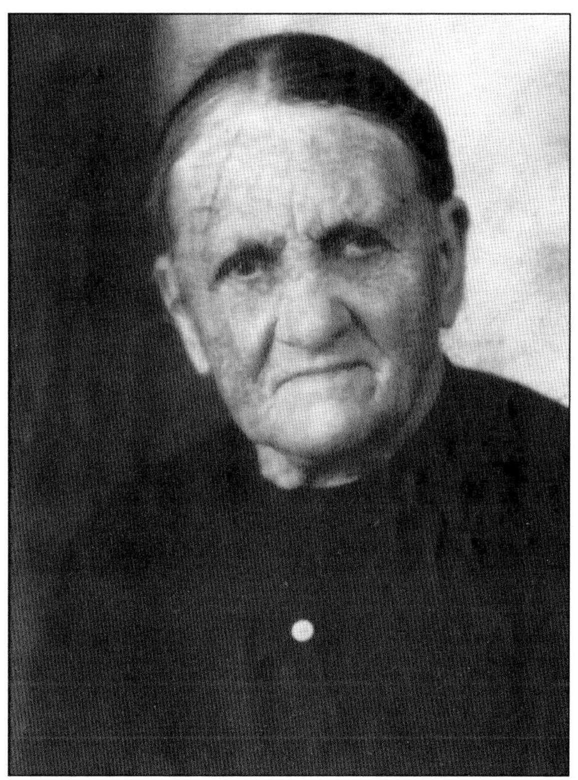

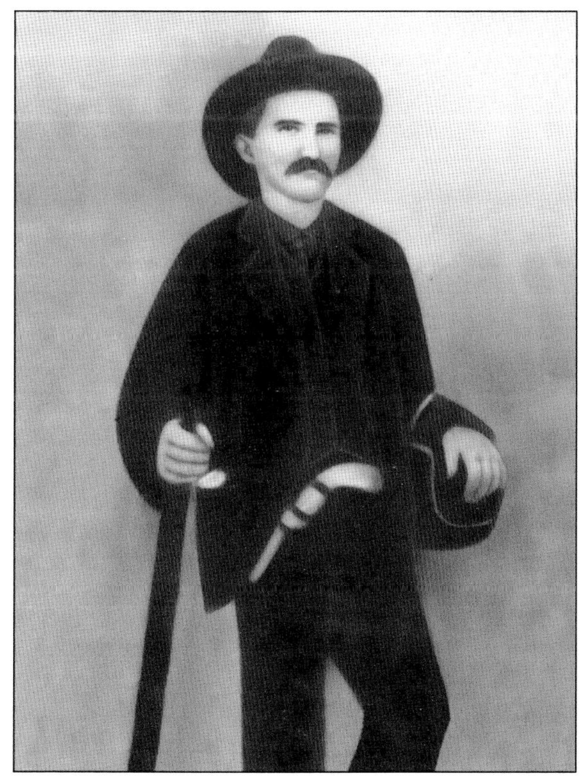

Anse feared Perry Cline's involvement and wrote Cline a letter trying to dissuade him. Hatfield's plea failed, as Cline helped elect Simon Buckner governor in 1887 and new warrants and bounties followed. A Cline ally named "Bad" Frank Phillips, pictured here, was among the most feared men in Pike County. He was deputized and began raiding into West Virginia. (Courtesy of the Big Sandy Heritage Center Museum.)

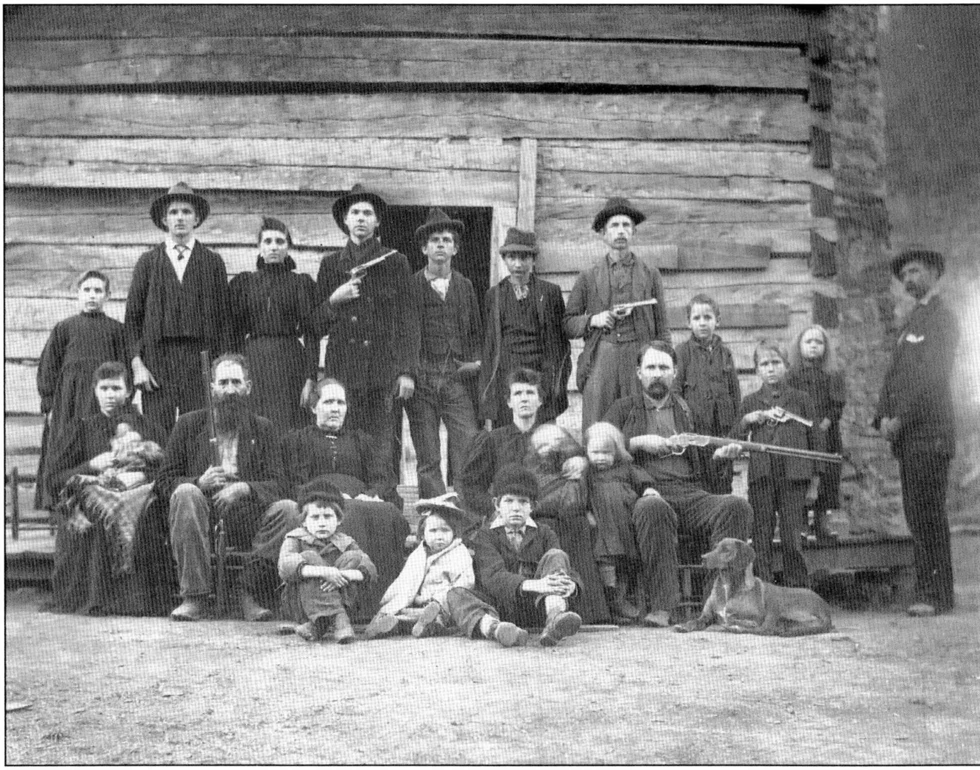

This c. 1897 photograph shows the Hatfield family with Anse (left) and his son Cap (right), each seated and holding rifles. The pressure that Phillips and his posse of over 20 men put on the Hatfields was immense. The Hatfields retaliated with a raid on the McCoy cabin. Then Phillips's men captured eight Hatfields and Hatfield allies to face Kentucky trials. (Courtesy of the Library of Congress.)

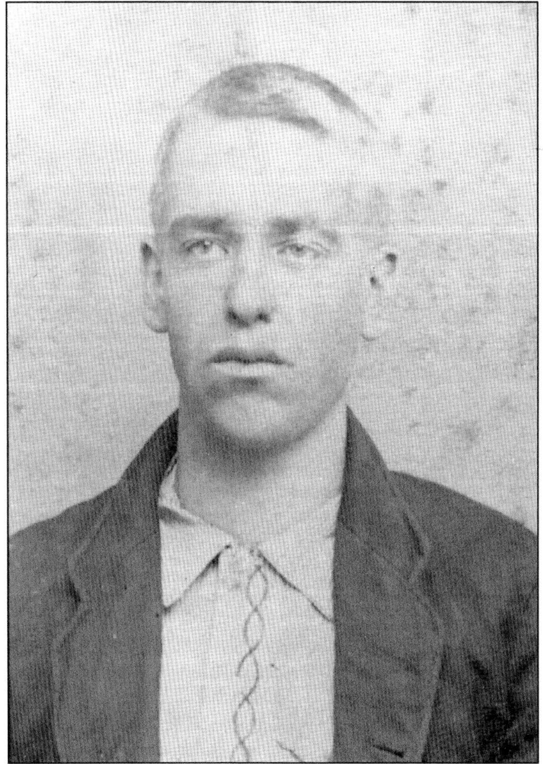

Though Pikeville attorney James York initially represented the Hatfields and Perry Cline represented the McCoys, Hatfield eventually replaced York with Cline. Among those on trial was Ellison "Cottontop" Mounts, pictured here, who may have been the illegitimate son of Ellison Hatfield. During the raid on the McCoy cabin, he shot and killed the disabled 30-year-old McCoy daughter Alifair. (Courtesy of the Big Sandy Heritage Center Museum.)

This was James York's former home, seen around 1962. Perry Cline and York were connected through Col. John Dils. Cline had been Dils's ward, and York was married to Dils's daughter Augusta. With Cline now representing the Hatfields and York representing Randall McCoy, the three men met here almost daily to negotiate an end to the feud. (Courtesy of the Pike County Public Library.)

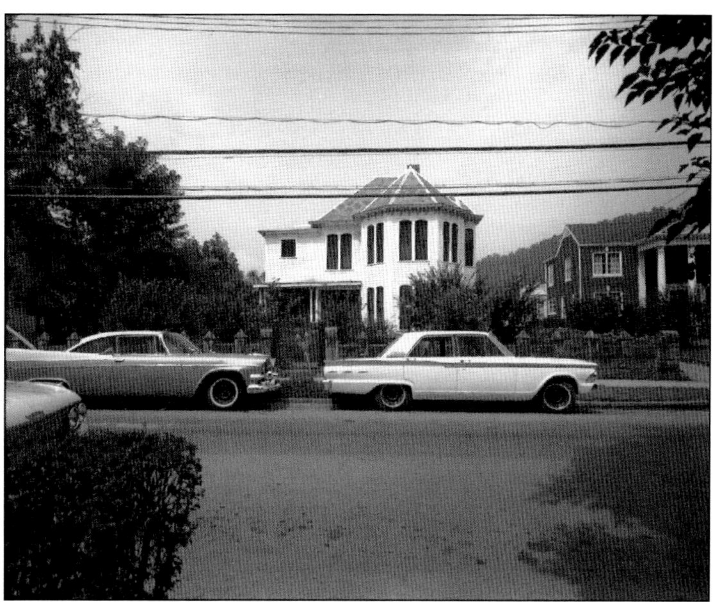

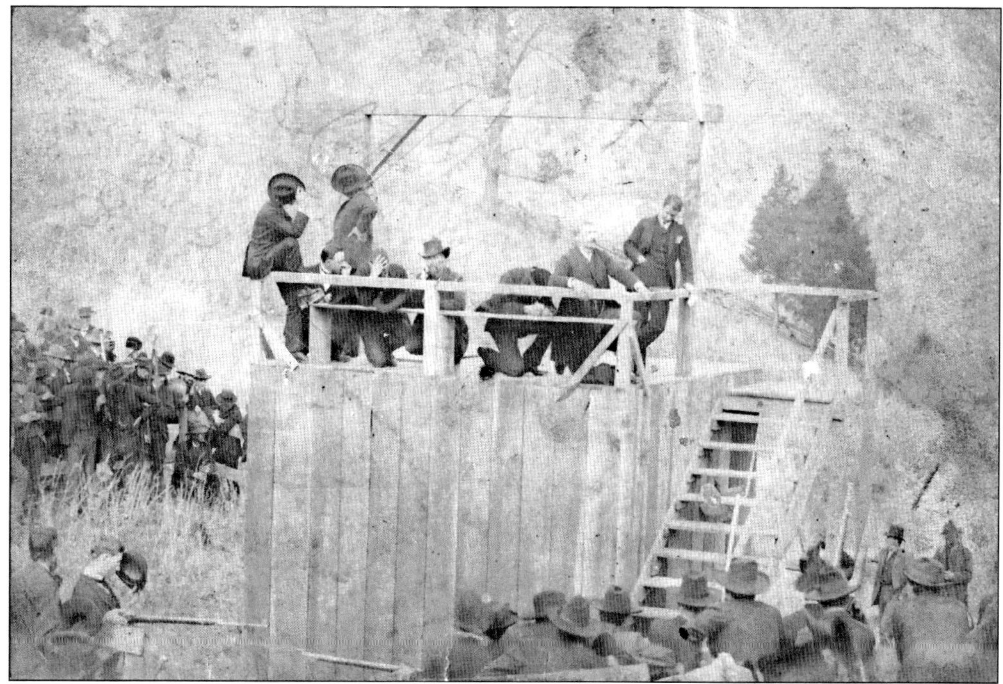

After confessing to killing Alifair McCoy, Ellison Mounts was sentenced to hang on these gallows in February 1890. He is kneeling, head bowed, next to Rev. John Glover who is also kneeling, hands on the rail, looking skyward. There were rumors of a Hatfield rescue attempt, so a local militia called Buckner's Rifles was called to stand guard and surround the scaffold. (Courtesy of the Big Sandy Heritage Center Museum.)

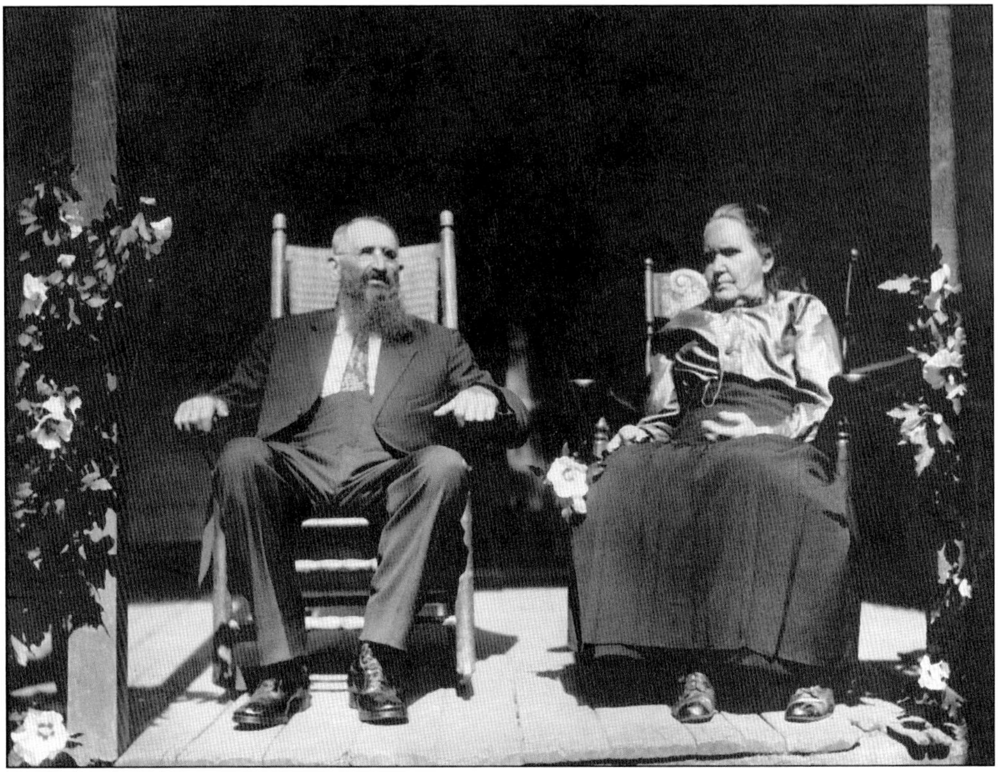

The Hatfields moved north to Logan County, and McCoy stopped pursuing them. In 1911, Devil Anse, seen here with his wife "Levisy" in about 1915, was baptized. Afterward, he was a man at peace, and his descendants went on to be respected members of their communities with many becoming professionals. A nephew was elected governor of West Virginia in 1913. (Courtesy of the Library of Congress.)

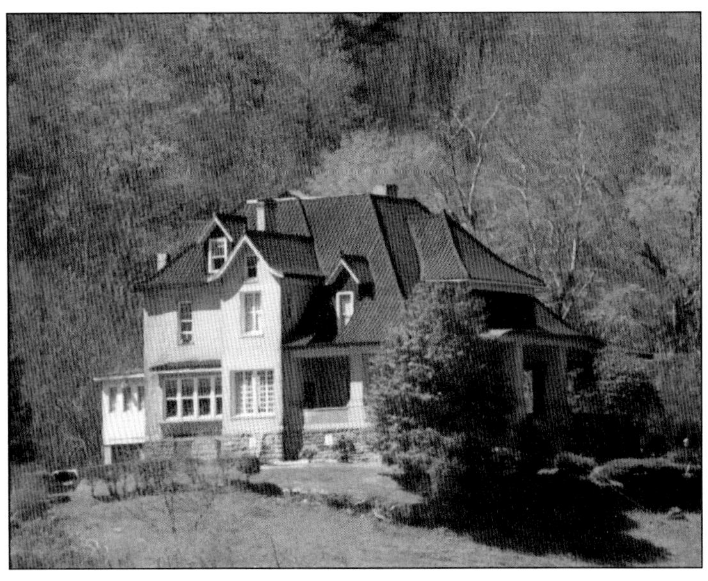

Perry Cline died in 1891, but James York went on to become Pike County judge. He and Augusta constructed this mansion between 1918 and 1933. It cost the equivalent of $2 million today. Augusta built a model of the home and then employed an architect to formalize the design. It still overlooks her beloved Pikeville College Academy Building. (Courtesy of the Frank M. Allara Library, University of Pikeville.)

Nine

Pioneering Leadership

Pikeville has been fortunate to have leaders who worked diligently to enact bold visions. We have mentioned Mayor Hambley, but he is not alone. The people in Pikeville and Pike County have often selected leaders based on ability rather than their origins, party affiliation, or whether they fit some preconceived mold.

One of the city's first mayors arrived from Bangor, Maine, in the 1890s and was a key player in the development of mining reserves and the arrival of the railroad. Another couple, William Harvey and Mary Elliott Flanery, arrived from the Ashland area in 1895. William also worked in the nascent coal industry, while Mary taught and wrote for Eastern Kentucky newspapers. They moved back to Boyd County in 1912, but kept their Pikeville home until 1919. Mary Elliott Flanery became the first woman elected to the Kentucky General Assembly—and any state legislature south of the Mason-Dixon Line—in 1921, just two years after women were guaranteed the right to vote.

Pikeville's Katherine Langley became the first woman from Kentucky or the South elected to serve in the US Congress, taking office in 1927. Six years later, Bessie Riddle Arnold—sister of John Paul Riddle—won the election for Pike County clerk. She held the position until her death 29 years later. A 1950 *Louisville Courier-Journal* article noted that Pike County had six women in public office, including Arnold and two of her former deputies. Another deputy eventually broke Arnold's record time as county clerk.

Pikeville's only governor, Paul Patton, was born in Lawrence County before moving to Pikeville in the 1960s. He was a coal operator, then Pike County judge/executive before serving as lieutenant governor and then governor. He was also the University of Pikeville's president and is now its chancellor. His accomplishments as governor were consequential for the entire state, but they were truly transformative for Pikeville and Pike County.

Though space doesn't allow for a complete list of this community's many successful leaders, the pages that follow offer a glimpse of some of their stories.

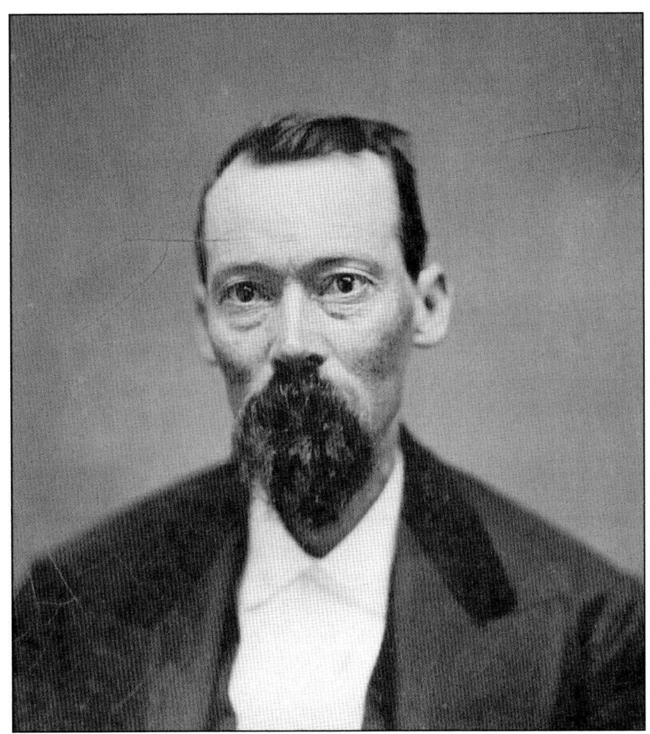

Perry Cline was not the character portrayed in many feud tales. He was orphaned at seven and raised by a Black family who brought him to John Dils in Pikeville to be educated. He was school superintendent, jailer, elected sheriff at 25, and elected state legislator at 36. He was devoted to his wife, Martha, until his death from tuberculosis at 42. (Courtesy of the Big Sandy Heritage Center Museum.)

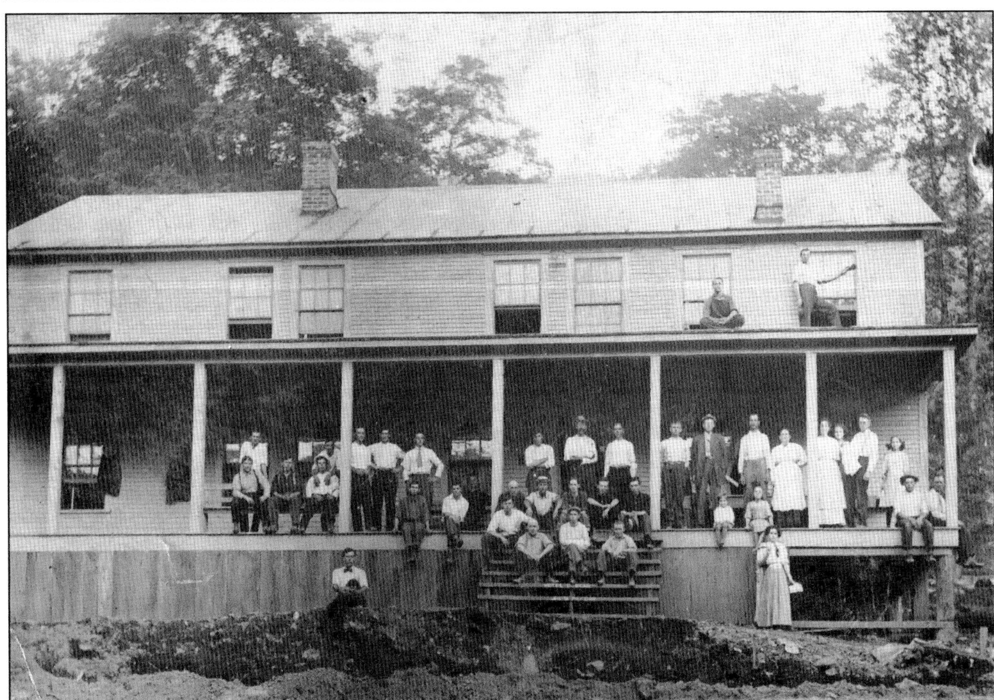

Ralph Hellier was Pikeville's first or second mayor and the general manager of the Pike Coal and Coke Company of Marrowbone when he died of the flu at age 36 in 1906. A company town built on Marrowbone was named in his honor and flourished until 1938. Pictured is a postcard of a boardinghouse there around 1911. (Courtesy of Brenda Hays, John Doug Hays collection.)

Mary Elliott Flanery was the first woman elected to the state legislature in Kentucky. She began her journalism career early in her 17 years in Pikeville and was a tireless champion of women's rights. It was Flanery who befriended Effie Waller Smith, marshaled a group of citizens to finance Smith's first book, and wrote the foreword herself. (Courtesy of the University of Kentucky Libraries Special Collections Research Center.)

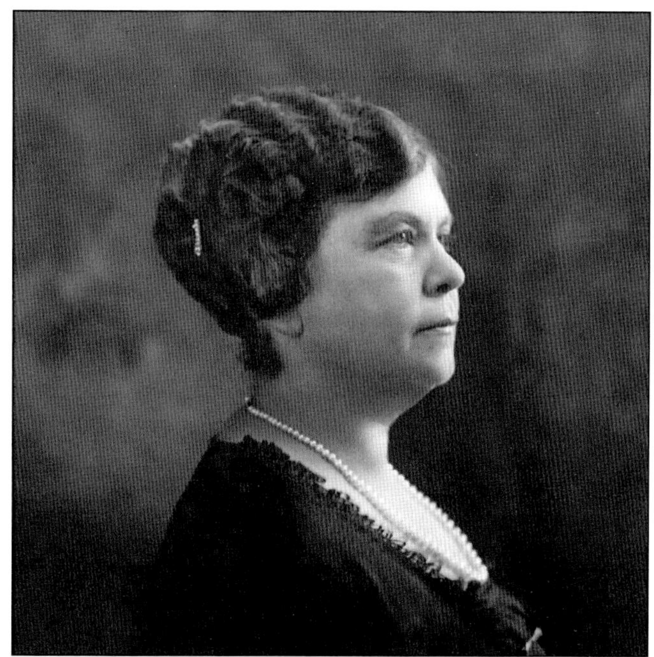

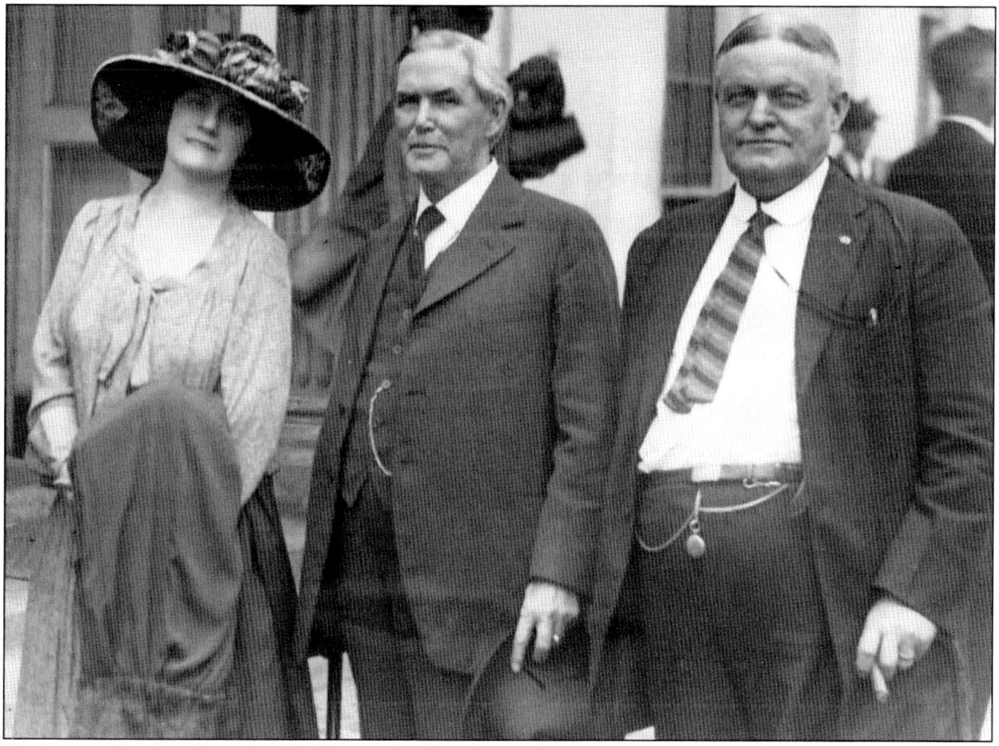

Katherine Gudger Langley (left) was the daughter of US congressman John Gudger of Asheville, North Carolina. She married Pikeville resident John Langley (right) in 1904. John was then elected to Congress, serving from 1907 until January 1926, when he resigned after exhausting appeals for his 1924 conviction for violations of prohibition laws. He entered Atlanta Penitentiary days later. (Courtesy of Brenda Hays, John Doug Hays collection.)

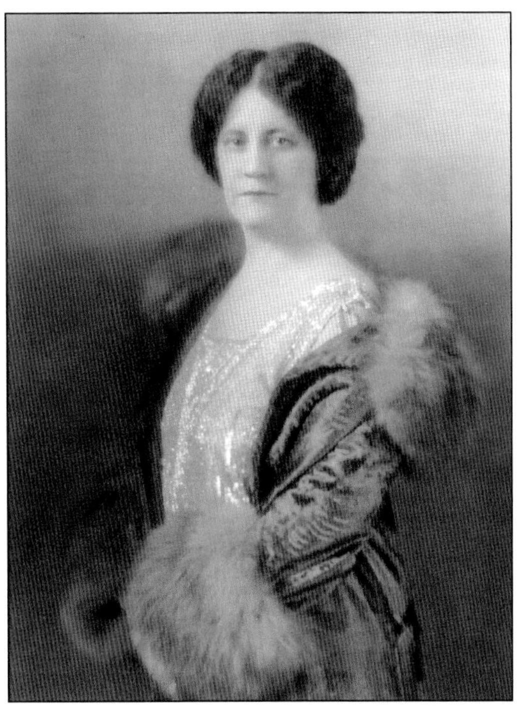

Paintsville judge A.J. Kirk was elected to complete John Langley's unexpired term, but Katherine Gudger Langley ran a "redemption campaign" based on John Langley's persistent claims of innocence. She defeated Kirk in the August 1926 primary before defeating Douglas Hays in November. In March 1927, she took office as the first woman to represent Kentucky in the US Congress. (Courtesy of Brenda Hays, John Doug Hays collection.)

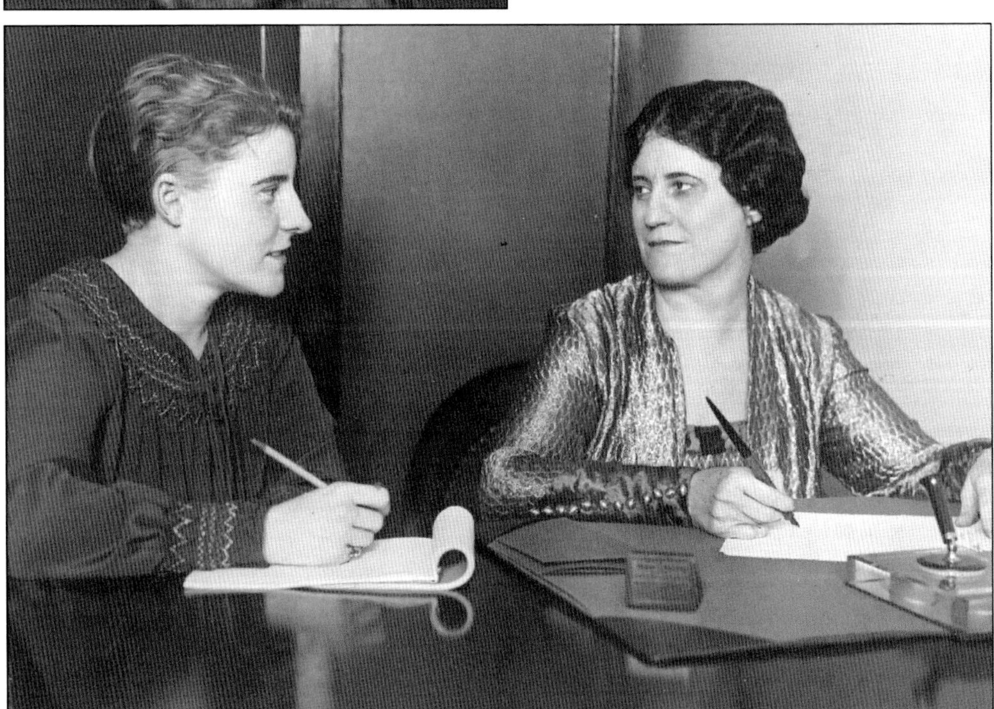

Decades of experience as congressional secretary for her father and husband along with a college degree and decades serving in various state Republican party roles prepared Katherine Gudger Langley (right) for legislative success. The congresswoman's daughter Katherine Bentley (left) worked as her mother's secretary. Langley served until 1931, when she was among 52 Republicans to lose their seats. (Courtesy of Brenda Hays, John Doug Hays collection.)

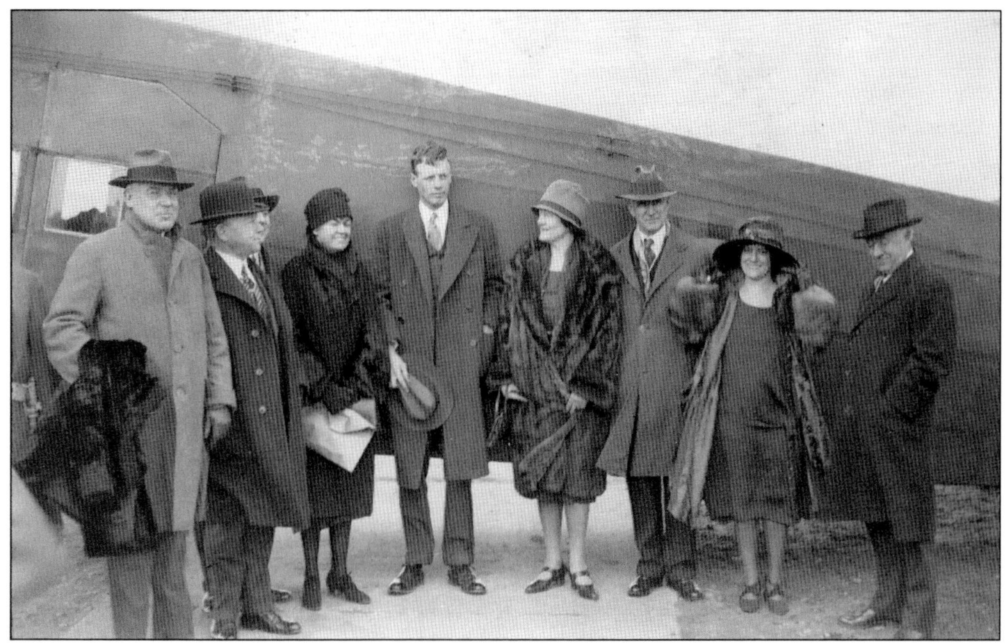

A year after his historic transatlantic flight, Charles Lindbergh (center) gave an airplane ride to six members of Congress, including Katherine Gudger Langley (second from right). It would be interesting to know if Pikeville native John Paul Riddle was discussed, as he and Lindbergh were friends. After Langley's 1931 loss, it was 66 years before Kentucky sent another woman to Congress. (Courtesy of Brenda Hays, John Doug Hays collection.)

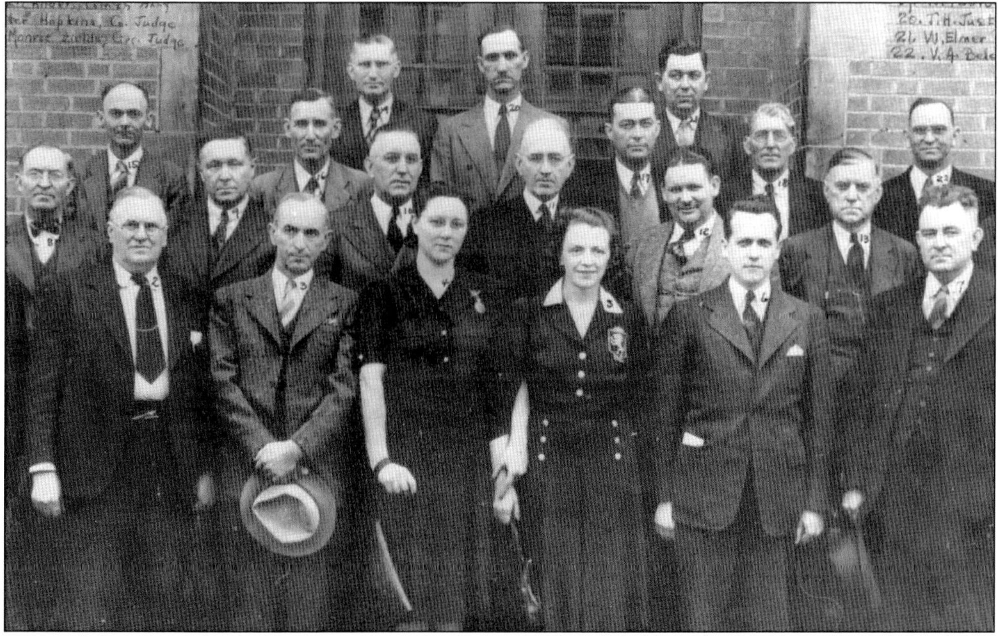

Bessie Riddle Arnold (first row, third from right) was the first woman elected to county office in Pike County, serving as county clerk from 1933 until her death in 1962. She won her first re-election by a larger margin than all other candidates on the ballot, a trend she continued. She is pictured here with county officials around 1945. (Courtesy of the Big Sandy Heritage Center Museum.)

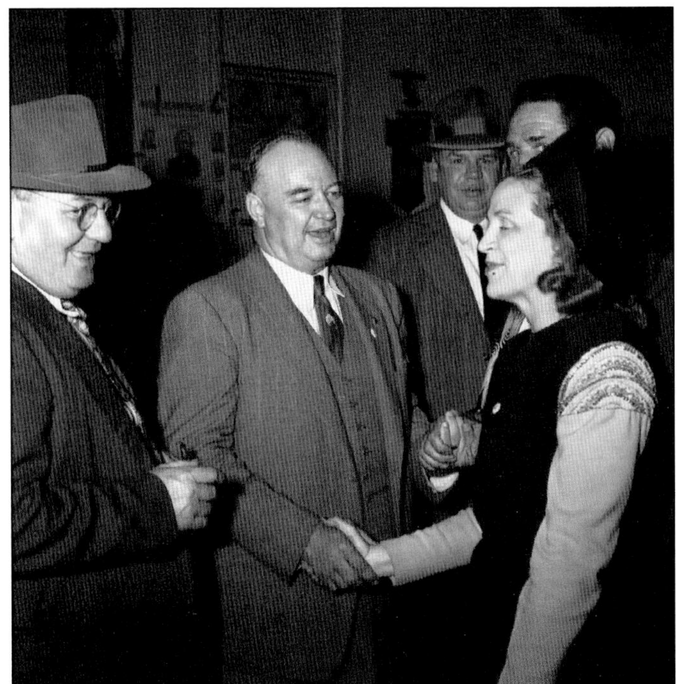

Arnold (right) is pictured shaking hands with Earle Clements (center) during his successful campaign to be Kentucky's governor in 1947. Arnold had various campaign roles in Democratic politics, including as local representative for Franklin Roosevelt's 1936 presidential campaign. Part of her legacy is the successful careers—political and otherwise—of the women who served as her deputies. (Courtesy of the Pike County Public Library.)

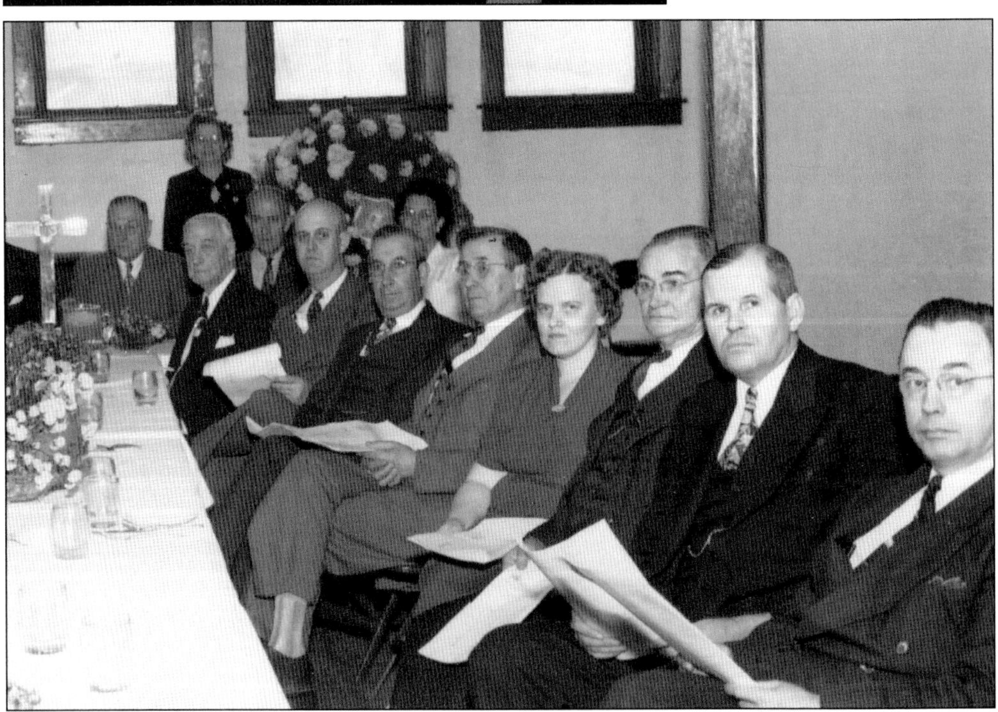

Kelly J. Day (fifth from right) is seen here at a Pikeville Methodist Hospital board meeting around 1945. Day owned Kentucky Wholesale Grocery Company and was Pikeville's mayor from 1934 until 1937. In 1937, he brought the largest gathering of conservationists the state had seen to Pikeville and helped form the Breaks Reserve Reforestation Association. (Courtesy of the Pike County Public Library.)

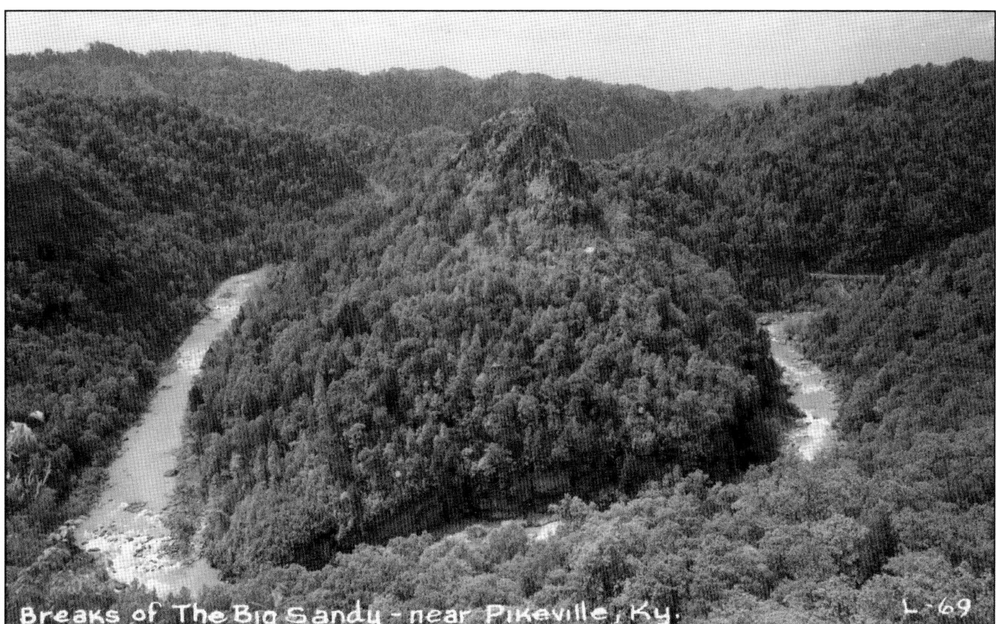

Breaks canyon was formed by five miles of the Russell Fork of the Big Sandy cutting through Pine Mountain, leaving nearly vertical cliffs. Mayor Day began advocating protection for the Breaks in 1926, but his 1949 visit with Virginia's governor was critical. Kentucky and Virginia built roads that met at the state line, and the newly created Breaks Interstate Park opened in 1958. (Courtesy of Sam Hatcher.)

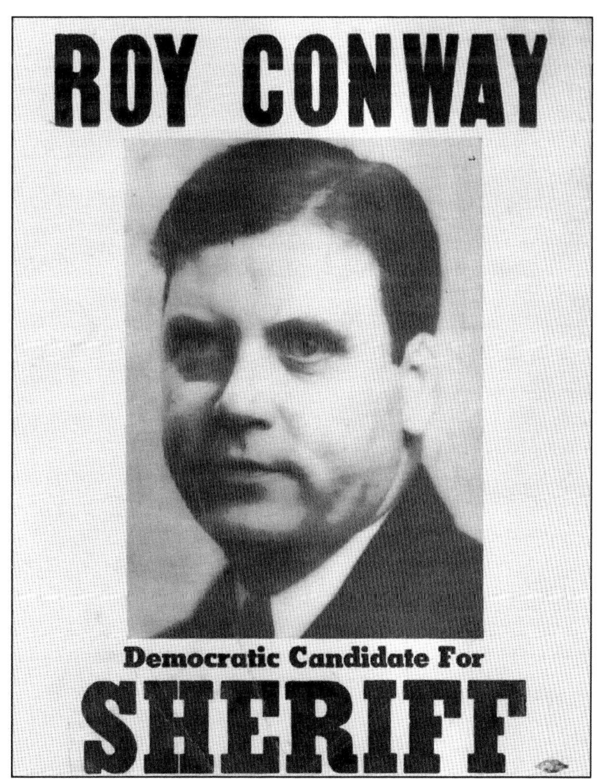

Roy Conway—father of former Kentucky first lady Judi Patton—was Pike County sheriff from 1949 until his murder outside his home on July 28, 1950. Sheriff Conway was previously a state representative with a reputation for fighting corruption. His abbreviated time as sheriff was active, with labor unrest, guarding a sequestered jury, and raiding gamblers and moonshiners. (Courtesy of the Big Sandy Heritage Center Museum.)

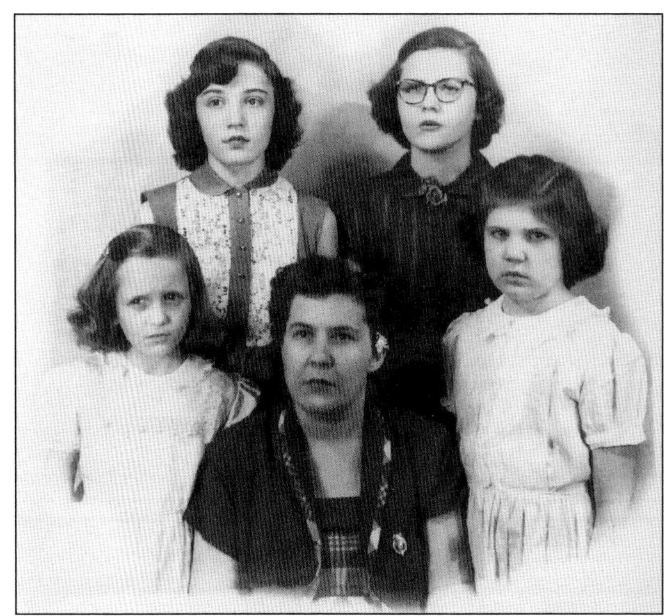

Roy Conway's wife, Esta, was appointed to replace her late husband as sheriff, and she served in the office until 1952. This photograph of Esta Conway surrounded by her four daughters (from left to right)—Nancy, Colleen, Anna Ruth, and Judi—was taken while she was the only woman serving as sheriff in Kentucky. (Courtesy of Gov. Paul Patton and Judi Patton.)

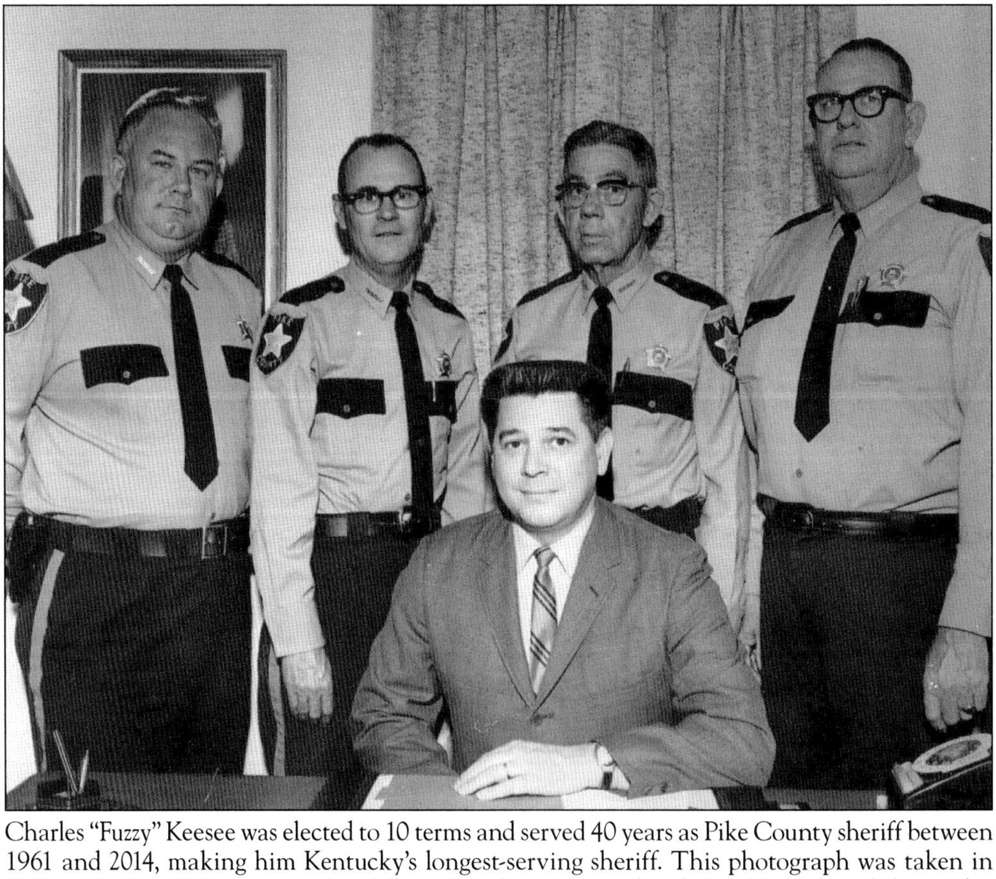

Charles "Fuzzy" Keesee was elected to 10 terms and served 40 years as Pike County sheriff between 1961 and 2014, making him Kentucky's longest-serving sheriff. This photograph was taken in 1962, with Sheriff Keesee seated and four of his deputies standing behind him, from left to right, Jack Banks, Junior Hatfield, Julius Blackburn, and Woodrow Runyon. (Courtesy of Easter Keesee.)

Lillian Pearl Elliott was a public servant for 71 years in Pike County, making her the longest serving in the county's history and one of the longest serving county clerks in Kentucky history. She served as a deputy clerk, first under Bessie Riddle Arnold, for 43 years before being elected herself in 1985. (Courtesy of John Elliott.)

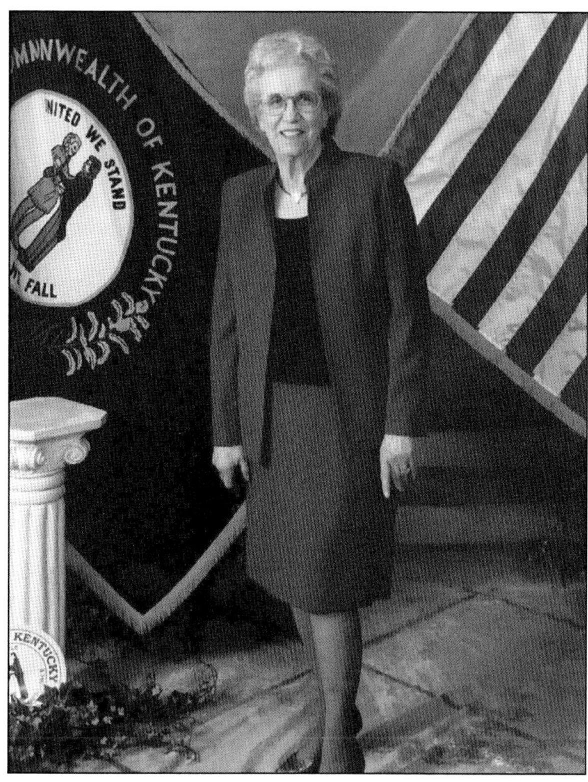

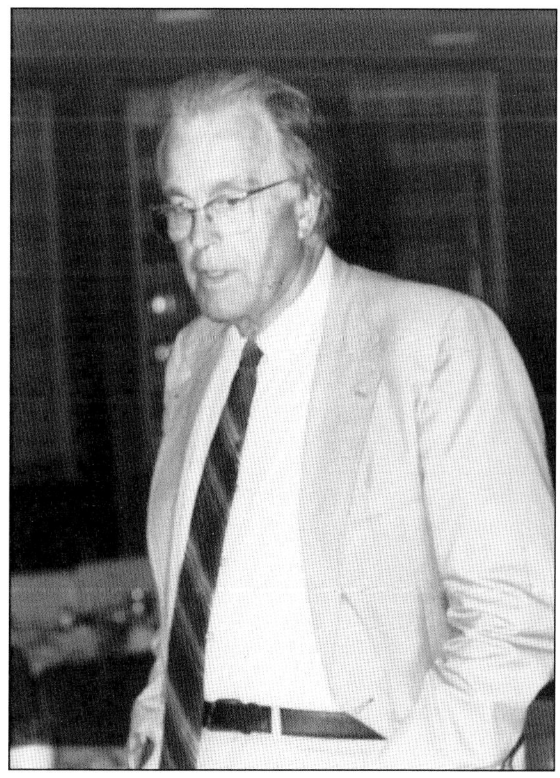

Mayor William C. Hambley—seen here in about 1989—graduated from Notre Dame and Northwestern University's medical school and was a surgeon in the Army and a Chicago hospital before returning to Pikeville in 1954. He is most remembered for the Cut-Through, but he also vastly upgraded parks and housing, among a number of other projects to improve citizens' quality of life. (Courtesy of the Pike County Public Library.)

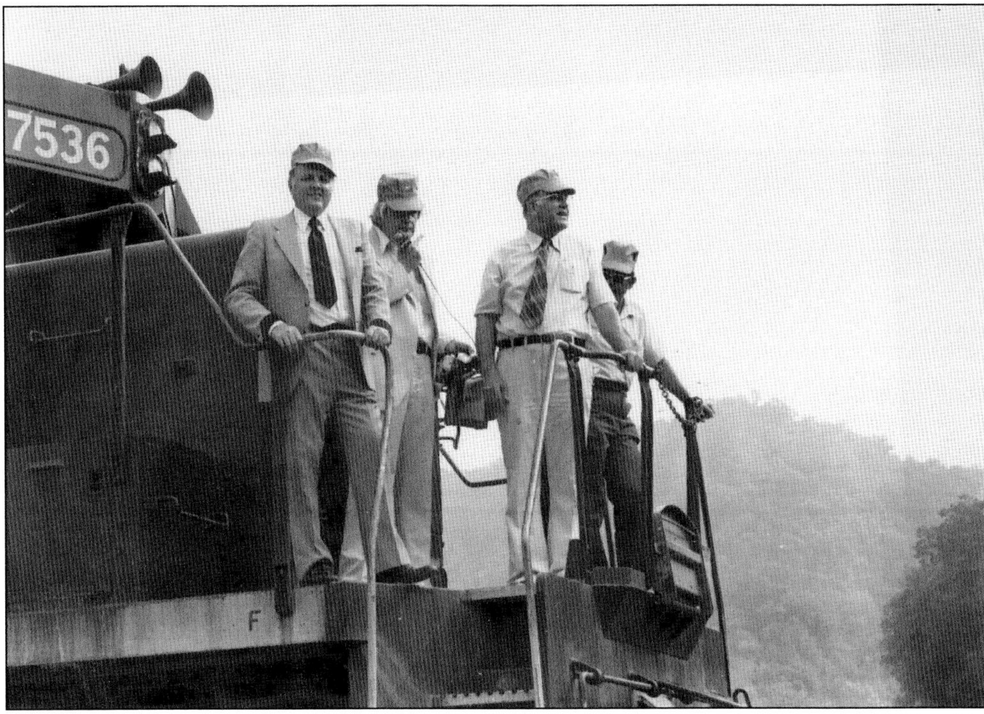

In July 1978, from left to right, Judge Wayne Rutherford, Walter May, and Mayor William Hambley rode the first train through the Cut-Through. Rutherford dedicated 41 years to public service, including six terms as county judge/executive. Among his many accomplishments, he led Pike County through the transition in the duties of county government brought about by the mid-1970s change in the Kentucky Constitution. (Courtesy of the Wayne T. Rutherford family.)

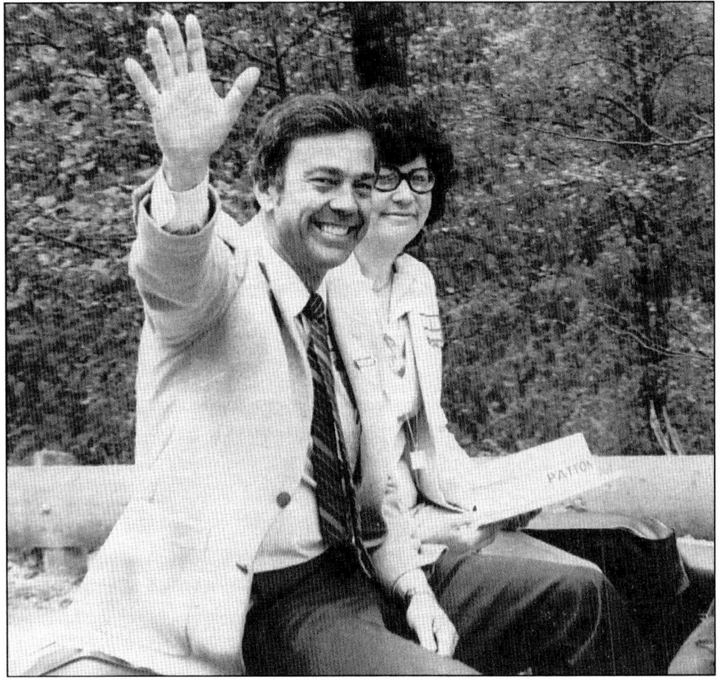

Paul Patton—seen here with Judi Patton around 1985—was a coal operator from the 1960s until 1978 and then entered politics. As county judge/executive, he started the county's solid waste program and paved nearly all county roads. Judi has been a tireless advocate for women's safety and the prevention of child abuse. (Courtesy of the University of Kentucky Libraries Special Collections Research Center.)

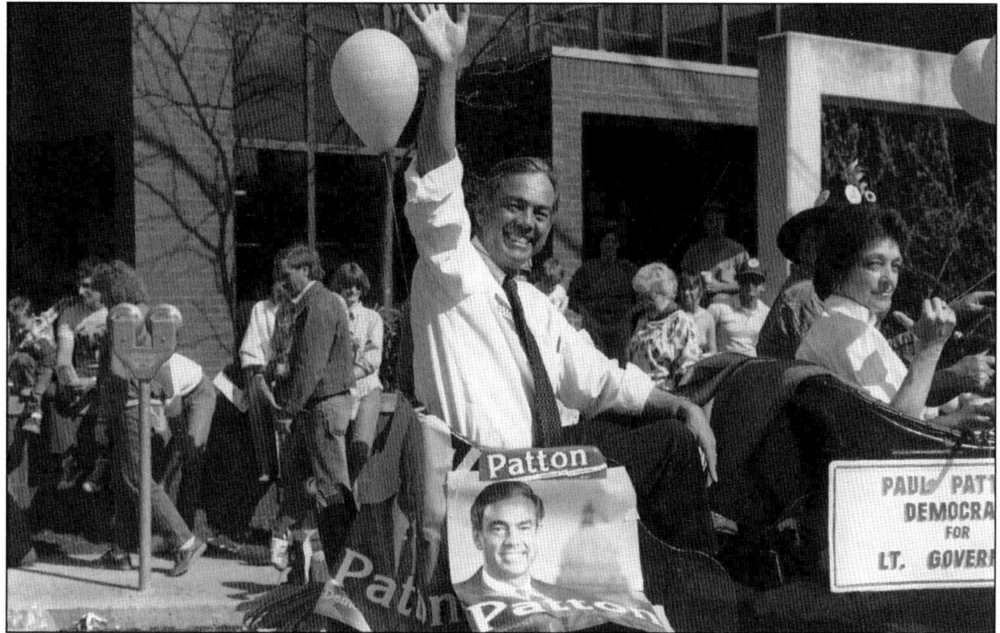

Paul Patton is seen here during his successful campaign for lieutenant governor in 1991 after serving as Pike County judge/executive for a decade. He became Kentucky's 59th governor in 1995. A change to the Kentucky Constitution allowed him to become the first Kentucky governor to serve two terms since 1800. (Courtesy of the Frank M. Allara Library, University of Pikeville.)

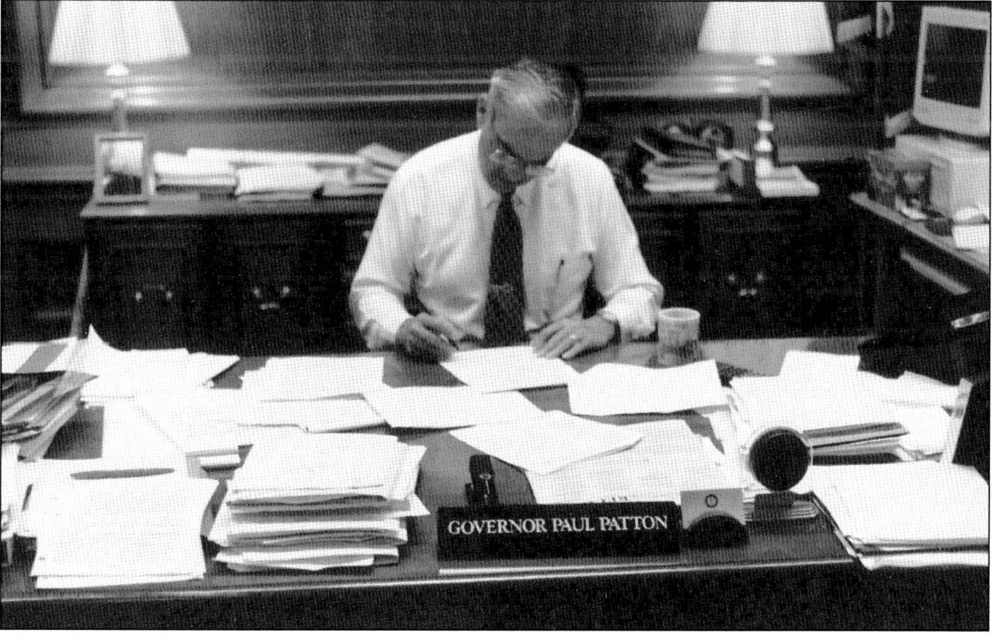

Patton became known as "the education governor" due to improvements to elementary, secondary, and post-secondary education under his administration. Closer to home, major road work through Pike County was completed, including all of US Route 119 and around half of US Route 460. During his two terms, the state government spent about $120 million in Pikeville, including moving downtown utility lines underground. (Courtesy of Gov. Paul Patton and Judi Patton.)

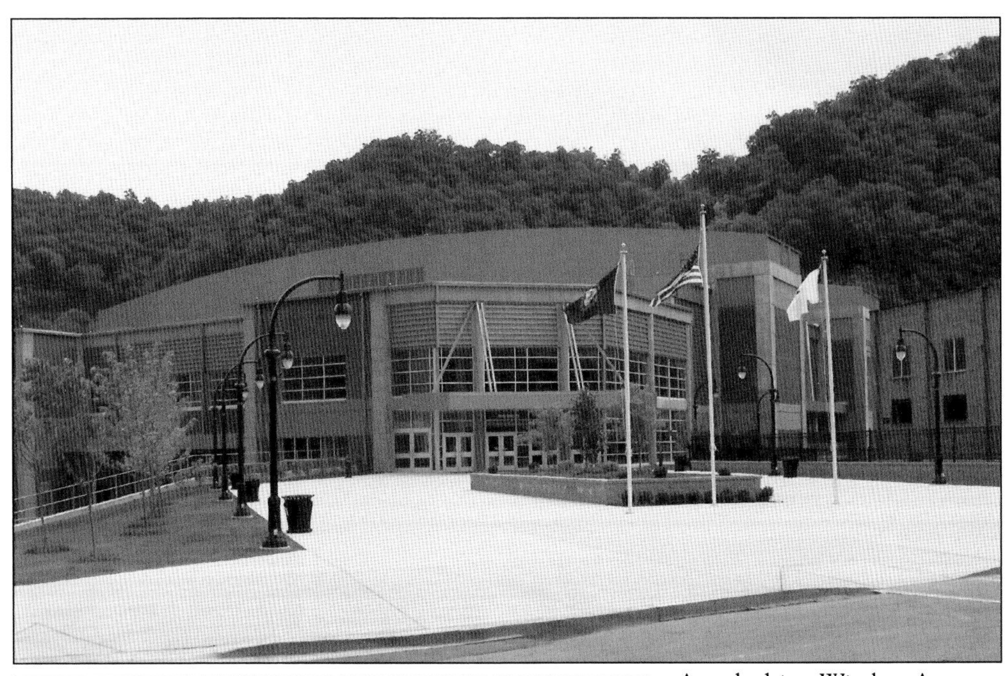

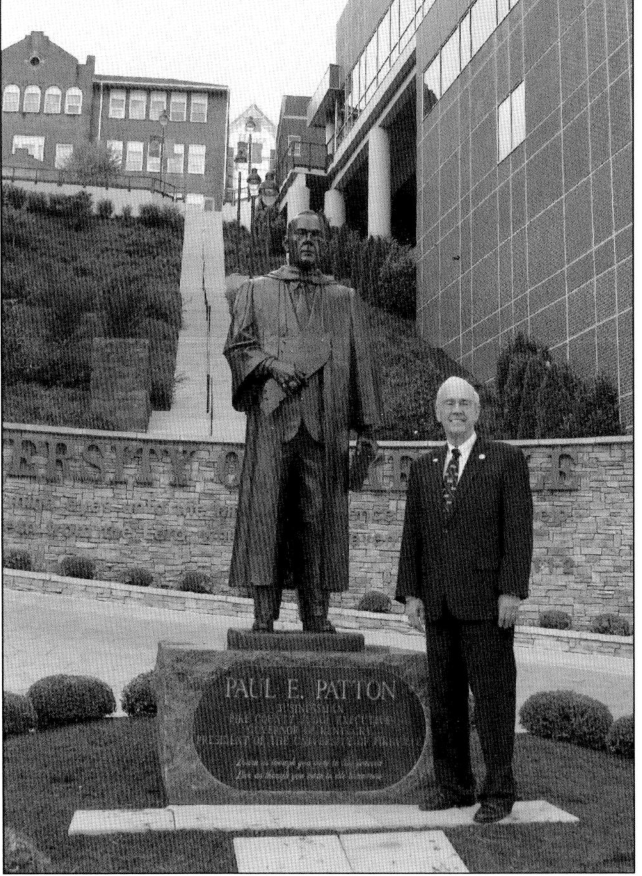

Appalachian Wireless Arena opened as the East Kentucky Exposition Center in October 2005. Governor Patton's 1998 executive order created a corporation to oversee the design and construction of the arena, and he secured almost all of the $29 million it took to construct it. The 7,000-seat facility continues to have a substantial economic impact on the city and surrounding area. (Courtesy of Dusty Layne, City of Pikeville.)

Governor Patton is pictured with a statue of him unveiled in July 2016 that stands at the bottom of the University of Pikeville's 99 steps. A longtime board member, he became the 19th president of the university in 2009 and served in that capacity until July 2013, when he was named chancellor. (Courtesy of Gov. Paul Patton and Judi Patton.)

Ten

Moving a Mountain

Pikeville is often called the city that moves mountains, and that is mostly true. In fact, it was only one mountain, and it took more than the city alone. Nearly 20 government agencies were involved in the Pikeville Cut-Through project. Dr. William C. Hambley, Pikeville's mayor from 1960 until 1989, was the driving force behind the project and saw it as a solution to several of Pikeville's most important problems.

First, the Big Sandy River seemed to leave its banks every other spring. Untold fortunes have floated down that river, and many more have been spent cleaning up county roads and city streets, rebuilding homes and businesses, or replacing possessions. Worst of all are the lives that have been lost—some washed away never to be seen again.

For decades, locals noted that the worst flood in recorded history came in 1862 while future president James Garfield was camped in Pikeville. A new standard was set in 1957 that is still unsurpassed in most locations along the upper reaches of the Kentucky and Big Sandy Rivers.

Then there was the railroad that ran along the path of today's Hambley Boulevard, with its numerous coal loadouts supplied by ever-present coal trucks driving through the downtown streets. The resulting traffic congestion, dust, and lack of land combined to stifle growth.

Funding was of course the primary challenge to building the Cut-Through. In 1965, Pikeville became the first town in Appalachia to win the All-American City Award, and then, in 1968, the city won a federal grant to become a Model City.

Construction on the man-made canyon through Peach Orchard Mountain began in November 1973. The Levisa Fork began flowing through its new channel in 1980—too late to avoid the damage the 1977 flood brought. At the 1987 dedication, Gov. Martha Lane Collins announced to some 2,000 people gathered that this was "perhaps the most remarkable engineering project ever undertaken in Kentucky." The project that had long been called "Hambley's Dream" was now a reality. Traffic started moving through the same day.

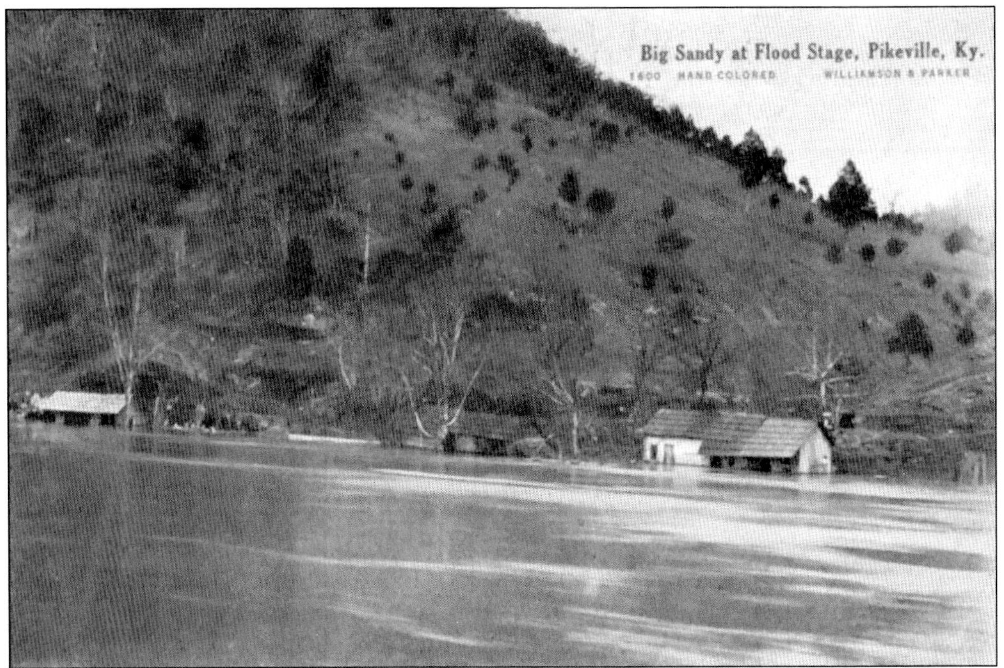

The earliest flood for which there is photographic evidence occurred in 1908 as seen in this postcard. There were also major floods in 1862, 1918, 1923, 1929, 1932, 1957, 1963, and 1977, all prior to the completion of the Cut-Through. (Courtesy of Brenda Hays, John Doug Hays collection.)

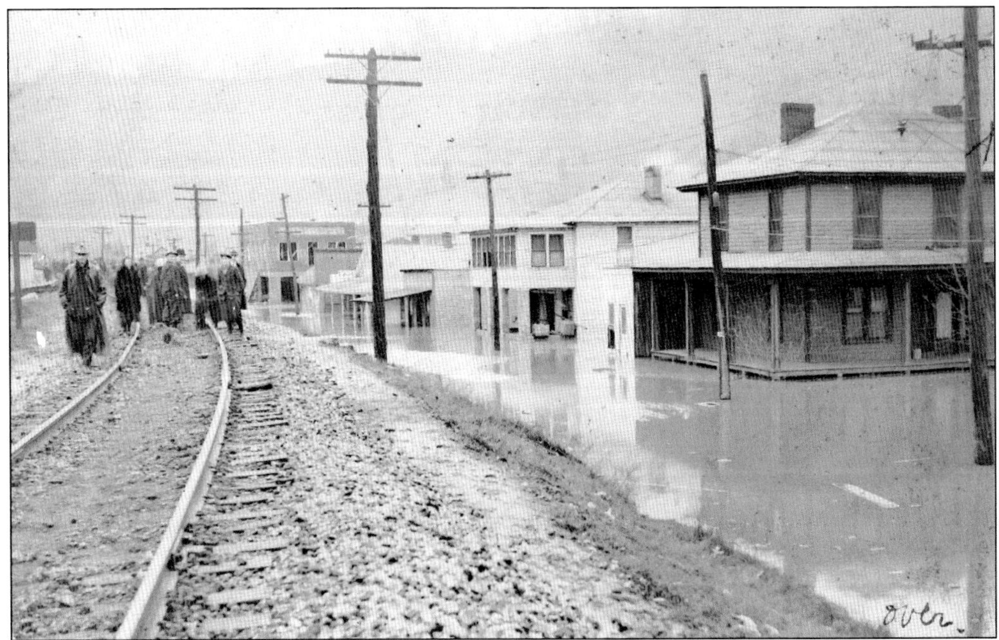

Several people can be seen walking along the railroad near Sixth and Cline Streets during the 1929 flood. The large brick building at center left was Hopkins Grocery, which sat at what today would be the corner of Hambley Boulevard and Seventh Street. (Courtesy of Brenda Hays, John Doug Hays collection.)

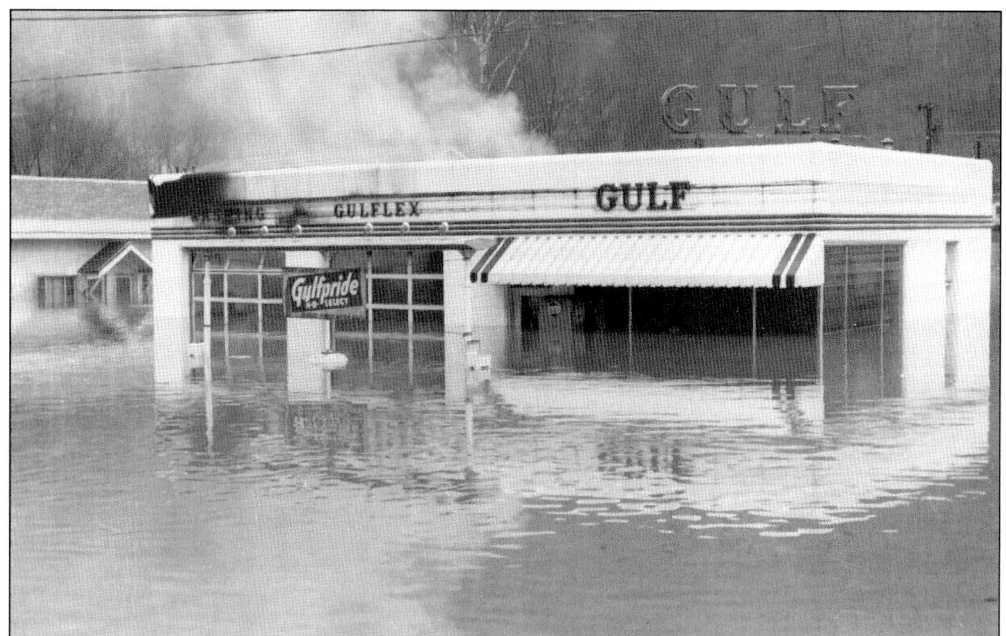

The 1957 flood crested at 52.72 feet, nearly a foot higher than the previous record set in 1862, and 18 feet above the flood stage. It appears fire may have damaged this nearly submerged Gulf station. In those years, there were several service stations throughout the downtown area. (Courtesy of the Big Sandy Heritage Center Museum.)

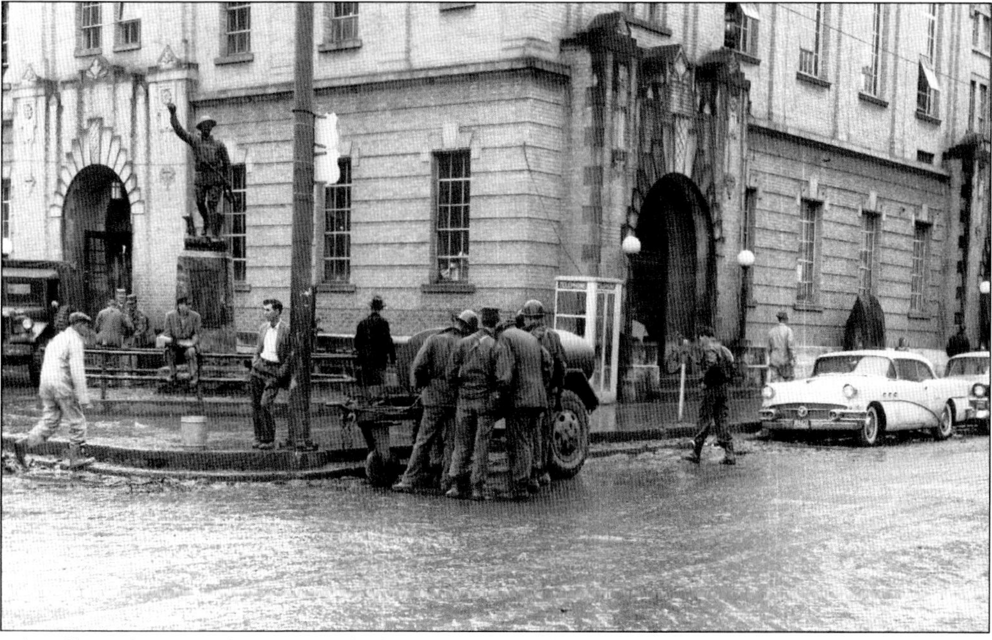

Pikeville and surrounding areas of Pike County were hardest hit during the 1957 flood. Pikeville was almost entirely underwater; in the city limits alone, estimates are that 400 automobiles were submerged, 250 homes destroyed, and another 2,400 homes damaged. When the National Guard was called in, the Pike County Courthouse served as the operations center. (Courtesy of the Big Sandy Heritage Center Museum.)

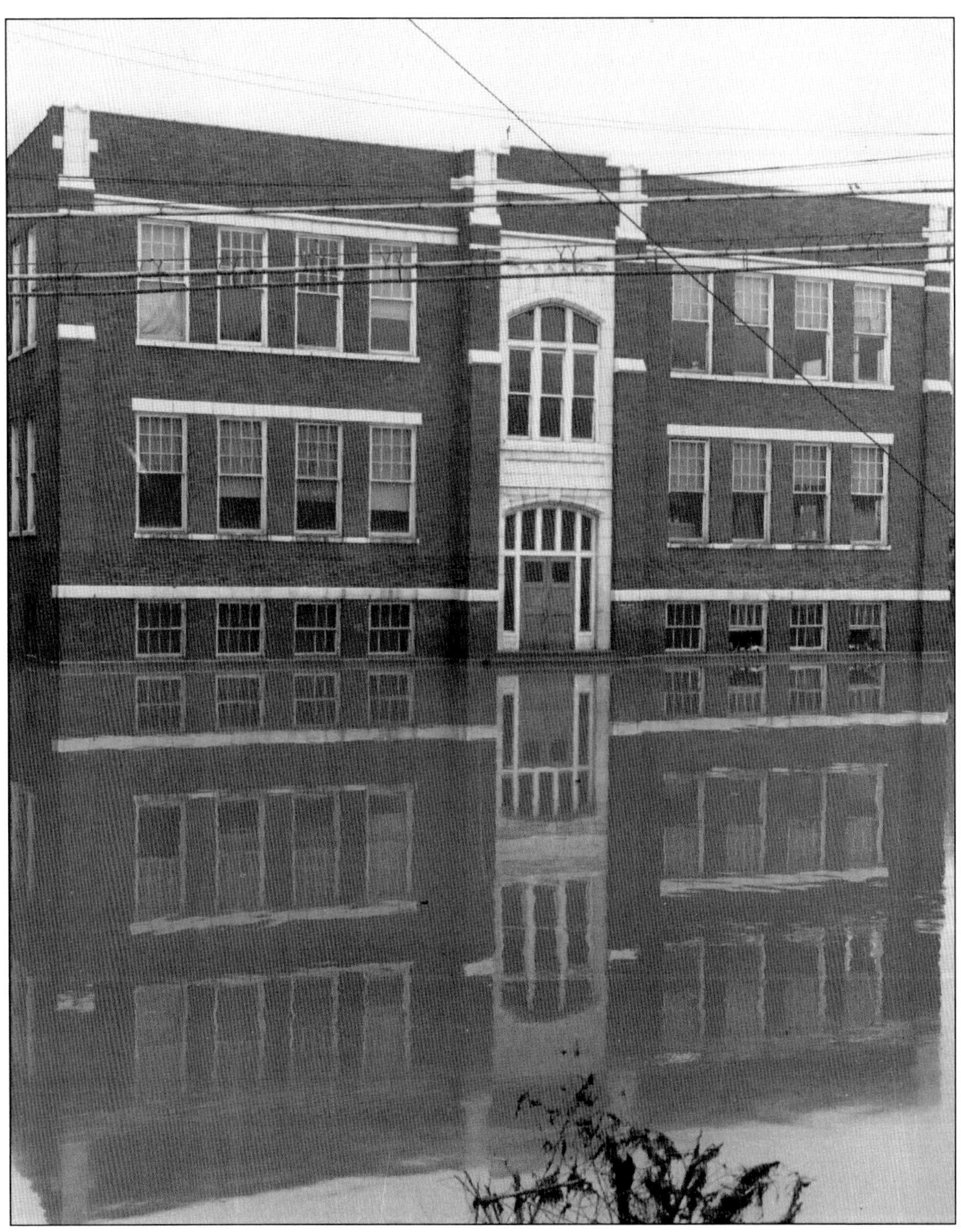

It is widely believed that the 1957 flood—which crested on January 30—was the worst disaster in Pikeville history. The original high school on Fourth Street was not spared. The high-water mark visible on the walls here shows that the flood reached at least the top of the front door. Reports from the time said that water reached the bottoms of chairs on the second floor, and nearby buildings on the campus were also damaged. In the elementary school building, the first-floor windows were overtopped, and in the adjacent gymnasium, the floor was destroyed. The basketball team was forced to travel to any place it could find for practices and games during the remainder of that season. It is a testament to the dedication of the community that school resumed in just three weeks. (Courtesy of the Big Sandy Heritage Center Museum.)

A congressional report following the 1957 flood stated that Main Street businesses had a minimum of three feet of water in them, with as much as nine feet in stores on other streets. The devastation seen here in a Pikeville clothing store was typical and likely cost many business owners their livelihoods. (Courtesy of the Big Sandy Heritage Center Museum.)

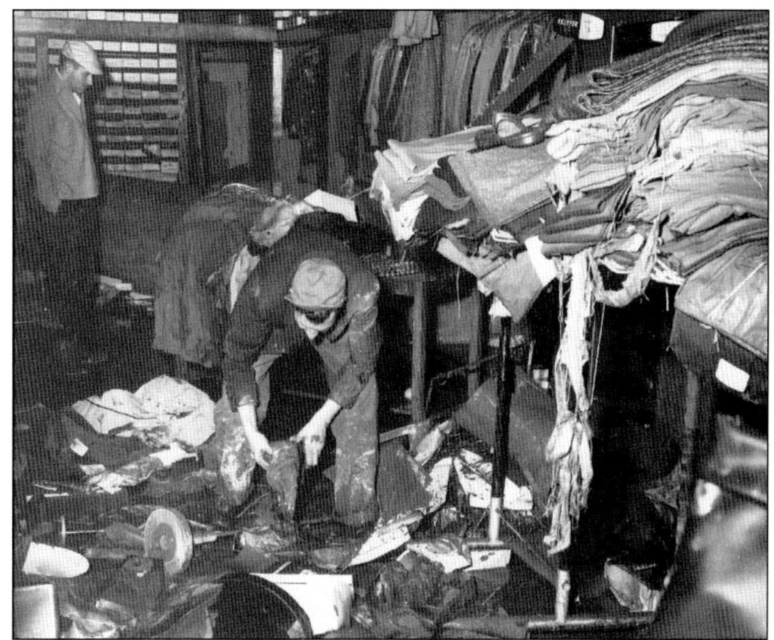

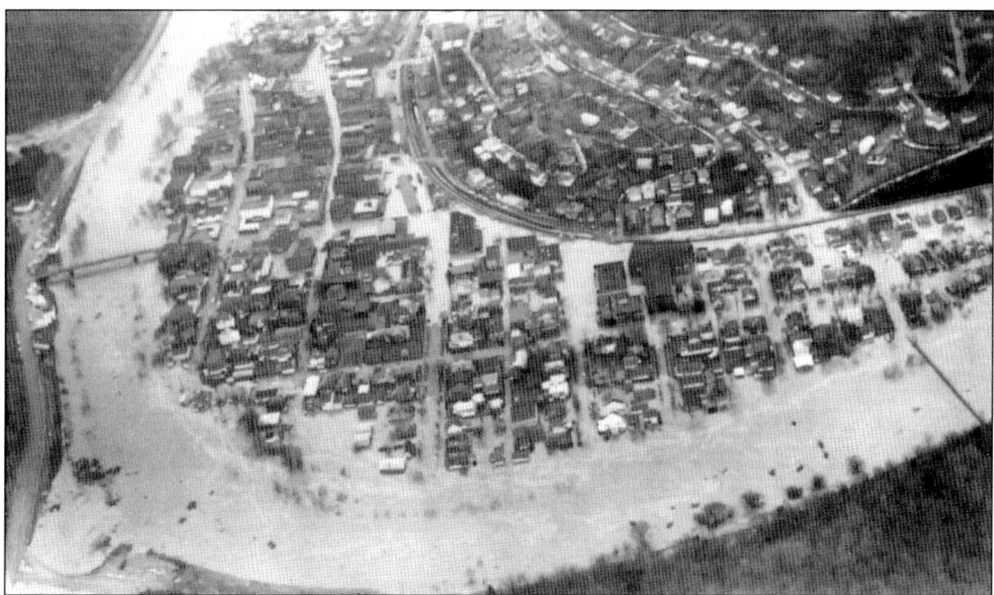

Just six years after the worst flood in Pikeville's history, March 1963 brought the flood with the fourth highest crest. This aerial photograph was taken after water levels dropped substantially. The river was flowing freely beneath the Middle Bridge; on the upper right, floodwaters had not yet drained from Kentucky Avenue, even though the railroad had reemerged. (Courtesy of Brenda Hays, John Doug Hays collection.)

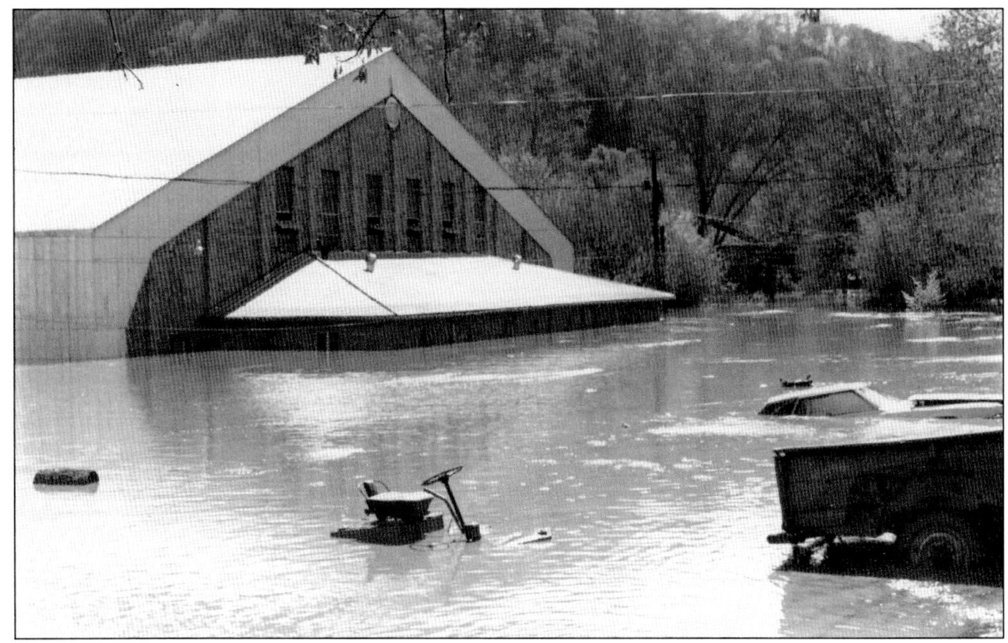

The 1977 flood was the third highest in Pikeville, even though it crested higher than the 1957 flood at nearly every gauge that was not downstream of Fishtrap Dam. Completed in 1968, that dam alone was not enough to prevent Pikeville buildings such as the University of Pikeville's gymnasium from once again sustaining flood damage. (Courtesy of the Frank M. Allara Library, University of Pikeville.)

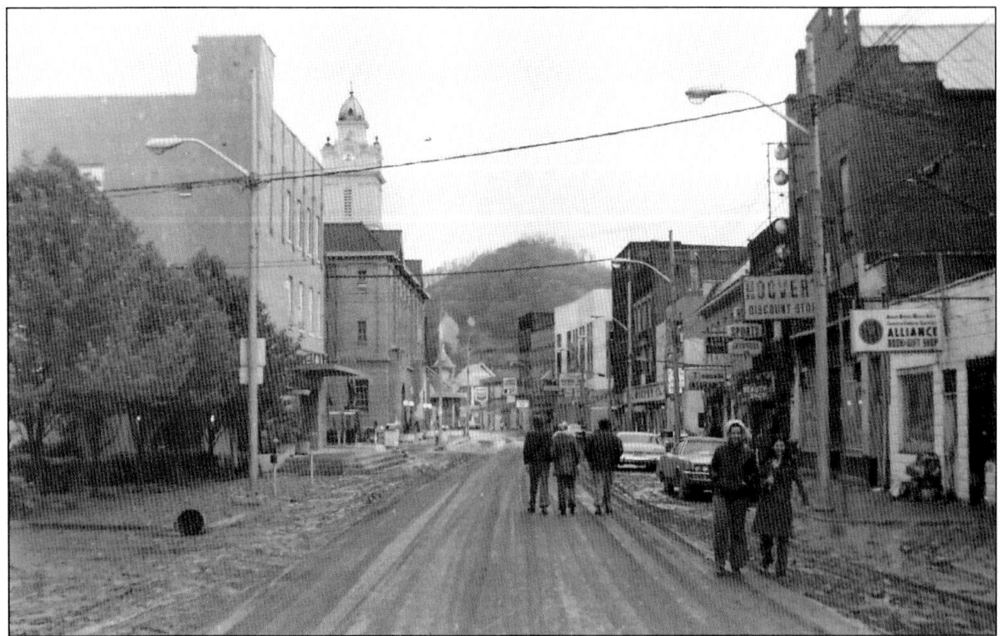

None of the buildings closer than the courthouse in this photograph are still standing. It was not the 1977 flood that eliminated them, but progress. The First National Bank building on the left was replaced four years later. The buildings on the right up to Division Street were demolished to make way for the Pike County Judicial Center in 2013. (Courtesy of Mayor James A. Carter.)

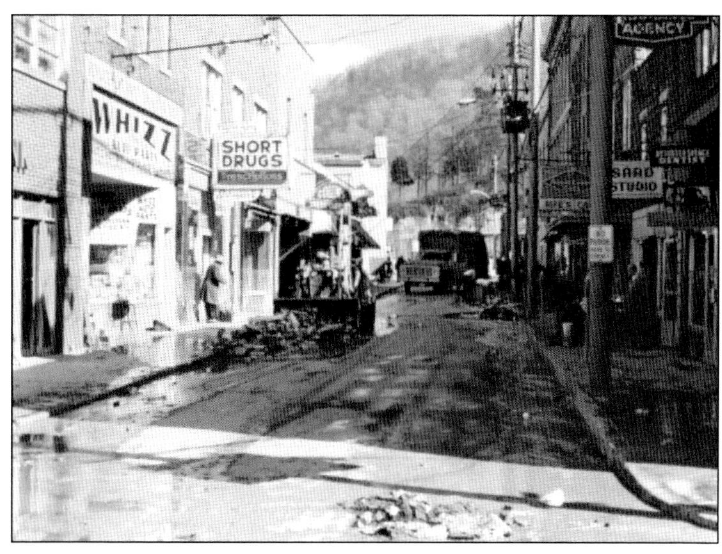

The community immediately got to work following the 1977 flood. The scene here on Division Street played out all across the city with backhoes, garbage trucks, and other equipment used to clean up the mud and debris left behind. Estimates were that $71 million in damages occurred in Pikeville alone. (Courtesy of the Frank M. Allara Library, University of Pikeville.)

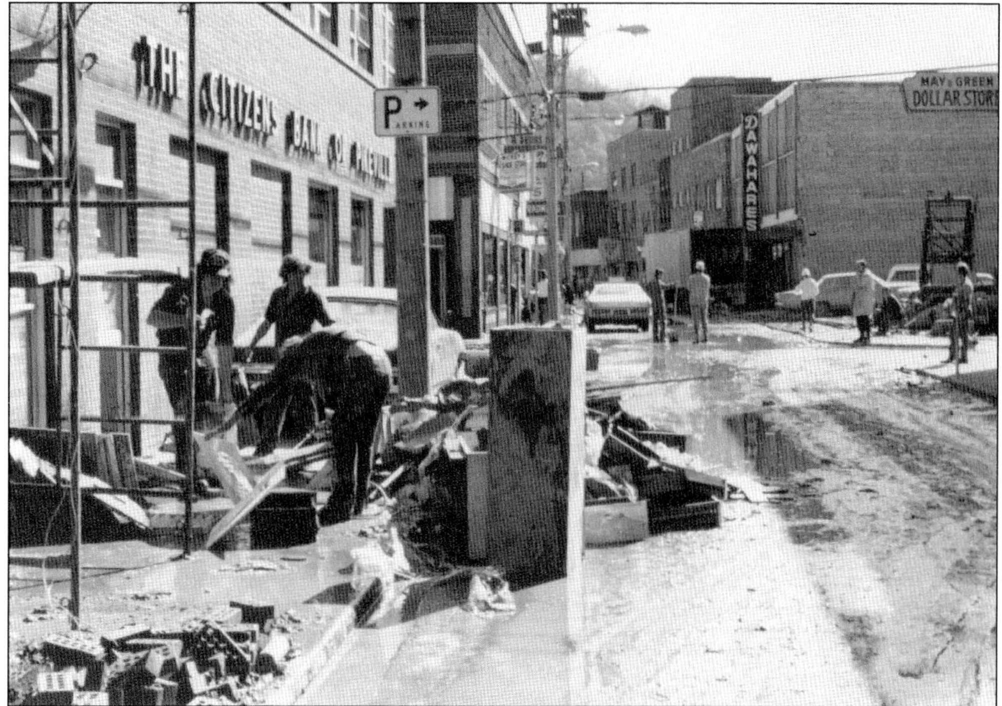

Workers removed damaged furniture and supplies from most downtown businesses, including Citizens Bank of Pikeville, seen here on the corner of Division and Second Streets. On the right, a delivery truck is parked in front of Dawahare's Department Store—where the Appalachian Center for the Arts now stands—likely to haul away damaged merchandise. (Courtesy of the Frank M. Allara Library, University of Pikeville.)

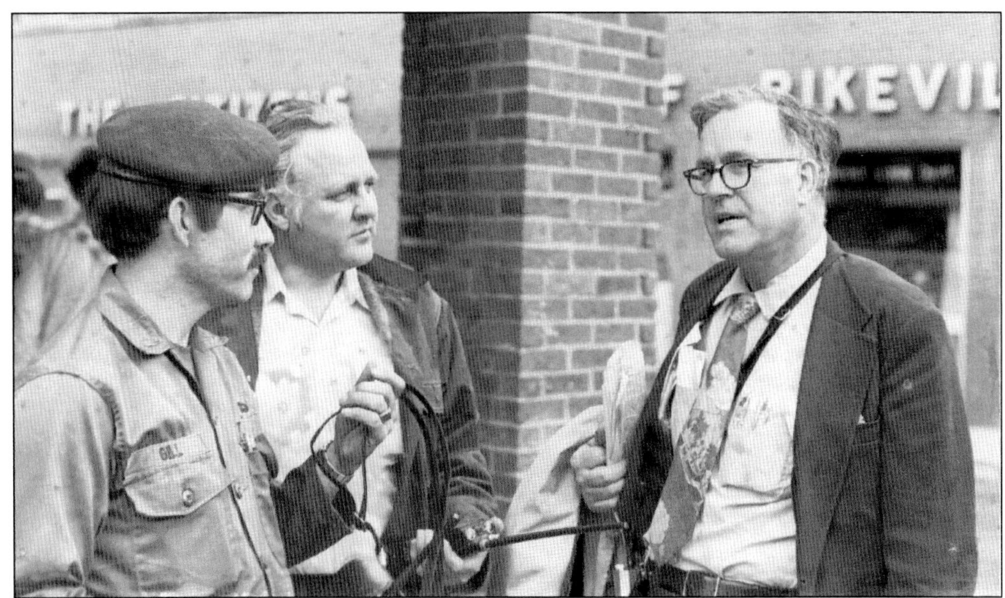

During the aftermath of the 1977 flood, from left to right, an unidentified National Guardsman, Pike County judge/executive Wayne T. Rutherford, and Pikeville mayor William C. Hambley were among those managing the immediate crisis. It should be remembered that Pikeville and Pike County cooperated extensively to make sure the Cut-Through project came to fruition. (Courtesy of the Wayne T. Rutherford family.)

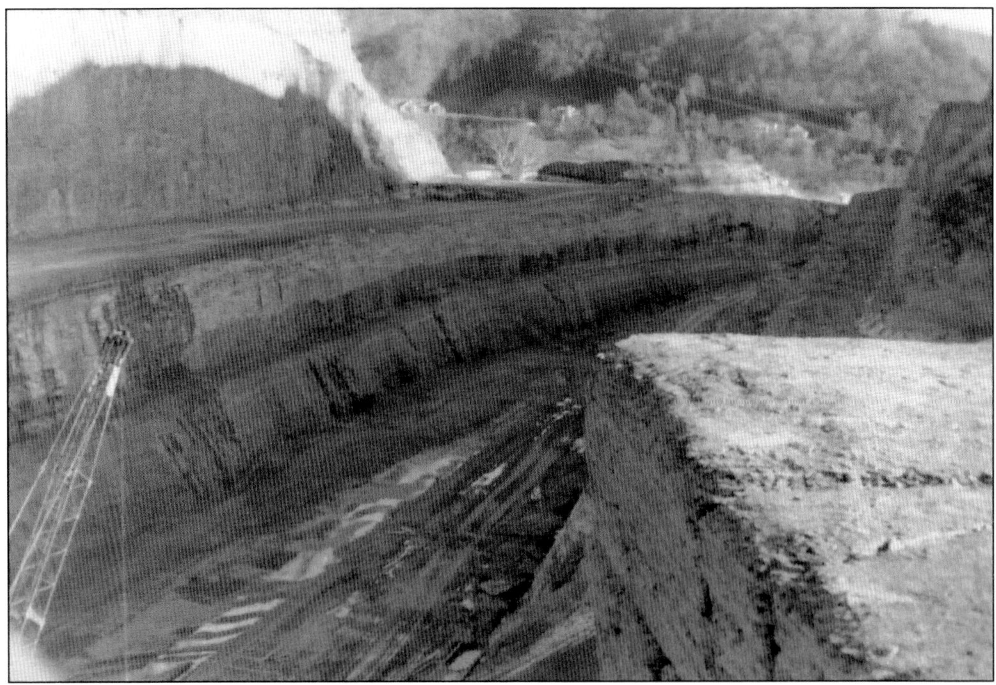

The first phase of construction on the Cut-Through began in November 1973, moving 13 million cubic yards of material to form the initial channel. The spoil from those cuts was deposited into Poor Farm Hollow and along Cedar Creek. Poor Farm Hollow was transformed into Bob Amos Park, and Cedar Creek is now a residential community. (Courtesy of Mayor James A. Carter.)

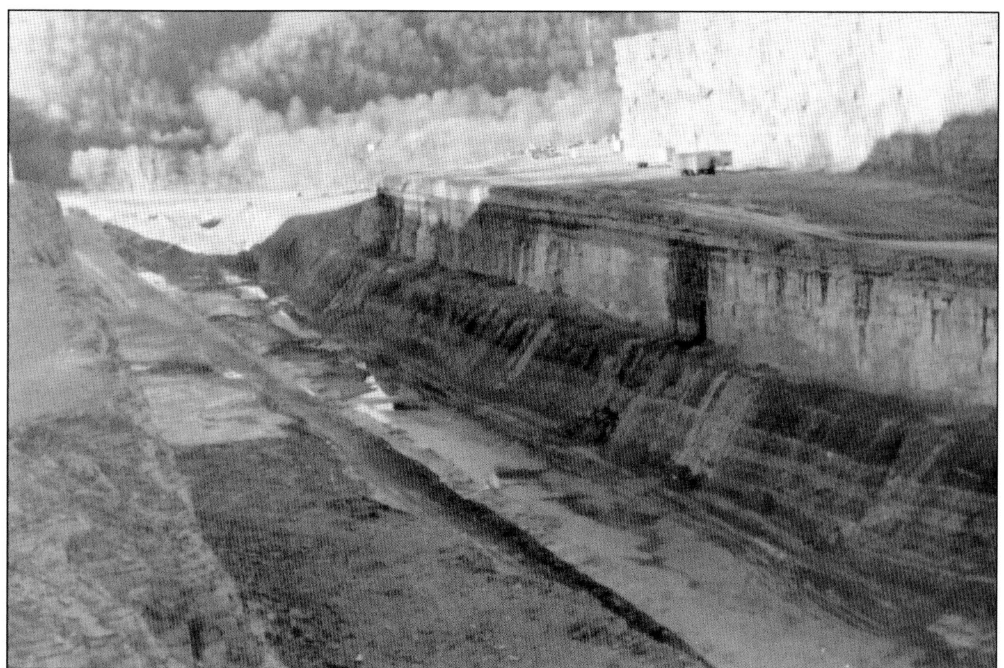

In September 1980, the temporary dams on either end of the cut were removed and the Levisa Fork began flowing through its new channel. After the river course was redirected, most of the old riverbed going by downtown was filled, though a section now called Pikeville Pond was kept for flood control and recreation. (Courtesy of Mayor James A. Carter.)

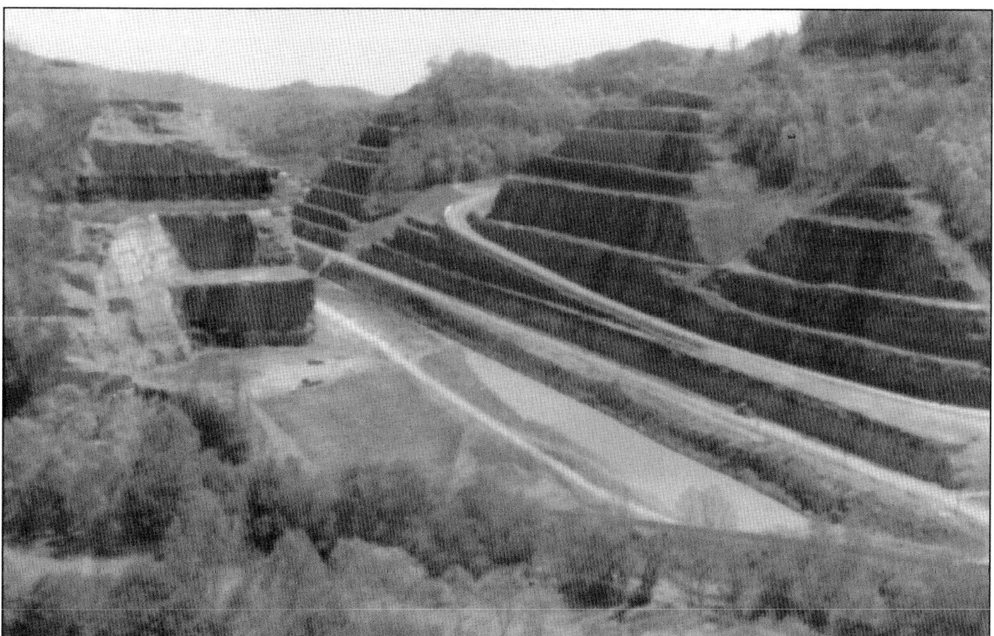

In 1977, as viewed from the north, the road cut on the left was still incomplete. It would take the removal of an additional five million cubic yards of material to complete. On the other side of the river, the rails were not yet placed, but the excavation for their path was completed. (Courtesy of Mayor James A. Carter.)

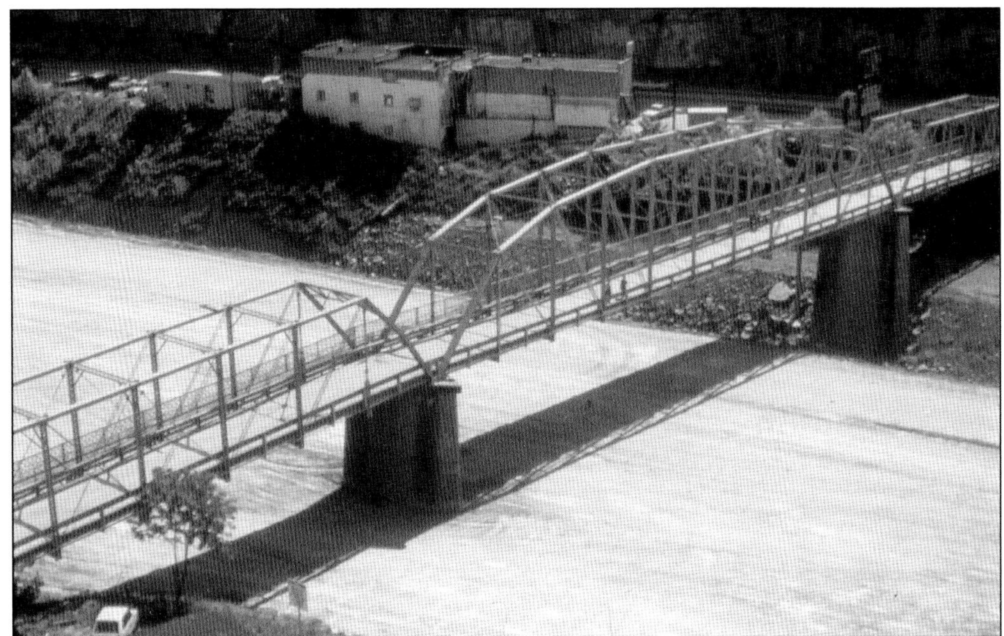

After the river was redirected, material excavated from Peach Orchard Mountain was deposited in the dry riverbed, creating over 100 acres of land in the downtown area. Here, the deposited material can be seen below the Middle Bridge, which would soon be removed. This area is now a parking lot next to the Riverfill 10 Cinema. (Courtesy of the Frank M. Allara Library, University of Pikeville.)

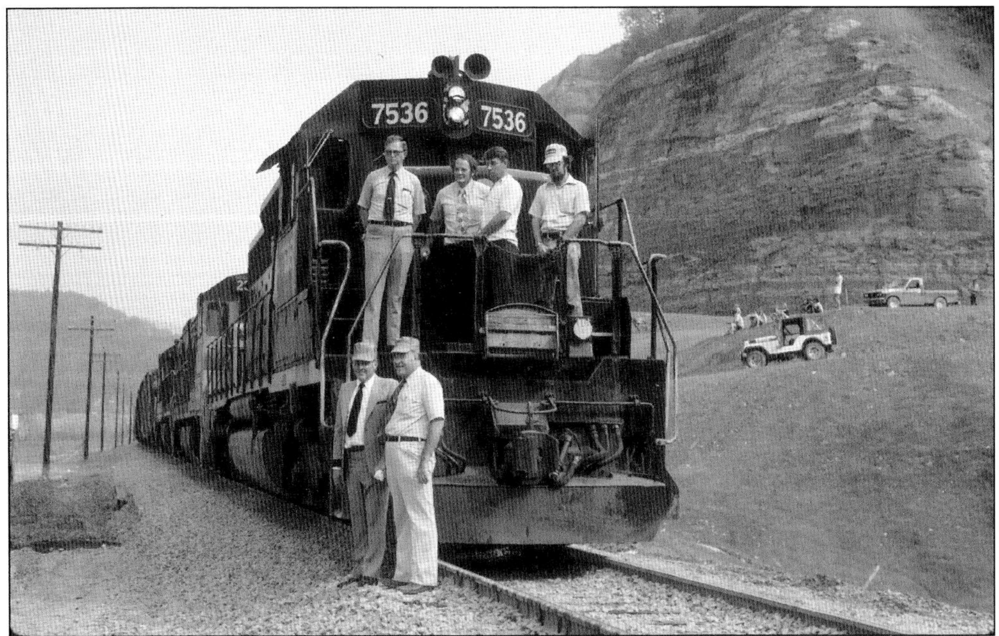

Following the final installation of the rails, the first train traveled through the man-made gorge on July 7, 1978, with Judge Rutherford and Mayor Hambley aboard. Here, they are on the ground having just completed the trip. Paul Kelly, who was the C&O road foreman of engines, is standing to the left on the train along with three rail workers. (Courtesy of Everett N. Young.)

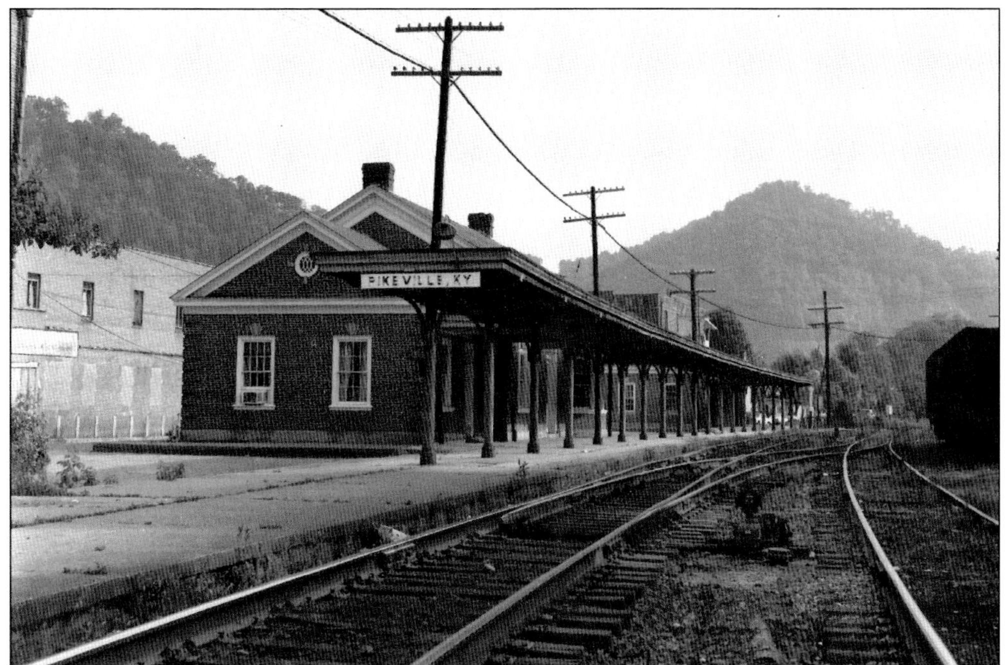

Beginning in 1983, Hambley Boulevard was constructed along the path of the old railroad and Cline Street. Hambley said once that the railroad's presence was the true inspiration for the project. He realized as a child that the tracks divided the town both literally and figuratively, and that to be truly united, the tracks had to go. (Courtesy of Everett N. Young.)

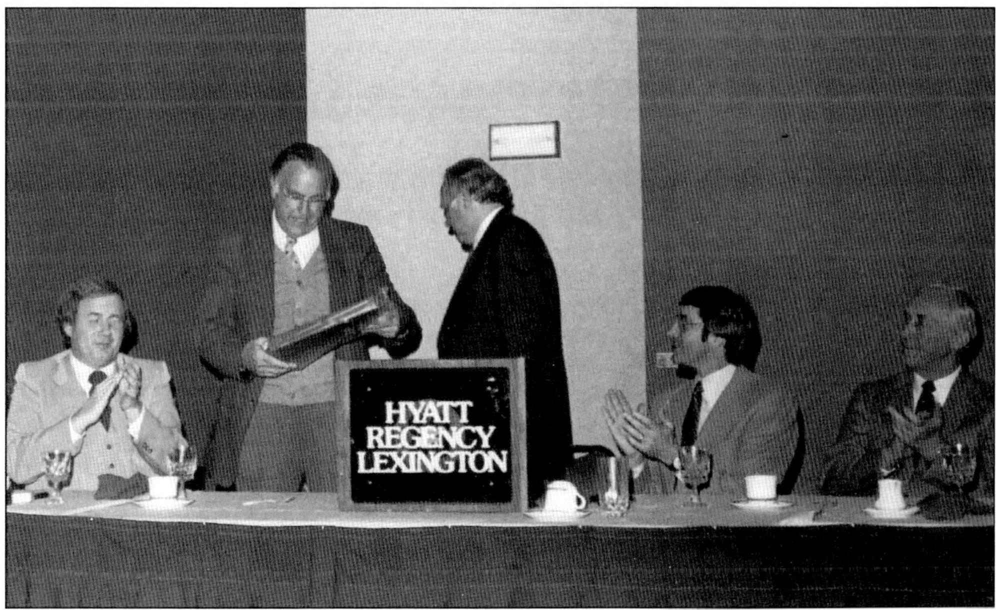

Mayor Hambley spent nearly 35 years planning, pursuing, and overseeing the construction of the Cut-Through. He was widely, and rightly, credited with spearheading the accomplishment. Hambley, though, always emphasized that he had help. At the 1987 ceremony opening the roadway, he said, "I am surrounded by the people who made this possible." (Courtesy of the Wayne T. Rutherford family.)

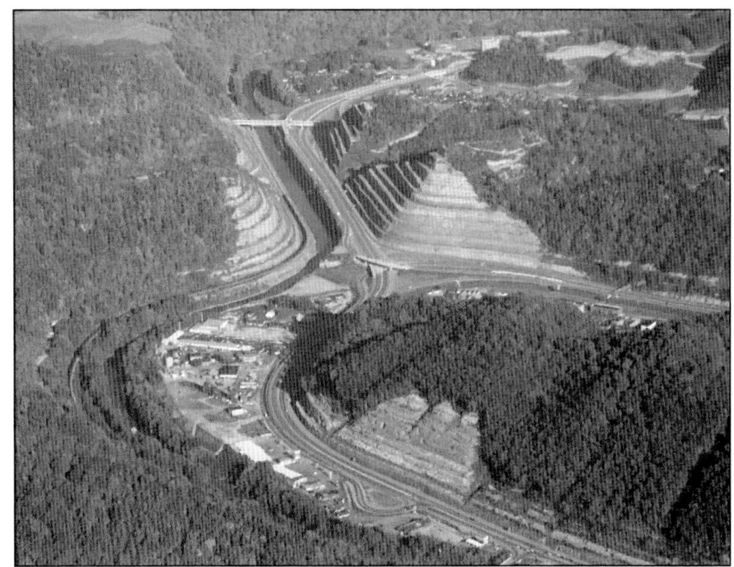

Traffic through the Cut-Through opened the same day as the dedication held on October 2, 1987. It had taken over 30 years and nearly 20 government agencies to plan, coordinate, fund, and complete the removal of 18 million cubic yards of rock from Peach Orchard Mountain at a cost of $77.6 million. (Courtesy of the University of Kentucky Libraries Special Collections Research Center.)

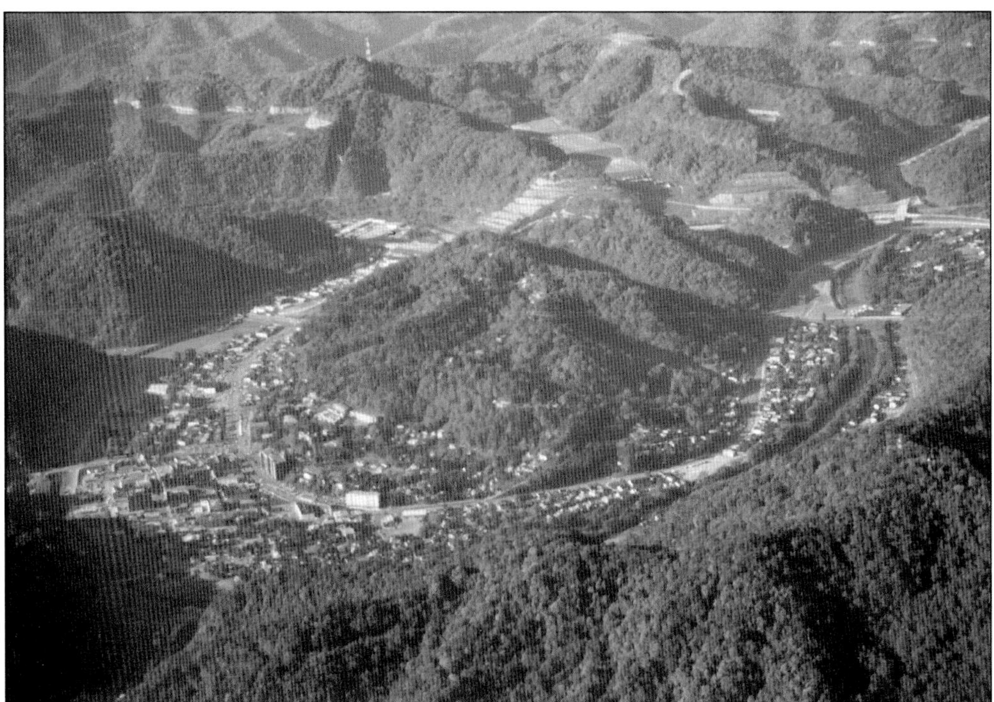

Today, the Levisa Fork—along with the C&O Railroad and 35,000 vehicles each year—travel 4,000 feet through the mountain rather than three miles around it. Without Hambley's dream, his hard work, and that of many others, the city's growth likely would have stalled. Instead, the people of Pikeville moved a mountain for progress. (Courtesy of the University of Kentucky Libraries Special Collections Research Center.)

Index